SHOOTING STAR

SHOOTING STAR

The Definitive Story of Elliott Smith

PAUL REES

NINE
EIGHT
BOOKS

NINE
EIGHT
BOOKS

NEB 019

First published in the UK in 2023 by Nine Eight Books
An imprint of Black & White Publishing Group
A Bonnier Books UK company
4th Floor, Victoria House, Bloomsbury Square, London, WC1B 4DA
Owned by Bonnier Books, Sveavägen 56, Stockholm, Sweden

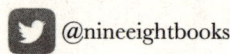 @nineeightbooks

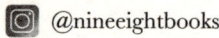 @nineeightbooks

Hardback ISBN: 978-1-7887-0582-0
eBook ISBN: 978-1-7887-0583-7

A CIP catalogue record for this book is available from the British Library.

Publishing director: Pete Selby
Senior editor: Melissa Bond

Cover design by Paul Palmer-Edwards
Cover image © Wendy Redfern/Getty Images
Typeset by IDSUK (Data Connection) Ltd
Printed and bound in Great Britain by Clays Ltd, Elcograf S.p.A

1 3 5 7 9 10 8 6 4 2

Nine Eight Books is an imprint of Bonnier Books UK
www.bonnierbooks.co.uk

MIX
Paper from
responsible sources
FSC® C018072

This one's for Mum.

'I'm the wrong kind of person to be really big and famous.'[1]

— Elliott Smith

CONTENTS

★

PROLOGUE

Memory Lane

Van Nuys, Los Angeles, California, the dead of a late winter's night in 2003. The neighbourhood sits in the heart of the San Fernando Valley, but it's an ugly, uninviting part of town all the same. The landscape is one of concrete, glass and asphalt. Air choked with smog. Car dealerships and single-storey, storefront-size buildings sprawl for miles along both sides of Van Nuys Boulevard. Still, silent and sodium-lit in this witching hour.

A concrete box of a building, the Valley Center Studios complex stands just off the Boulevard. The previous year, Elliott Smith, perhaps the most beloved singer-songwriter of his generation, shelled out to buy one of Valley Center's self-contained studio subdivisions. Smith's was a smallish room split again in two. The studio control room was in one part, the tracking room in the other – its walls angled and ceiling sloped so as to better capture sound.

Kitting his new studio out, Smith spent thousands more dollars indulging his passion for vintage recording gear. He bought Neumann tube microphones, a Fairchild Tube Limiter compressor and his pride and joy, a Triad Trident A-Range recording console for the control room. The exact same Trident model his beloved Beatles had once used and one of only seventeen ever made. Already, though, he was finding the Trident troublesome and temperamental. The wiring was faulty, dilapidated and couldn't be made to work. Fearing he'd been sold a dud, he began to pore over recording manuals, looking to find fixes. Soon enough, the act would consume and torment him.

The demons raged within him these days. Dredging up all the horrors of his childhood. Smith claimed he had been abused by his stepfather, Charlie Welch, while being raised in Texas. He shared the details of his secret shame with his closest intimates, but also on occasion with complete strangers in bars. Towards the end of his too-short life, he was remembering even more repressed memories from that time and seeing a retinue of therapists to help him try to manage his trauma.

He was plagued with self-doubts and paranoias, his always low levels of self-esteem plunging to uncharted depths. Not three years ago, one might have perceived Elliott Smith as having the world at his fingertips. True, his record sales remained relatively modest, but he was beloved, revered even. With his intimately intricate songs, he had enraptured both his audience and his peers. Each one of these songs was a billboard display for the vastness of his talent.

Back in the spring of 2000, Smith had just completed a new record, his fifth and most ambitiously mounted to date. With a year-long world tour lined up to promote it, his major label record company anticipated he was on the verge of breaking through to a new and more rarefied strata of success and acclaim. Things didn't pan out that way. The studio album, *Figure 8*, failed to ignite. It was simply too artful and too demanding of a listen to ever operate as background music to fit mainstream tastes. Throughout the supporting tour, Smith drank heavily and was taking a cocktail of hard and prescription drugs.

He came home to Los Angeles in bad shape and proceeded to rollercoaster downwards into a hellish personal abyss. Wracked and poisoned by combinations of booze, heroin, cocaine, speed, crack-cocaine and the litany of psychiatric drugs he was being prescribed, Smith shut himself off from the world at large. He kept on making music. Haphazardly, chaotically most of the time, but with a vaulting purpose still. What he aspired to was his magnum opus. A double album filled with the wildest, most unbound, but also loveliest and most desolate music he had ever made. It was to be the sum of all his parts.

By now, he'd been engaged at this task, on and off, for the better part of two years. During this time, he'd worn down, fallen out with, cast aside or else left despondent so many of his friends, lovers, collaborators and fellow musicians. As mercurial as he was, he could also be utterly self-absorbed. A loyal and generous friend at times, he was prone, too, to being selfish, cold and cruel. Demanding and exhausting with his torments and neediness.

He was burning up a lifetime's bridges and without anything approaching a finished new record to show for it. When he was able to work, it would often as not be for entire days at a time and going without sleep or sustenance. He had filled boxes of tape reels with hour upon hour of tracks, a rag-bag of crazily bold ideas, yet even so there was no solid, clearly defined shape to this heaving mass of material.

On this winter's night, he arrived at the studio late, as was his custom, and with a newly acquired friend in tow: Andrew Morgan, a budding young songwriter. Physically, Smith looked frail. He was pale, drawn and cadaverous. Taking a guitar, a twelve-string acoustic borrowed from Morgan, he settled in among the detritus littered about the studio – cables, scrunched up Post-its, overflowing ashtrays – and began to pick at a tune. A lilting, folkish song he titled 'Memory Lane'.

Eyes closed, head bowed, he sang it in a near-whisper, his voice rasping. With his lyrics to the song, he was telegraphing all his miseries. The core of his life's story in a single take, it was heartbreaking to see and hear. Yet at the very same time, it was to bear witness to his ongoing wonder. No matter how broken down he became, Smith could always make magic and in the act of doing so find a state of grace.

He sang: 'This is the place you end up when you lose the chase; where you're dragged against your will, from a basement on the hill.'

★

'Memory Lane' brought to mind nothing so much as 'Black-bird', Paul McCartney's most decorative song with the Beatles. This was no accident of happenstance. Smith cherished and evoked the Beatles over and above all others. Seeking to make his defining statement, it was the Beatles he was most especially measuring himself against. Specifically, the White Album, their own wildly erratic, self-indulgent but frequently brilliant double album of 1968. The crucial difference being there was a Fab Four to shoulder the Beatles' load and three of them stellar song-writers. Smith did all of his own heavy lifting – the totality of the music, lyrics, arranging and singing, and most of the playing. He was every bit a solo artist, a true one-man band.

Besides the Beatles, other comparisons were habitually drawn to his work. Bob Dylan's wordplay, Neil Young's wilfulness, Ray Davies' flourishing melodies, Brian Wilson's vaulting pop sym-phonies, Nick Drake's delicate fragility, the ragged beauty of Alex Chilton's most self-reflective moments with Big Star . . . Not a surprise among them. They are, after all, the stock-in-trade ref-erence points for just about every half-decent singer-songwriter seeking to follow in their footsteps. However, uniquely in Smith's case these weren't merely idle remarks. They were entirely accu-rate, fully justified. The body of his work did indeed stand at the shoulder of giants.

Like John Lennon, McCartney, Dylan, Young or Wilson, Smith used his inspirations as a launching point. They were not the whole deal. From the raw elements he took from each of them, he fash-ioned a sound all his own making. Listen to his finest songs – God, listen to *any* of his songs – and they're instantly recognisable as being him, and only him. The near-whisper of his voice, the virtuosity of his guitar playing, in his later work particularly, the dexterity and complexity of his arrangements and the acute sense he was pouring out his innermost being. Added up, he was among the same special breed as each of them, which is to say he was a rare, precious and one-of-a-kind artist. An artist who left a vivid, lasting and all-too-deep impression on the people who got closest to him.

'I can't begin to tell you how extraordinary he was,' says photographer JJ Gonson, his former girlfriend, who had managed Smith's post-college band, Heatmiser. 'He was crazily, impossibly talented. He could play rhythm and lead guitar all at the same time. His tunings are bizarre. His words are bizarre. His songs are incredibly complicated to play. He just could breathe music. I knew the first time I ever saw him I was watching a brilliant songwriter. I had a whole physical response. He was *that* good.'

Margaret Mittleman picked up the reins of managing Smith's solo career. Prior to going to work with Smith, she had steered Beck through the coronation period of his 'Loser' single and *Mellow Gold* album (1994). 'Elliott was the greatest artist I've ever worked with,' she says. 'As far as how his mind worked and how he wrote songs. I really felt like Elliott was going to pull his shit together and was always going to re-invent himself. I thought he'd have that ability to keep things fresh and to write his own rules.'

★

Briefly, Elliott Smith was made famous by just one of his songs. A sad, lovelorn tune, he put 'Miss Misery' to tape during the late winter of 1997 and while living up in Portland, Oregon. It wasn't even his best song, but it found its way onto the soundtrack of an Oscar-winning film, Gus Van Sant's *Good Will Hunting* (1997), written by two young actors, Matt Damon and Ben Affleck. 'Miss Misery' was Oscar-nominated, too. The following year, Smith performed the song at the Oscars ceremony in Hollywood. He didn't win on the night, but a record-breaking TV audience of 55 million was exposed to him – shy, awkward and reticent-seeming, greasy-haired and uncomfortably attired in an ill-fitting white suit.

As it always does, the gaining of mass exposure extracted a heavy price from him. An entirely reductive view of him persisted. From then on, he was commonly perceived as a sad sack with a guitar, doomed to having audiences shout out for 'the Oscar song'. Try as he might, he was never wholly able to get out from under the shadow of 'Miss Misery'. In this sense most of all, so it also went with the crushing weight he bore from his childhood traumas.

From Smith's own account, by what he said and wrote throughout his life, he regarded his formative years growing up in Duncanville, Texas, with his mother, Bunny Welch (née Bunny Kay Berryman), and stepfather, Charlie Welch, as a chamber of horrors. He was to carry the mental scars with him all of his life. The drinking and the drugging numbed the pain. Likely, there were other, physical manifestations, too. Such as his lifelong affliction with irritable bowel syndrome (IBS), which at regular intervals made it all but impossible for him to eat. At all events, the toll of his earliest memories, the extent to which he believed he was betrayed, never left him. There was hardly ever a time he wasn't battling against, or else running to get away from, the damage done. He fled Texas for Portland, left Portland for New York, and New York for Los Angeles. He ran until he could run no more, to the point of exhaustion and utter despair, and when he simply gave up altogether.

Along the way, there was the cycle of friends and associates he had made and then abandoned, vanishing from out of their sight. From one stop to the next, one person to another, he might be seen to have taken on a completely different character. Forever in the act of trying on a different skin and putting on a new face. It was as if he were never at ease with the ones he was given, nor ever fixed on who it was he wanted to be.

Garrick Duckler befriended Smith during their time together at high school in Portland and when they played together in the band Stranger Than Fiction. Elliott stayed in touch with him almost to the bitter end. He wrote me: 'I think everyone who knew Elliott well felt hurt by him, injured and put down by him at some point.'

Then again, there were all the other sides and aspects to Smith. The parts of him not scarred or broken, how he appeared in his moments of release. At such times, he would blaze and dazzle. Intellectually bright and relentlessly curious, he was serious-minded and sensitive, but also witty, funny, playful and mischievous. He could be strong-willed and bull-headed, but gentle and considerate to others. He was complex and complicated, a whole person.

'Thankfully, the first thing that comes into my head when I think of him is his big, beautiful smile,' says Dorien Garry, whose

New Jersey apartment Smith crashed in when he first moved out to the East Coast. 'His smile is something I feel like people didn't get to experience enough, because he's not smiling in so many of the photographs taken of him.

'That smile of his and his incredible laugh. His laugh was unmatchable. It was so big and so infectious, and so wildly genuine. It came from so deep within him. It was just as beautiful a sound as any music he ever made.'

Pete Krebs was another friend and fellow musician of Smith's from Portland. He says: 'If Elliott was still with us and if I could get a straight answer out of him, I'd ask him what would make him happy. Like, what does happiness look like to him? I don't know if he ever experienced happiness or not. I'd hope so.

'I wonder if Elliott felt like a short life was predestined for him. Was all the heartache worth it? I mean, what did he give up to get all of that acclaim? Would he have rather made art for art's sake and eased into a life of quieter pursuits? Man, parts of getting older are tough. These are things he hasn't had to experience. To put it in a broader, existential context, is it better to fade away, or go out in a white-hot flash? I don't know if he came out ahead, or he didn't.'

Elliott Smith is gone. He departed this world at thirty-four years old and in the most shocking way imaginable. He left behind him a treasure trove of celestial, transfixing music but there are also still left hanging questions as to what exactly happened in the kitchen of a small house, halfway up a hillside on Lemoyne Street, Los Angeles. It was in another neighbourhood of the city, Echo Park, and around midday on 21 October 2003 that Smith may well have shared with us one last hard and uncomfortable truth.

Once more, the scene is a marathon studio session, the spring of 2003 now. He was bent on experimenting. On the last tour he did with his backing band in 2000, he had begun performing a new song he'd written and first put down to tape at the Beatles' preferred studio, Abbey Road in north London, 'Brand New Game'. Afterwards, a fan sent him a cassette of them performing the song in Cleveland, Ohio. The tape's mix was muddy, indistinct, but he fixated on putting it to use. So far as it's possible to explain his thinking on the song, Smith wanted to record himself in the studio re-playing all the instruments – guitar, bass, piano and drums – and singing along to the live tape. Then, he meant to have the two versions mixed together into a kind of psychedelic-sounding soup.

This much he managed over the course of a single day and night. Improbably, the result was extraordinary. The whole ebbing, swooshing gloop had somehow or other coalesced and flowed as one. At the centre of the tumult was Smith's own voice. Worn down to a husk, it seemed to radiate all the pain and hurt in his world. His words slice through the viscous music. At first, striking, scattershot images leap out – an 'ape man in a cave', a 'glass eye nature made' – until we arrive at the closing verse when he cuts to the heart of the matter: 'Everything's impossible . . . Push the point to oblivion and keep turning the blade.' . . .

PART 1

Duncanville, Texas

CHAPTER 1

The Eyes of Texas

He never really was Elliott Smith. He was born Steve Paul Smith on 6 August 1969 at Clarkson Hospital in Omaha, Nebraska. His parents, 24-year-old Gary Smith, a Vietnam vet who was studying medicine, and Bunny Smith, twenty-five, a school teacher, had been married for three years by then. Gary was a Nebraskan and Bunny native to Texas. They were wed in Dallas, but set up home together in Omaha and in a nondescript apartment block downtown on 41st Street in sight of the I-80, the main arterial route out from the city and away into the epic expanse of the Great Plains of America, more than a million square miles of nothing but flat sod and dirt.

That summer of 1969 was one for the ages in President Richard Nixon's America. By any measure, it was a monumental time to be alive – a savage and brutish one, too. In the month before Gary and Bunny Smith welcomed their son into the world, Neil

Armstrong and Buzz Aldrin walked on the Moon. Nixon ordered the first war-ravaged US troops home from Vietnam. Senator Edward Kennedy drove poor Mary Jo Kopechne off a bridge and to her doom at Chappaquiddick on Martha's Vineyard, Massachusetts. During just the first twelve days of little Steve Smith's life, the Woodstock Festival happened in upstate New York and in degrees of mud and chaos. Under cover of darkness on two hot, black Los Angeles nights, Charles Manson sent members of his Family out into the city to rampage and slaughter.

Sadly, the Smiths' marriage wasn't made to last. Bunny filed for divorce in 1970. Gary Smith completed his MD and in time moved up to Portland, where he was to establish a psychiatric practice. Bunny reverted to her maiden name of Berryman. She won custody of their boy and took him back with her to Texas. To Duncanville, to be precise, a suburb of Dallas and a small town with a population of under 30,000. It was a place of predominantly white, mostly middle-class folks. There were good schools, church on a Sunday and Stars and Stripes flags fluttering from row upon row of fresh-cut lawn. A railroad line bisected the town, demarking the more affluent and downtrodden sides of Duncanville.

There was music running through Bunny's family. Like her mother, Margaret, Bunny played piano and sang in a church choir. Her father, Bill, was an ordained minister and a signmaker by trade, but would moonlight playing drums in Dixieland jazz bands. Whenever they babysat their grandson, Bill and Margaret would play and sing harmony to him, little Steve sat up at the piano. Gary Smith took his boy one week out of every year. Steve Smith was three years old when his dad played him the Beatles for the first time. In Gary's apartment, father and son danced around together to the whole of *Sgt Pepper's* . . . However, the song little Steve was most delighted by was 'Rocky Racoon', a whimsical Paul McCartney piece from the White Album.

In July of 1973, the month before her son turned four, Bunny re-married. Her second husband, Charlie Welch, was a travelling salesman, hocking insurance to farmers. Welch played golf at the weekends and was a dab hand at cards, bridge and most especially poker. To begin with, he settled his new family into a neat house, red-bricked with a white-columned façade, on East Center Street. It was a good, quiet and respectable part of town. Later, with his business flush, Welch moved them out to a bigger place, a farmhouse on four acres of land in Cedar Hill, a couple of miles south-west of Duncanville. It had a barn, stables and a basketball hoop in the front yard.

In time, Bunny bore Welch two children of their own – a boy, Darren, in 1975 and a daughter, Ashley, the following year. Soon after, Steve turned seven. By most accounts, Welch was a strict, unbending and devout parent. Not the type to dance around a room to the Beatles. The family attended a local Methodist church every Sunday without fail. Bunny's first-born wasn't too bothered with the Bible teaching, but the fire and brimstone sermonising he was subjected to, at home as much as in church, sure enough left its mark. Even many years later, Smith admitted: 'Church still scares the shit out of me. It just made me really scared of Hell. If you grew up being threatened [with going to Hell], it's really hard to be like, "Oh, it probably doesn't exist."'[2]

To all outward appearances, Steve Smith otherwise seemed a regular, happy little boy. Those days, he had a mop of sun-bleached blond hair. Bright-eyed, a chatterbox, he liked nothing better than to sing at the top of his voice and to shoot hoops. He passed through Duncanville's Central Elementary School without alarm or incident. At ten, Bunny paid for him to take classical piano lessons. He practised at home on his mum's electric piano, pieces by Tchaikovsky, Debussy and Rachmaninov. Occasionally, he was interrupted by the piano's habit of picking up CB radio transmissions from passing truck drivers. In time, he progressed to composing a piece of his own. He called it *Fantasy* and won a prize for his work at a local musical festival. Smith stopped going to the piano lessons after a year, but he continued to play at home and also took up the clarinet.

Sat at the piano, blowing the clarinet, or skipping along to the Beatles, it all amounted to one and the same thing, which is to say Smith's complete and utter immersion in music. What joy he found in music from such an early age, but comfort and sanctuary as well. Music was his escape from the cruel wrath and temper of his stepfather. From the fearful things shouted out in the family home and which also passed unspoken. Terrors he would be haunted by for all of his too-short life. Horrors he would go on to reference, time and again, in his lyrics. Open wounds he didn't, or wasn't ever able to, conceal.

'You learned early on about his upbringing,' says Margaret Mittleman. 'That he was betrayed by people and his trust issues for that.'

'The first year of college, during one summer, Elliott decided to read Freud,' recalls Smith's high-school friend Garrick Duckler, now a psychotherapist himself. 'He showed up on my doorstep with a copy of *The Interpretation of Dreams* and said to me: "Why does everyone hate Freud so much? He has such provocative things to say about the most private parts of ourselves. And such important ideas about how we might understand ourselves."

'Clearly, I was talking to the eight-year-old in him. When you're eight, things matter in life. He always was connected, however tenuously at times, to that part of himself, buried as it got under the layers of drug use, claustrophobia of fame, depression and despair.'

Back there and then in Duncanville, Texas, the fun-loving, smart kid who lit up and sang along to 'Rocky Raccoon' seems also to have been a time bomb being primed. A scientific study published in 1998, *The Adverse Childhood Experiences*, identified ten traumas potentially inflicted upon children or young adults. These include physical abuse, verbal abuse, sexual abuse, physical neglect and emotional neglect. 'There is,' the study states, 'a powerful, persistent correlation between the more ACEs experienced and the greater chance of poor outcomes later in life . . . drastically increased risk of . . . depression, substance abuse, smoking, early death.'

Dr Leah Quinlivan is a Chartered Psychologist and Research Fellow at the University of Manchester. She says: 'There's a lot of research now suggesting an association between adverse life events and future self-harm and behaviour. Nothing is ever deterministic, [but] what you find with people who do come from

7

abusive backgrounds particularly, there is a very strong association with future adverse outcomes. It's often cumulative in a lot
of senses. So with someone who has experienced a lot of abuse,
they may continue to experience difficulties. They might get bullied, for instance. Or they might fall into drugs and alcohol.'

Steve Smith first got drunk when he was eleven years old. One
of the older kids in the neighbourhood invited him round to his
house to shoot some pool. The kid's dad happened to make
his own moonshine and the two boys raided his stash. Smith
recalled the moment to Keith Cameron of the *NME* in 1999:
'But I didn't have a hangover. Too young,' he concluded.[3]

CHAPTER 2

Permanent Waves

When Steve Smith started at William H. Byrd Junior High, the Welch-Smiths were only recently moved into the school's catchment area. For the most part, his fellow sixth-graders came up together from the same elementary schools within the well-heeled neighbourhood. A stranger among them, he arrived at the school with his armour-plating on. The first impression he gave his new peers was of someone who was easy-going, quick to laugh, something of a class clown. Momentarily, he might even have passed himself off as a jock. Basketball, he had always loved. Now he successfully tried out for the football team.

Soon enough, though, he began to lay out another pattern for himself at Byrd. Using music to navigate by, he found his true bearings and a mooring point. Typical of Duncanville, the school was small-'c' conservative and the faculty generally a pretty buttoned-up bunch. The exception to the rule was Miss

Burton, the music teacher. Liberal-minded and outwardly passionate about her subject, Miss Burton encouraged each fresh intake of sixth-graders towards the school band she presided over. At any given time, this group was made up of around seventy aspiring young musicians – all of them brass or woodwind players, since it wasn't possible for the school to incorporate a string section. Playing clarinet, Smith sailed through Miss Burton's sixth-graders' audition.

Miss Burton was a taskmaster, too. She drilled her charges with daily practices and sometimes twice a day. Through the course of these sessions, Smith struck up fast friendships with two other sixth-grade kids. Kevin Denbow also played clarinet and was sat at the stool next to him. A soft-spoken heavy metal fan, Denbow stood out for having let his hair grow down to the neck of the Ozzy Osbourne T-shirt he habitually wore. Steve 'Pickle' Pickering played saxophone in the band and also piano. This other Steve shared Smith's birthday, 6 August. 'Pickle' was skinny as a pipe cleaner and short-sighted. His eyes loomed like saucers from behind the bottle-thick lenses of his glasses and so he seemed in a permanent state of surprise. They made for an odd-looking group, like disparate souls shipwrecked together and bound to form their own island.

'All three of us were a little less conformist than the rest of the student body, I think,' says Kevin Denbow. 'That's kind of what sparked our relationship. We all had a tendency to grow our hair long and to wear rock 'n' roll T-shirts. At band practice, we'd come up with wind arrangements to songs not necessarily promoted by Miss Burton. On one occasion, we did a saxophone and clarinet arrangement for "When I'm Sixty-Four" by the Beatles. We definitely had our own little quirks and inside jokes, things we found funny that no one else seemed to.

'We never really played any sports together. Steve did some running back then and we occasionally passed the time shooting baskets in front of his house, but Pickering wasn't very athletic at all. Steve and I had some issues with the jocks in the school – the more machismo guys. It was everything from running our mouths off back and forth in the parking lot to the odd fist fight, but nothing more than typical adolescent behaviour. For the most part, we got along.'

Outside of school, the three of them met up on their pushbikes and rode over to play arcade games at the local 7-Eleven. Weekends, they went bowling or to see a movie in town. Or else they would chip in to rent a clutch of videos from the neighbourhood Blockbuster store. Their staple choices were music films and serially the same ones over and again – Pink Floyd's *The Wall*, the Who's *Tommy* or Jimi Hendrix's . . . *Plays Berkeley*.

Music was by far the strongest bond between them. From the outset, the glue was the records they all listened to. There was the Beatles, of course, but also Led Zeppelin, Floyd, AC/DC and Rush. Their other regular destination as a group was the Red Bird Mall, which was home to Duncanville's sole record store, the Melody Shop. Even as an adolescent, Smith's tastes were eclectic. He was as enthusiastic about discovering German hard rock band the Scorpions as he was Big Star, the Clash, Elvis Costello or R.E.M.

'Steve had the first Walkman I ever saw,' says Denbow. 'He used to live with those headphones on. Man, he'd be like, "Here, listen to this!" He'd put the headphones on you and have you listen to six bars of a Zeppelin song he was obsessed with. Then he'd go home and try to play it on piano.'

★

For his twelfth birthday, Gary Smith presented his son with his first guitar, a Martin Sigma acoustic, and to go along with it, a Peavey amp. He started off on the guitar working out the basic chords to Beatles' songs from the White Album, 'Julia' and 'Sexy Sadie', and then how to finger-pick them. In short order, he progressed to actually playing and making music with his friends. Mostly, they gathered at the Pickering house and where there were delights for Smith. Pickle's dad was a hobby musician. He owned a 1970 black Les Paul guitar, a 1964 Fender twin reverb amp and a four-track recorder. There was a fourth lad joining them now, too: Mark Merritt, another band kid and Rush fanatic.

Merritt also had a guitar of his own, a cheap electric with a $10 amp. Over at Pickle's house, he and Smith would put their two amps one on top of the other. Stacked up like Rush's amps on the gatefold cover of their double live album, *All the World's a Stage*. Denbow was a third guitarist. Pickle went on piano despite Smith being the better player. They began teaching themselves to play their favourite songs. Smith lobbied strongest for a George Harrison song, 'Old Brown Shoe'. Unsurprisingly, the Beatles,

Zeppelin, AC/DC and Floyd featured heavily in their repertoire. They made a stab at every track on another Rush album, *Permanent Waves*, and even took a pass at 'Amazing Grace'. As none of the others could much carry a tune, Smith was pressed into becoming their lead vocalist.

'He was always a bit reticent to sing,' says Denbow. 'We had conversations about it numerous times in my bedroom over at my house. He wanted to be able to record his own songs onto a four-track, but he just didn't like the sound of his own voice. We had a discussion about him doing "Cry Baby Cry" by the Beatles, but to try out kind of whispering it. When he did that, it seemed to open up a door for him. He could hide a little behind the whispery voice.'

For a lot of the time, Smith seems to have been hiding in plain sight in Duncanville. He was popular enough to be elected band president in his senior year at Byrd. Hanging out and making music with his friends, he might appear to them fun-loving, light as air. They gleaned he had a difficult relationship with his stepfather, and he even let slip some of the details. The list of chores he was expected to do. How Charlie Welch, a keen runner himself, would rouse him from bed at seven on a Saturday morning and order him off on a 6-mile run. He showed up at Pickle's house one day with the neck of his Martin acoustic broken and told his bandmates it had happened during an argument with his stepfather. And he only ever intermittently invited any of them over to his house.

'The times I can remember going over to Steve's house, his mum was really nice and very welcoming,' says Denbow. 'Charlie was more standoffish. Steve was a bit private and mostly kept us in the dark about what happened when everybody went home. I know there was a strict religious theme running through their house. There was not a lot of playing on Sundays. I knew when Steve had his chores to do he wasn't going to be hanging out with us. There was no getting around those with Charlie, he always had a yard tool for Steve.

'All of us had in common the brooding adolescent depression that goes along with growing up. Steve kind of grew out of it a little bit later than the rest of us. He was definitely fascinated by the depths he could go to. He could be kind of morose and brooding. He was fun to hang out with, too. We'd sit and laugh about stuff for hours, but there wasn't a whole lot of filler with Steve. When Steve spoke you paid attention, because he didn't mince his words.'

By the time they were in their senior year, Smith was the strongest and most influential driving force in the band. The summer of 1983, he visited his father up in Portland and brought back with him to Texas a red Gibson SG electric guitar, just like the one Angus Young played in AC/DC, and to go with it a couple of effects pedals. The new guitar appeared to spur him to take control. He manoeuvred Mark Merritt over to bass guitar and organised a first public performance for the band in Duncanville. It was a talent show at the Trinity Methodist Church over on Clark Road – his stepfather's church.

For this auspicious occasion, the friends recruited two additional members from the school rank. The first was a drummer, Tim Hunt. Since Smith was beset with stage fright, the second was a singer. A pretty girl from the school year below theirs named Kim McCommas, whose mother was the sixth-grade math teacher and who Smith had a serious crush on. All of their parents turned out for the show, Charlie Welch among them. They got to play just two songs, each one a small act of rebellion on Smith's part. The first was a surf-instrumental 'Tequila', a number-one hit for the Champs back in 1958. The other was Led Zeppelin's 'Stairway to Heaven', with Smith taking on Jimmy Page's centrepiece guitar solo.

'It was the only time I ever performed live with Steve,' says Denbow. 'We were laughing as we were playing "Stairway to Heaven". We found it side-splitting. I don't know how the adults in the congregation took it. Most of the kids in school who went to the church were like, "Right on!" Even today, old schoolmates bring it up with me on occasion. Evidently, it made an impression.'

For his part, Smith got an ever bigger kick out of trying out Pickle's dad's four-track machine. The first homespun recording sessions he undertook were with his friends and beginning in the autumn of 1983. They cut a couple of Rush tunes together, 'Closer to the Heart' and 'Subdivisions', and also five of Smith's own compositions, each an instrumental. In a flash, he moved on to churning out songs with lyrics, too. Although in respect of the latter, he may have had an ulterior motive to begin with at least. They cut alternate takes of one of his songs, 'Ocean'. He took the lead vocal on the first pass, Kim McCommas taking over for the second.

'Kim was a pretty good singer and she also played acoustic guitar,' says Denbow. 'She was a really nice girl and she and

Steve had a clandestine thing going on for a while there. They took it very seriously at the time and her parents were extremely protective. In retrospect, they probably weren't really boyfriend and girlfriend, but they hung out together a lot.'

As with most adolescent infatuations, this one would likely have cooled off in any circumstance. Smith's utter immersion with writing and recording his own music doubtless made it inevitable. At home in Cedar Hill, he convinced his mother to shift her upright electric piano into his bedroom. Once this was accomplished, he could shut his door and retreat into his own world. Along with his Gibson SG, a boom box and a mic, too, he spent hour upon hour locked away in his bedroom, writing, arranging and recording his own songs, filling up piles of cassette tapes. Sometimes he'd ask Denbow or Pickle over to play.

'He got obsessed with John Lennon's *Shaved Fish* album,' says Denbow. 'He learnt all the songs from it on piano. Then he took what he'd figured out from Lennon's songs and started to incorporate it into his own. I think this was probably the true genesis of him being a songwriter and of him moving towards doing something more original.

'Those times were probably the highlight of my childhood, and hopefully, his as well. I can still see him in my mind's eye, sat there on the bed with his spiked blond hair and his Gibson SG, and us playing songs together in his bedroom. Those are the images I kind of hang on to.'

So it was they passed through junior high. Sitting together knee to knee on a bed and playing music. Yet even then, there was something that set Steve Smith apart. His friends and bandmates, each of them bright and inquisitive boys, were as lit up as he was by those Saturday afternoon taping sessions. It was just that when Steve got his teeth into a thing, his appetite for it would be unquenchable.

'I don't think Steve ever really entertained the thought of doing anything else but being a musician,' says Denbow.

Dr Rachel Gillibrand is a chartered psychologist. She offers another perspective. 'That degree of focus is interesting,' she says. 'One of the things you see with an addiction is what is termed a "stunted dopamine hypothesis". The things that make the rest of us feel good actually don't make some people feel so good. They feel almost flat instead. They're driven to do more simply to get the same buzz as other people.'

The very same autumn of 1983, Smith went up with his friends to Duncanville High School. There, they carried on together in much the same vein. They all joined the Duncanville High School band, even though it was a marching band and too rigid and formal for their tastes. On the side of it, they broke off and formed their own more experimental ensemble of twelve brass and woodwind players. In the ensemble, they set to work rearranging one of Rush's most byzantine prog-rock epics, the eleven-minute-long 'Xanadu'. With this piece, they trained their sights on entering the Texas State-wide Inter-Scholastic League music competition, set to go ahead down in Austin at the start of the next year.

They recruited a sophomore girl named Michelle to play lead clarinet in their ensemble. Michelle was smart and sassy, but best of all, she drove her dad's muscle car to school. A deep sea-blue Pontiac GTO with a Grim Reaper figure spray-painted on the hood, no one missed seeing Michelle coming. Smith was smitten and the two of them hit it off. Michelle began running him and his friends around town. One night in mid-November, she drove them all over to Dallas to see the Police play the Reunion Arena on the Synchronicity tour. Michelle looked old enough to pick them up a six-pack of beer for the ride home, the GTO roaring its 370-horsepower symphony as they cruised through that long, dark Texan night.

How present and free Smith must have appeared to the rest of them just then. He was sat up front, next to Michelle, a can of Bud in his hand, smiling and laughing and radiant-looking. As if he was right where he needed to be and they would go on driving down those Texas roads together. Except, and although none of the others knew it just yet, he was already gone from them. On another long, dark and lonelier night, he had called his father up in Portland to plead with him. Told him he simply couldn't go on living in Charlie Welch's house and how one of them was sure to wind up dead if he did.

Whatever it was compelled Smith, he never did say publicly. It might have been a single, eruptive incident, or else a culmination of things. Either way, Gary Smith heard and heeded his fourteen-year-old son. He consented to have his boy move 2,000 miles cross-country to live with him and neither his mother or stepfather stood in the way of him going. The date set for his departure was just after New Year's, 1984. He wouldn't be competing with his friends down in Austin after all. Two weeks before he was due to go, he broke the news to them. He didn't make a big deal of it and they didn't press him for any deeper details.

His last Saturday in Duncanville was spent with Kevin Denbow. They went to a local water park, swam and joked around. Afterwards, they sat in the parking lot listening to a bootleg Beatles' tape Smith had mail-ordered. On it was an alternate version of 'Old Brown Shoe'. He persisted in winding the tape back to play it on repeat, as if Harrison's song were telling him a secret. That night, he slept over at Denbow's house. The two friends stayed up late, talking about music and vowing to stay in touch with each other. Before they drifted off to sleep at last, Smith suggested leaving behind with Denbow his beloved, broken Martin Sigma acoustic, telling him he didn't have a travel case for it.

'He said to me, "If you can fix this thing and get it to play, then you can have it,"' says Denbow. 'My dad had a little workshop out behind the house. I took it out there and worked on it. And I fixed it up to where it would pretty much play in tune. I still have it now. Over the years, the parts have worn down. It wasn't made of real bone but I suspect I could have it restored for $200 and it would play just fine again.'

PART 2

Portland, Oregon

CHAPTER 3

New Frontiers

You couldn't escape much farther from Texas and still be in the United States than Portland. All the way up there on the very tip of the Pacific Northwest. Sixty miles to the west of the city, there is nothing but ocean. Only Washington State and a 300-odd-mile drive due north separates Portland from the vast Canadian land mass. Just 50 miles to the north-east of the city limits, the ominous volcanic bulk of Mount St Helens rears up. Close enough to have powdered Portland in corpse-grey ash when it last erupted on 18 May 1980.

At one time, this was the outer limits of the American frontier. The first white settlers didn't begin fetching up at this far-flung point until the 1840s. A hardy band, they had hauled their wagons all the way across the country, 2,170 unforgiving miles along the length of the Oregon Trail. The town they gave rise to was just as teak-tough and weather-beaten as they were. Soon, its saloons, bordellos and gambling dens were filled with sailors, trappers and gold prospectors, the lot of them roistering and brawling and blowing off steam before heading back out into the wildernesses.

For more than a century, it was outsiders – industrialists and entrepreneurs from the East Coast, by and large – that prospered from exploiting Oregon's abundant natural resources. Timber, beaver pelt and salmon most particularly. It was Portlanders who did all of the grafting and the city sprang up, blue-collared and callused – until each of those resources got to be ruinously depleted, or else exhausted altogether, and then the money too drained out of the place. By the mid-1980s, Portland was also beginning to feel the full, ravaging, boom-to-bust effect of Reaganomics. High unemployment, swingeing cuts to social services, hollowed-out buildings and homelessness, not yet the gentrified city of today. It was six years out from the first Nike store throwing open its doors downtown. There were more dive bars than coffee shops. A trickle of tech companies, but this was a way off still from the stampede towards Silicon Forest.

In total, Portland in 1984 was a provincial, somewhat sleepy, out-of-the-way-seeming kind of place. Summers in the city are warm, but short. The rest of the year tends to being overcast and rain-drenched. Outwardly at least, Portlanders in general appeared unpretentious and no-nonsense. Commonly, they wore jeans, T-shirts, sneakers and work boots, and with a Docker Hat *de rigueur* for warding off the damp and cold – the very look Elliott Smith would go on to make his own.

Up to this point, the rock 'n' roll the city served up fitted the same overall picture. The best of it was hard-edged, abrasive and thoroughly uncompromising. In the '60s, Portland threw up a couple of primal-sounding garage rock combos, the Kingsmen, and Paul Revere and the Raiders, both of whom cut feral, yowling versions of an R&B standard, 'Louie Louie'. Throughout the late '70s and '80s, the city gave rise to such ferocious punk and hardcore bands as the Wipers, Neo Boys (actually four teenaged girls) and an imposing bunch named Poison Idea, who looked like renegade lumberjacks, or else backwoods serial killers.

As a matter of fact, three years down the line, it was Poison Idea who might even have best summed up all of the thoughts whirring in fourteen-year-old Steve Smith's head on the dull, wet day in January 1984 he landed in Portland. This was on a splenetic rant titled 'Lifestyles'. The band's hulking singer, Jerry A., vomited out these lyrics: 'I take the good with the bad, the bad with the bad, but I wish the bad would stop.'

Elliott's father, Gary Smith, had also remarried, to Marta Greenwald, a fellow psychotherapist. They lived with their baby daughter, Rachel, in a colonial-style house on the south-east side of the city. Portland was separated and demarked by the Willamette River, a major tributary of the Columbia River, just as surely as Duncanville was by its railway tracks. Traditionally, the west side of the river was seen as the prosperous side of town and in particular, the affluent hillside neighbourhoods rolling to the north-west. Up in the hills, a myopic view prevailed of the eastside, and especially the south-east, as the rough part of Portland.

In actual fact, there were plenty of leafy, upper-middle-class neighbourhoods on the so-called 'wrong' side of the river and the Smith-Greenwalds were comfortably off. Even so, west-side kids feared crossing the river and venturing into these supposed no-man's lands. Meanwhile their east-side counterparts carried the chip of this ignorance on their shoulders.

In certain ways, Smith was growing up to be a mirror image of his father. They were the same build physically, both quietly spoken but expressive with their facial expressions and idiosyncratic characters. His father and new stepmother sent him to a high school north of the river. Founded not so long after Portland itself in 1869, among Lincoln High's alumni were the renowned abstract artist Mark Rothko, Matt Groening, creator of *The Simpsons*, Mel Blanc, the voice of Bugs Bunny, Daffy Duck and Porky Pig, and a Space Shuttle pilot, S. David Griggs. Plenty of well-off west-side families sent their offspring to Lincoln High, but the school drew in kids from across the city through its International Baccalaureate language programme. Doubtless these east-siders were acutely aware it was they who were seen as interlopers in this territory.

As it would be throughout his life, Smith's entry point into Lincoln was through music. He joined Lincoln's marching band on clarinet. There was a kid in his chemistry class, Jason Hornick, who played guitar. Along with his friend Garrick Duckler, Hornick posted a note on the school noticeboard, looking to start up a band. Smith answered their call and Hornick invited him over to his parents' house one day after school to try out with them. Hornick and Duckler were both from West Hills families, but each of them wore it lightly. The three boys eased into a comfortable rhythm playing along with each other, Smith and Hornick trading guitar licks and Duckler plonking along with them on bass. According to Duckler, he formed a strong instant impression of Smith even before then.

'We were climbing the stairs to Jason's bedroom at a rapid pace,' he recalls. 'Why we always ran up and down stairs, and why we always washed our hands in cold water, became one of the topics the three of us discussed. I'd said something to Jason and Steve said from behind me, "You have a deep voice." It had a simple, direct and observational quality.

'I remember turning around and smiling at his comment. Thinking back on it now, there was something in it consistent in Steve throughout. An asocial impulse, language used to describe rather than provoke, a kindness in tone, a simple thing noted in plain sight and, if you listen closely, a very slight invitation to see what the other would do with his comment – like tossing a ball. I'm not sure if other people got this, but a lot of what Steve said had an undercurrent of relational communication.'

Another of Hornick's friends, Tony Lash, played flute in the school band and the drums, too. A year ahead of them at Lincoln, Lash was an acolyte of Neil Peart, Rush's virtuoso drummer, and fascinated also with the whole process of recording music. Inevitably, he also made an instant connection with Smith. One afternoon at band practice and for their own amusement, the two of them tried arranging a dissonant, out-of-key version of Robert Johnson's Delta blues standard, 'Hot Tamales'. But they were stopped in their tracks by an appalled trombone player threatening to beat the pair of them up.

'We thought it the most hilarious thing, but it drove everybody else insane,' says Lash. 'Steve was hilarious. He had a really dry sense of humour and he was very smart academically. I wasn't otherwise massively social in high school. I only kept a few friends, so I didn't necessarily have a good barometer on how he compared to other kids. To me, he was just always there doing his own thing and writing songs. It's only in retrospect I can look back and appreciate how talented and ambitious he was with music.'

Smith quickly fell into writing songs with Duckler, who penned lyrics. Besides music, the two of them shared a mutual love for reading and a predilection for scrutinising the inner workings of their own minds. As Duckler sees it, 'Calling ours a friendship doesn't quite fit. It was more like we were living in each other's psycho-emotional worlds.' Through Duckler and Hornick, Smith was drawn into a small, radiant set at Lincoln. The members of their creative, intellectually minded clique would subsequently go out into the world to become doctors, writers, professors, artists and a renowned singer-songwriter.

The others in their orbit were Glynnis Fawkes, Duckler's girlfriend, Shannon White, Smith's girlfriend for a while, Susan Pagani, Shauna Hannibal and Alice Vosmek. Together, they were self-enclosed, insular, revelling in their own company. When he was with them, Smith felt among his kind of people and yet even so, apart and unknowable at the same time, too.

'Steve really had no friends other than the rest of us,' says Duckler. 'If anything, people at Lincoln actively were put off him, or else treated him without much notice. He wasn't prickly, but was often unsmiling. He wore kind of beat-up clothes and always seemed to be looking to see if anyone was giving him dirty looks. Jason's mum said some disparaging things about his clothes once, but his ripped jeans and nylon shirts always were in stark contrast to Jason and me, the goody-goods.'

'I don't think I ever got to know anything quickly about Steve,' says Glynnis Fawkes. 'I can remember he got a tattoo on his arm that read, "Don't mess with Texas", which I thought was outrageous. Mostly, he was understated and would be on the edge of things. It wasn't like he was a rock star walking down the school halls and the crowd would part for him.'

CHAPTER 4

Strange Days

To begin with, Smith and his friends back in Duncanville were able to keep to their promises to each other to stay in touch. During Smith's first spring break at Lincoln, Pickle flew up north for a visit. He brought with him his keyboards and the two of them resumed playing together in Smith's bedroom. The same summer of 1985, Smith made the return trip down to Texas. On this occasion, Pickle arranged for their Duncanville band to reassemble and so Smith got to sing a bittersweet harmony one more time with pretty Kim McCommas.

He went back to Duncanville the summer following, too, and Kevin Denbow recalls being his chauffeur around town. The two of them idled away those long, hot days riding around in Denbow's pickup truck, Pink Floyd's *The Wall* cranked up on the cassette deck. It was as if nothing had changed between them – except, of course, in reality the only thing not to ever change was the very reason Smith fled from Duncanville in the first place: he didn't want to be around his stepfather for any longer than he had to. Soon enough, the gaps between his trips home to Texas got longer and the length of his visits grew shorter.

'We still saw him at Christmases when he'd come home to see his mum,' says Denbow. 'He just grew further away as time went on. We'd speak by mail or phone, but there would be years in between.'

The first year he was living in Portland, Smith forged ahead with the new band he'd joined alongside Jason Hornick and Garrick Duckler. They arranged to borrow a four-track tape machine, an old Tascam with knobs the size of door handles, and a pretty good mic, a Shure SM57. Smith fell back into the steadying rhythm of recording sessions at one or another's house. For the purposes of these the three friends employed a drum machine they christened 'Dr Rhythm'. Smith played guitar and piano and sang. By the end of their first school year at Lincoln, they had given their band a name – Stranger Than Fiction. They were also satisfied with enough of the songs they'd put to tape to grandly conceive of making an album all of their own.

They were good and ready to send this out into the world – or distribute it around Portland at least – by June of 1985. Altogether, they made up a couple of hundred or so cassette tapes, each one replete with a white inlay card upon which was a photocopied black ink depiction of an array of cartoon hens and a scrawled title, *Any Kind of Mudhen*. For the major part, they handed this batch of tapes out to friends and acquaintances at school, although they also persuaded the manager of a downtown record store, Django's, to put a few copies out for sale at the princely sum of $3.99. As for the actual music . . . well, it sounded tinny and muddily mixed to be sure, but the dexterity of the playing is clear enough and likewise the pronounced Rush influence. The thirteen tracks included on the tape were twitchy, spasmodic and with a surfeit of lunging tempo changes. As for Smith's vocals, he pitched his voice high like Rush's lead vocalist Geddy Lee and keening.

At the beginning of their sophomore year, they talked Tony Lash, their senior by a year, into throwing his lot in with them on drums. The four of them were now diligent about rehearsing. At Lincoln, there were practice rooms out the back of the main music classroom, with a drum kit and a piano to hand. Daily, they would gather in one or other of these rooms, during whatever free time they could grab before or after school band practice. Outside of Lincoln, they assembled at one of each other's houses, or else piled round to a West Hills friend of Lash's, Eric Hedford, who would go on to drum with another band out of Portland, the Dandy Warhols. Set up in Hedford's bedroom or his parents' basement, the whir of the old Tascam was their other constant accompaniment.

'It was earnest, and also fun, but it could be stressful, too,' says Lash. 'With the complexity of the songs, this was very ambitious stuff for a bunch of sixteen-, seventeen-year-old kids to be taking on. We'd be playing a really long, complicated song and then right at the end of it, I'd do a big drum flub and we'd have to go back and repeat the whole thing all over again. Recording meant going over to Eric's house, because he had drums, a piano, mics and a mixer. I remember Eric's parents in the main, because their patience got to be worn pretty thin.

'In general, we meshed pretty well. We definitely all shared a certain kind of humour. Everyone was really smart. Garrick wrote all of the lyrics, he always seemed to me to be more distant than the other two. My seriousness was towards the production aspect. Even then, this chafed at Elliott – Steve – a bit. I was really into Trevor Horn and all of this highly produced music. He was into rawer-sounding stuff such as Elvis Costello or the Clash. I hated the sound degradation you get from bouncing tracks on a cassette four-track. There would be tension between us, he could be frustrated with me at times.'

During the autumn semester at Lincoln, they completed their second cassette album, titled *Still Waters More or Less*. The thirteen songs featured were still schizophrenic-sounding but had better honed arrangements, as if they were moving towards a point of light. There was another two-tone, black-on-white print on the inlay card cover and this time a portrait of the band. Four unsmiling, inscrutable-looking young men pictured stood behind, or else climbed up onto, a set of steel railings. As if here also they were striving to break out, to run free.

Duckler's girlfriend Glynnis Fawkes took the photograph. 'I ended up taking lots of pictures of them,' she recalls. 'They always did look serious in their photographs, but I also remember them often joking around. Steve was stoic in front of the camera. I seem to recall him wearing sunglasses a lot. He had a way of looking down and a very slow smile. It was always great to see him smile when he was playing. The four of them would share these looks and you'd know they were communicating with each other.'

They made their public debut one lunchtime at Lincoln. It was an inglorious occasion, their schoolmates left nonplussed by their vaulting progressive rock. Their short, jittery set was met with smatterings of polite applause, but more shuffled feet and blank looks. This, after all, was a year in which the sounds reigning on MTV and American FM radio were of airbrushed pop and blow-dried soft-rock – Madonna and Janet Jackson, Mr Mister and Starship.

'The other kids just didn't know what to make of us,' says Lash. 'Certain people, I think, were impressed by the level of technical accomplishment, but it wasn't as though we got elevated within the general population of the school. We were too nerdy for that.'

Between times, Smith revealed certain other parts of himself at Lincoln. As in Duncanville, he was at his most animated whenever he happened to be playing, listening to, or talking about music and which he did more often than anything else. These were the channels through which he gave himself over. Outside of music, he retained his passions for reading, video games and basketball especially. Though joyful, he looked awkward and ungainly around a basketball court.

He grew close to Jason Hornick, but tightest of all with Garrick Duckler. Duckler's father was a psychologist. The bookshelves in his bedroom at home were every bit as crammed as Smith's. In

neither of their cases were these more regular teenager staples –
J. R. R. Tolkien, say, or Stephen King – but, rather, heavyweight
volumes on psychology and literary classics. Both of their tastes
extended to Russian literature in particular, and in Smith's case,
the works of Fyodor Dostoevsky most of all. His attraction to
Dostoevsky was instant, intense and obvious. Dostoevsky, too,
grew up in a devoutly religious household, raised by a strict and
unbending father. His greatest works – *Crime and Punishment, The
Idiot, The Brothers Karamazov* – are not only the most profound
literary examinations of the human condition, but were just as
much exorcisms for his own demons.

'Dostoevsky was, to Steve, like a mirror into his soul,' says
Duckler. 'His need to create a morality in an immoral universe,
the author's powers of psychological evaluation, the relationship between sadness and fear, the hysteria of throwing oneself
at one's love immediately followed by a whole bunch of rash
things, the abusive relationship with his father . . . Everything
about him was so perfectly Steve.

'There was one time Steve was over at my parents' house and
we were hanging out in my room. He picked up my copy of
Nabokov's *Lectures on Russian Literature*. He saw from the table of
contents one of the lectures was on Dostoevsky. In this lecture,
Nabokov said a bunch of terrible things about Dostoevsky. Steve
was torn apart by reading it – so much so that he lay down on my
bed and fell asleep. I was very affected by this at the time, how
deeply personal it was for him. When he woke up, he apologised
to me. I told him his falling asleep was a compliment. Safety was
not exactly easy for him.'

In all of Smith's interactions, there was always this other, more troubling aspect. Occasionally, one might catch a passing glimpse of it in plain sight. Mostly, it remained under, but still not so very far below the surface. There like a nag or an itch, or something scuttled to a dark corner. It was a persistent sense of everything not being right with him. The feeling there was a weight pressing down upon him and with it, however indistinct or subconscious this sometimes was, a reason enough to fear for him.

One might catch his mood shifting or see him cloud over, the light dim or go out altogether in his eyes. Or then again, be a witness to one of his rarer eruptions. Just as in Duncanville and with the jocks in the parking lot at Byrd, at Lincoln and in spite of his slight stature, he wouldn't back down from a confrontation. Then there were those times he even appeared to want to initiate one.

'It would be wrong to say Steve got into fights at school really,' says Duckler. 'Or at least, to say he would want to get into fights, although on the surface this is what it looked like. To take one instance, Steve played on the basketball team with me at Lincoln. During one game and somehow through a series of dirty looks, he got someone on the opposing team to foul him and which he then retaliated to on court.

'When we were driving away in his Datsun after the game, a rock was thrown at the car. Steve circled the parking lot. As we drove around, I noted he was fighting back his impulse to attack his attacker, tears in his eyes. Not wanting to become the same kind of monster who'd done things to him. I believe this pattern of having people attack him was a deeply unconscious impulse to recreate an early childhood scenario. His incumbent feelings of wanting to retaliate, but also wanting to flee, staving off the worry he'd brought on such an attack. This was replayed over and over again in his life.'

Mark Buchanan, like Tony Lash, was a year ahead of Smith and his friends at Lincoln. He, too, was a budding musician and played guitar in another of their high school's bands, Danny and the Originals. Their stock in trade was '50s and '60s covers, which is to say they were a lighter-hearted group one might sing and dance along to and so nothing at all like Stranger Than Fiction. Buchanan recalls speculation even then about what made Smith tick. Why it was he would fall to brooding and the air surrounding him got to be heavy. Why he wasn't ever quite as easy as the others to be around.

'It was clear there was something he was grappling with, but it also never made us not like him,' Buchanan says. 'The whole of his school group was focused on this question of making meaning in a variety of ways. In this respect, Steve fit right in.

'In a sense, we had the beginning of a notion Steve had grabbed onto some pain. Whether or not this pain was something the rest of us could understand or relate to, it defined the universe for him. It informed his choices. His art, like a pearl, was built like a kernel around his resignation, resentment, anger and his hurt. He constructed a narrative he didn't share with us, except through the music, and so you didn't know what the grit was really, you just saw the pearls.'

'There were outward examples of what I would consider to be some of the many paradoxes he contained,' recalls Duckler.

'Namely, those of a person who dreaded, feared, wished for and brought about attacks on himself and whose involvement in literature and philosophy had a reality all of its own.

'He seemed to me like someone who was given respite from all of this by forming the friendships he had in our band. Recently, his father, Gary, told me the first time he saw Steve with Jason and me he thought to himself, "Oh boy, I hope these guys like Steve. They seem so nice." We did – deeply.'

All the while he was at Lincoln, Smith went on making music with Stranger Than Fiction. They completed their third cassette album in the autumn of 1986. It was titled *Waiting for the Second Hand* and their four faces once again adorned the cover art. Superimposed onto a clock face, they were studious-looking and unsmiling. The songs balanced the same mix of vaulting ambition with gauche cliché. On this occasion, Glynnis Fawkes contributed lyrics to one of the more ornate songs, 'Egypt'. It was, she says, 'a very silly song and no, I'd never been to Egypt.'

Another track, 'Fast Food', was a wholly different matter. A powerhouse of a song Smith worked up in his bedroom, it was set to an urgent, rolling rhythm and demonstrated his sharpening sense of melody. As it unfolds, the stronger the impression grows that this is Smith truly beginning to open up his wings as a songwriter and metamorphosing. A good enough song at any rate for him to have revived it twenty years later and for the last album he would ever get to finish.

'There are some songs he wrote back then that are as good as any he did, in my opinion at least,' says Mark Buchanan. 'Clearly, he had some inherent gifts. He was already very good as a musician and a songwriter. He was somebody to pay attention to.'

As a band, Stranger Than Fiction were also starting to get out of their bedrooms and basements and play more to actual audiences. They performed at a couple of private arts colleges in the city, Reed and Lewis & Clark, the second of these shows along with Danny and the Originals. They did a west-side Jewish synagogue's youth club dance, punctuating their set with a cover of the Beatles' 'Blackbird', and another dance at a West Hills elementary school, Ainsworth. At Ainsworth, Smith sang Bob Dylan's 'Ballad of a Thin Man' with such intense conviction he found himself afterwards surrounded by a gaggle of chirping sixth-graders wanting his autograph.

Headier still, they were invited to play at Lincoln's homecoming dance. For this auspicious event, they served up another Beatles' song, 'Lucy in the Sky with Diamonds', and one by Genesis, 'Abacab'. The robotically parping Genesis song brought their schoolmates rushing onto the makeshift dancefloor.

'The cafeteria at Lincoln was dismal, but I remember having the best time dancing to "Abacab",' says Glynnis Fawkes.

At such moments, visibly Smith's load might also appear to lighten and lift from him. He would start to stand straight-backed and not as he did more typically, slouching over and shrunken inwards. At first, there would be just the flicker of a smile playing at the corners of his mouth. Then, as gradual but wondrous as the sun coming up, this would turn into a full-watt, beaming grin, his whole face transforming. This much happened at another show he got lost in with the band. It was organised for the Russian Club at Lincoln and went ahead at Glynnis Fawkes' family home up in the West Hills. Especially for this show, they choreographed a routine to go along with the Beatles' 'When I'm Sixty-Four'. A funny little kick-dance Smith performed mid-set with Duckler and Hornick, and as Lash sat behind them rat-tat-tatting Ringo Starr's shuffling beat.

'When I saw those three guys doing their dance together, it was almost like, "Well, we're not hung up on what the gender norms are for American high school boys,"' says Mark Buchanan, who was in attendance. 'We didn't have those precise words yet, but we felt it. I'm not saying we were ahead of gender curves in any way, but there was nothing macho or toxic about it. It was both confident and comfortable. There was rather so much joy of music and love of friendship, and solace, too.'

In other snapshots from his senior year at Lincoln, Smith seemed to fit in just as well as he did the Texas night he thundered home from Dallas, riding shotgun in a deep-sea blue Pontiac GTO – three years and a lifetime ago. There was the Halloween party his father and stepmother let him throw at their house. His friends crossed the river for it in their fancy dress. They ended up shrieking and running around the gravestones of a nearby cemetery. Midnight struck to the sound of their wild, careless laughter. Whatever hauntings and horrors Smith carried around with him were momentarily forgotten and left to lurk in the shadows.

There were nights too when Hornick took them out cruising in the shiny big Suburban he'd learned to drive in. Circling the blocks downtown, Smith sat up front or else wedged in the backseats with Duckler and the girls. It was another small act of rebellion, since the city operated a 'no cruising' policy. Nothing left to do if the cops pulled them over but get out and walk.

'One of those nights, I ended up walking around with Steve, Jason and Garrick, being bored,' recalls Glynnis Fawkes. 'There was a shop sign Steve pointed out. It read, "Orthodontics for Adults". He went and stood in front of this sign and broke out into song, singing the words on it, over and again in different voices. I was doubled over laughing. Steve was so quiet usually, but there he was, suddenly not afraid of whoever heard or saw him.'

Once more, though, Smith had plotted his route out and far away. After Lincoln, he was bound for the opposite side of the country, to Amherst, Massachusetts, and Hampshire College, a prestigious institution for the academically gifted. Although just then perhaps the strongest force pulling him east was the fact he'd be following his girlfriend Shannon White, who'd accepted an offer from Hampshire first.

His final term together with Hornick and Duckler at Lincoln, he cut one last tape with Stranger Than Fiction. They called this one *Menagerie* and it, too, marked a leap ahead. The songs were sharper-pointed, Smith's singing voice more confident and forceful-sounding; the sum of it grasping towards the taut arrangements and baroque flourishes of Smith's favourite Elvis Costello album, 1982's *Imperial Bedroom*. On the inlay card, he credited himself as 'Johnny Panic', as if he was testing out a new skin already ahead of his next move.

'Changing his name was a laugh, but serious at the same time,' says Mark Buchanan. 'What seemed like the obvious part of his struggles was he never settled, he was always moving. Changing one's name calls attention to oneself. Was it an act of defiance? Like, "I get to choose who I am and to reject the pieces of my past".

'At Lincoln, being a seeker was part of our collective identity. We cared about why things were the way they were and where we fit in the mix. We cared about how the personal fit with the universal. I suspect there are kids at every high school who raise those kinds of questions. Part of the reason Elliott Smith took off, I think, is enough people recognised themselves in what he had to say, what he struggled with and in his pain.'

CHAPTER 5

Still Waters

A smallish, leafy town with a population of around 35,000, Amherst sits among the rolling hills, lush forest glades and fertile farmlands of the Pioneer Valley. The Connecticut River flows along the town's western borders. The city of Boston lies 90-odd miles and a couple of hours' drive to the east. Attractive and welcoming, Amherst appears to the first-time visitor genteel, easy-paced and an altogether pleasant place to have pitched up at. Or, as the poet Emily Dickinson, born in Amherst in 1830, felt moved to write: 'Oh, a very great town this is!'

The economic lifeblood of the town is drawn from its famed Five Colleges – Amherst College, Smith College, Mount Holyoke College, the University of Massachusetts and Hampshire College. Collectively, each of these institutions burnished Amherst's reputation as a hotbed for free, liberal and radical thinking. Founded in 1970, Hampshire was the newest and most out-there of the five. From its inception, Hampshire set itself at the vanguard of an alternative brand of education. At Hampshire, there were no academic departments, tenured faculty or grades given out. Hampshire's students were entirely free to study what they wanted, how they wanted and for as long as they wanted.

Fast becoming one of the hardest colleges in the country to get into, Hampshire was able to prize-pick the most gifted applicants. There was a pretty price to pay for being gilded with entry though. With annual fees of $20,000, Hampshire was at the time one of the most expensive colleges in the country to attend. By the end of the decade, around half the student intake required financial support from the college with their fees. Smith was among the class of 1987 to take up grant aid. With its verdant grounds and avenues of trees, the whole atmosphere the Hampshire campus gave off was one of privilege and exceptionalism – 'The school had a silver spoon in its mouth,' Chip Brown, a Hampshire graduate, wrote in a *New York Times* article published in June 1990, Smith's third summer of college.

'[The] students look the same, too,' Brown continued. 'Backpacks and sneakers, blue jeans with holes in the knee, a certain scruffy air . . . Clothes, intellectual positions and even behaviour are governed by the code of the "politically correct", which is to say antisexist, antiracist, anti-homophobic, anti-speciesism.'[4]

Smith was enrolled to study for a degree in philosophy and political science. He was shape-shifting almost upon entry into this rarefied world. Steve Smith was simply too much of a dull, run-of-the-mill ordinary, jock-sounding name for him to go by at Hampshire, he decreed. Neither was 'Johnny Panic' any more suited. Together with Shannon White, he dreamed up a second joke name for himself. He was digging at Hampshire's sense of entitlement in the process with 'Elliott Stillwater-Rotter'. The additional 't' in Elliott was White's shout. Perhaps he was taken with how different and not quite right it looked written down. At all events, he soon enough paired this new Christian name with his given surname instead to become Elliott Smith. He never got around to making the change official though. On his passport, bank statements and in all of his other personal documents, he was to forever remain 'Steve Smith'. It might have been he didn't want to let go of his true self altogether, or, more likely, it was indicative of his carelessness for such everyday details.

His first few weeks at Hampshire were otherwise eventful. His relationship with White didn't survive the jolt of landing and quickly petered out. They were to stay platonic friends, but not nearly so close and never again boyfriend and girlfriend. As soon as the very first week, Smith was beginning to form the strongest, and most enduring, attachment of his college life.

As a first-year student, Smith was housed in one of the apartment blocks on campus, Enfield House. His four flatmates were Carl Germann, Jane Weatherbee, Mandy Daramin and Neil Gust. Born in New York but raised in Iowa, Gust was gay but not yet out. Tall, gangling and good-looking, he couldn't help but make an instant impression. He too was a music nut. Like Smith, he'd grown up listening to the Beatles and Led Zeppelin and gone on to become a disciple of Elvis Costello's. Gust's mother also had paid for him to take classical music lessons, albeit on guitar, and he had passed through high school making his own four-track recordings. Needless to say, the two of them were immediately drawn to each other.

With Gust, Smith started up at Hampshire the exact same cycle familiar from his time in Portland and Duncanville before. The pair of them began testing out their common ground through long, excited conversations about music. They took trips together into nearby Northampton, Amherst's next-door town, to browse the racks at Main Street Records, renowned as the best record store in this western corner of the state. The clinching stage was next and the more intimate act of sharing songs of their own with each other. They sat knee-to-knee on a sofa, or on either of their beds, a couple of acoustic guitars propped in their laps, the songs passing back and forth between them like relay batons.

'Elliott would play me one of his songs, or I'd play him one of mine, and the other would join in and play along,' Gust told David Greenwald of *The Oregonian*. 'We would show each other our lyrics and point out what we liked. I always felt I was on the right track if I got him interested.'[5]

Inevitably, following on from this stage, Smith and Gust got around to putting their music to tape. They were able to hire a four-track machine and mics from the college. These taping sessions went ahead in their dorm room, or on one occasion in the stairwell of Enfield House, the better to capture a reverbing sound. This last, impromptu bout of recording was curtailed by a group of their block-mates who, riled by the noise, made off with all the mics the pair had set out at strategic points up the stairs.

Going into their second semester at Hampshire, Smith thought up a name for their acoustic duo – Swimming Jesus. Saddled with this unedifying handle, they played their first few shows together, at the coffee shop on campus or else one over in Northampton. Smith and Gust both sang and they peppered the original songs in their short sets with covers – the Beatles, Elvis Costello and Tom Waits. For Smith, these outings with Gust were a blessed relief from his studies.

In certain respects, he seemed the model Hampshire student. Just as self-disciplined and laser-focused in regard to his course work as with his music. He even looked the part, with his ever-present worn-out jeans, backpack and bed hair. The trouble was he didn't, or else couldn't, let up on himself. He wasn't so much taking his chosen subject as utterly immersing himself in it, precisely as he had gorged on Dostoevsky in high school and as if it were the be-all and end-all. Specifically, he devoured the writings of two radical feminist activists, Catharine A. MacKinnon and Andrea Dworkin. MacKinnon, who led crusades against sex discrimination and pornography, affected him the most deeply: 'If you're a straight white man, she made it impossible to live your life without constantly doing something shitty,' he told R. J. Smith of *Spin* in 1999.[6]

Up to Hampshire, Smith's depressive episodes appeared fleeting, passing clouds blown off in a breeze. Now, they got to be heavier, darker, longer-hanging. There were whole days at a time when he would shut himself away in his bedroom. He complained more readily of stomach aches and wouldn't eat. At a balanced point, he would be quiet going on silent, self-effacing and with a tendency to fade into the background like a Polaroid in reverse. So withdrawn, blank-faced and not-quite-right, he could make his fellow students feel uncomfortable being around him. His upswings were also appearing more extreme. Those nights, his was the loudest, most drunken voice at a party on campus. This was how Garrick Duckler found his friend when he visited him at Hampshire.

'The only time I ever saw Elliott dancing was when he uncharacteristically dragged me onto the dancefloor at Hampshire, saying, "Come on, Garrick, bust a move, just bust a move!"' Duckler recalls.

'He wasn't drunk, or even taking drugs that much yet. Looking back on the moment, I can see why I felt so confused. There was a quality inside his plea I didn't know how to react to, something scary. Like someone who doesn't know if he's living in a nightmare. Or else, if he *was* living in a nightmare and things were different now.'

At the end of his first college year, Smith caught up with Duckler and also Jason Hornick, back in Portland. This was the summer of 1988 and they spent the better part of it once again cruising downtown. Hornick at the wheel, an R.E.M. album, *Lifes Rich Pageant*, blasting from the stereo, Hornick and Smith dissecting Peter Buck's chord progressions, Duckler and Smith fathoming Michael Stipe's oblique lyrics as the neon night turned to a pink-hued dawn. Inspiration enough for Smith and Duckler at least to slip back into making music with each other. They called upon Tony Lash, working as an apprentice engineer at a local studio, to oversee their latest round of recording.

It was a different kind of music they made now, and from a changed perspective. More assured, more questing, these new songs of theirs were alternately quirky and fitful, Elvis Costello-style, or else angular and obtuse like R.E.M., or, then again, prettily attired and folksy, but also harder-hitting. Smith aped Costello, too, with his singing, and in particular by approximating his strangulated kind of upper range. His Costello voice is to the fore on a song Duckler wrote the words to, 'Condor Avenue'. The title refers to a Portland address and where Duckler's older brother was at the time working as a lawyer. The song's finger-picked acoustic intro, meanwhile, set a course Smith was bound to follow.

They went by the name A Murder of Crows on the resulting cassette album, *The Greenhouse*. The cover of the tape featured two photos taken by Glynnis Fawkes once again: one a portrait of Duckler wearing a white jacket and the other of Smith, his hands clasped tight to his head, his hair long, unruly and blond. On the inlay card, Smith reverted to crediting himself Elliott Stillwater-Rotter. One song in particular stood out from the pack once the tape was circulating among their Portland friends. It was another acoustic track, titled 'Shotgun'. A desolate ballad, with Smith's vocal pitched low and seeming disconnected, it closed with a mantra all the more menacing for sounding so matter of fact: 'Shotgun, I got a shotgun . . . Oh, little boy, I've got a shotgun.'

'Even today, those lyrics pop straight into my mind,' says Mark Buchanan. 'They're ominous and terrifying still, and damn, they're hard to forget. They haunt me.'

For his second year at Hampshire, Smith moved off campus with Gust and out to Northampton. He fretted over the rising scale of his student loan, a dead-weight millstone around his neck, and took odd jobs in town to go towards paying it off. For a time, he worked as a laboratory assistant, charged with taking care of the lab dogs being experimented on at the facility. Not the kind of labour to shout about among the anti-speciesism activists at Hampshire and where he continued for the most part to keep his head down, a ghost figure in their midst.

Even Neil Gust wasn't made privy to all his machinations. Outside of Swimming Jesus, Smith started up another musical project. This one was a full band, loosely arranged at this point around three or four other Hampshire lads and hinged upon intermittent practice sessions. It was months before he brought this activity to Gust's attention and invited him into the fold. Gust's entry to their ranks spurred Smith to think of a name for this new group as well. He christened them Heatmiser, after a brand of thermostat – better than Swimming Jesus, but not by much. The sound they began aiming at was also louder, electric, more abrasive and not nearly so easy on the ear.

Their push towards this came from a loosely aligned collection of bands percolating in the fecund undergrounds of American music. These bands carried on out of sight of the mainstream, but their records were fast becoming staples of college radio and in the racks at Main Street Records. At any rate, theirs was an altogether rousing distraction from the regular rounds of poetry readings, student demos and panic-and-stress workshops going on at Hampshire.

The principal outriders for this movement were two bands from opposite sides of the country. Rampaging out of Southern California in the late '70s, by the mid-'80s the boiling rage at the core of Black Flag's blunt-force anthems was stoked by their own grinding poverty. This, and the seething angst of their charismatic frontman, Henry Rollins, a heavily tattooed, musclebound human pit bull transplanted to them from Washington, DC. As a teenager coming of age in his hometown, Rollins buddied up with a wirier, but just as intense kid named Ian MacKaye. It was MacKaye who went on to form the second of these trailblazing bands, Minor Threat, and whose warp-speed songs were as tightly wound as their leader.

Following in the footsteps of Black Flag and Minor Threat, a fleet of like-minded groups had sprung out from cities all across America. There was Hüsker Dü and the Replacements from Minneapolis and arty Sonic Youth from New York, sheathing their droning, dissonant songs in blizzards of distortion. More local to Hampshire, there were the Pixies out of Boston and Dinosaur Jr. from Amherst itself. Back up in the Pacific Northwest, Mudhoney in Seattle and an awkward-looking bunch from the logging town of Aberdeen, Nirvana, whose debut studio album, *Bleach* (1989), was to land at Main Street Records as Smith was finishing up his second year of college. Most of all, Smith was struck by Ian MacKaye's next band, Fugazi, just then finding their feet. Fugazi's attack was still fuelled by MacKaye's own righteous anger, but there was a more precise edge to their weaponry, their songs complex, angular and as sharp-pointed as razor wire.

Nevertheless, Smith left these new templates to one side when he returned to Portland for summer break and to form one last collective with Duckler, Hornick and Lash. This one they called Harum Scarum. They rehearsed and recorded at a studio complex housed in a re-converted old warehouse, a couple of blocks west of the river, the Palace. For the most part they were easy with each other, but the mood spiked whenever it was time to put the songs to tape. Once more, it was Smith and Lash who butted heads.

'There was that same tension again between us,' recalls Lash. 'I'd worked on more guitar-band records by then and I was getting more versatile. Elliott would still want things to be less polished than I did. He had, though, definitely made great strides with his songwriting.'

They titled the finished cassette *Trick of Paris Season*. For the first time on the liner notes, Smith listed himself as 'Elliott Smith'. Nine of the ten songs are credited to Smith and Duckler, the remaining one to all four of them. The range of these songs, the assurance with which they cover ground, bears out Lash's assertion. 'This Bed' is a crepuscular ballad. 'Bald Faced Lie' has a half-spoken vocal from Smith and the whirring musical air of a fairground. Most captivating of all is the urgent, driving

'Catholic', sung by Smith in his best Elvis Costello sneer. These were songs by someone racing ahead.

'Catholic' was another song Smith was to rekindle further on down the line and under a different title, 'Everybody Cares, Everybody Understands'. He would pen a new set of lyrics for it, too. One of the lines he was to write nine years later actually sums up precisely where he was at right around then and also where he was primed to go off to. As he was to sing it in 1998: 'You've got a pretty vision in your head, a pencil full of poison lead.'

CHAPTER 6

Teen Spirit

Smith spent two more years at Hampshire. Out in the wider world during this time, the first McDonald's was opened in Moscow. On their TV screens, Americans watched four LAPD officers beat a black man, Rodney King, and Operation Desert Storm unfold as if it were a video war game. Detectives in Milwaukee discovered the brutalised remains of eleven men and boys in an apartment belonging to Jeffrey Dahmer. One of the hot topics on campus was a sexual harassment case brought by *Boston Herald* reporter Lisa Olson against the local gridiron team, the New England Patriots, and three of its star players.

At Hampshire, Smith carried on playing with Neil Gust in Swimming Jesus and Heatmiser. With both groups, he practised often but performed intermittently and at a rate of about one show each semester. He didn't go home to Portland at all during the summer break of 1990, staying on in Northampton to work odd jobs and chip away at his student loan. By his own account, it was a dispiriting time for him.

'Over the summer, all of the rednecks would come out in Northampton,' he told a fanzine writer seven years later. 'They would drive down the street calling me a faggot.' Even still, he added, 'it wasn't as bad as actually being on the college campus.'[7]

Conceivably spurred to get himself out of Hampshire, Smith kept up a certain level of self-discipline with his studies. The Hampshire ethos allowed students an elastic time-frame to work towards their degrees. He successfully completed his BA in a relatively rigorous four years. By the following summer, he was contemplating his future away from Hampshire. Principally, he was scheming with Neil Gust on where best to strike out for next and for them to go on being in a band together. Their options narrowed to either Portland or Chicago. They picked out Chicago at least in part because it was home to one of their favourite new bands, Urge Overkill.

There was, too, one thing nagging at Smith: there was, he felt, an obstacle to their friendship, a barrier Gust put up and which he hadn't been able to breach. He finally confronted him about it at a Fourth of July party in Boston. Gust recalled the moment in 2007: '[Elliott] asked me why sometimes I would act like I wasn't his friend. I knew exactly what he was talking about. I realised, "Okay, if we're going to live together, then I have to tell him I'm gay and he is going to be the first person I've told."

'It's hard to explain. We had a roommate, a gay guy who had a crush on me. I didn't reciprocate his feelings. Then he and Elliott became really close friends and I sometimes thought they were friends at my expense. As a result, I would sometimes act like an asshole to Elliott. We were nineteen, twenty years old. Not fully developed emotionally. We went outside for a walk and I just blurted it out. I started to cry and he was completely amazing. We sat down on the kerb and talked for a very, very long time. He was the only person who knew for another six months.'[8]

The two of them eventually settled on Portland as their destination after Hampshire. Gust's was the casting vote. In the main because he had liked Tony Lash's drumming on the Harum Scarum tape Smith played him. Along with Gust, Smith returned to his adopted home city in the late summer of 1991. They arrived on the cusp of a new music scene bubbling up in Portland. The independent spirit firing it was drawn down the Pacific Northwest coast from Seattle, where the grunge sound was fermenting on local indie label Sub Pop and even more acutely from another Washington State city, Olympia.

Specifically, it radiated out from a second radical and free-thinking college institution, Olympia's Evergreen State. Fugazi and Nirvana both played early shows at Evergreen and the college's radio station, KAOS, was a well-established bastion of alternative music, the more obscure the better. Olympia's version of Sub Pop was K Records, founded in 1982 by an Evergreen student, Calvin Johnson. As Sub Pop was majoring in the bludgeoning likes of Soundgarden, Mudhoney and Tad, K Records leaned towards more offbeat fare.

In Portland, the nascent scene popped around a few blocks of downtown and a handful of dimly lit clubs. Principally, these were La Luna, the X-Ray Café, EJ's and, scuzziest of all, Satyricon, with its peeling paint, glutinous floor and reek of stale sweat and piss. If these venues best befit Seattle's grunge, the bands forming to play at them were by and large quirkier and more like their Olympia counterparts. In the space of a year, their ranks included a punk-pop trio, Crackerbash, Pond, Sprinkler, the Spinanes, and Trailer Queen, an all-female band fully reflective of a fanzine launched out of Olympia the same summer, *Riot Grrrl*. Perhaps most typical of the Portland bands was Hazel. Their breakneck brand of noise-pop was augmented on stage by the presence of their bearded dancer, Fred Nemo, who delighted in prancing about dolled up in a pink tutu. A disparate lot all told, but collectively they set off the low-hum crackle of *something* going on in Portland.

'Up to this point, Portland was a sort of musical backwater,' says Pete Krebs, singer and guitarist with Hazel. 'It was a place for bands to stop between Seattle and San Francisco when they were doing a West Coast tour, but it wasn't known for much of anything.'

'Portland's was a scene started out of innocence,' adds Chris Slusarenko, bass player with Sprinkler. 'None of us had any expectations. If you were going to be played on your local college rock station, it amounted to total success.'

At a stroke, one record released on 24 September 1991 changed everything for the indie-rock bands sprouting in Portland and in cities and towns all over the country. On the back of it, their underground rumblings were raised to a full-throttle, airborne clamour. The previous New Year's Eve, Nirvana had played a show at Satyricon. Their frontman, Kurt Cobain, saw in 1991 wrestling on its rancid floor with a woman he had only just met. She was a loud, brattish, sometime denizen of Portland by the name of Courtney Love. Nirvana was at the time still touring their *Bleach* album for Sub Pop, but in the process of moving over to major label Geffen Records to make their follow-up. Upon arrival, *Nevermind* didn't so much kick down doors as scorch the whole earth. It was certified Gold in a matter of weeks. The second week of 1992, it displaced Michael Jackson's *Dangerous* at the top of the *Billboard* Hot 200 chart.

Newly back in Portland, Smith could hardly avoid being exposed to *Nevermind*. Doubtless, he favoured Nirvana's primal-scream, supercharged take on the Beatles. As likely, he saw something of himself in their slight, troubled and preternaturally gifted songwriter. Like him, Kurt Cobain was the product of a broken home. He was stricken with a debilitating stomach complaint, as Smith would also be. Cobain's placebo was to send out into the world the sum total of all of his anguish, pain and mental torture – this likely struck the most resounding chord of all with Smith.

★

To begin with, Smith and Gust found an apartment to rent outside of the city in Beaverton, 7 miles west of Portland. Nike's headquarters were sited just outside of the Beaverton city limits, but there wasn't much else going on there to distract them from their stated aim of getting another band up and running. Smith, however, simply couldn't be roused to the task. He was still poring over his college texts, principally Catharine MacKinnon's treatises, and sunk into a torpid state. Subjecting himself to the full force of MacKinnon's damnation, he complained of being drained of energy, not able or inclined to do anything but mope and mull.

Obsessing over the matter gave him a purpose at least and eventually a route out of his inertia, albeit an unlikely one. He announced to Gust and other friends his resolve to abandon music and frivolous pursuits and instead to make something more useful of himself as a man. All things being equal, he considered the best way of doing this was to become a fireman. Characteristically, he committed himself to a forensic scrutiny of a firefighter's lot. Before the clouds lifted once more and not nearly so listless, he fell back into the comforting cadence of writing songs with Gust. They collaborated like writer and editor, going both ways. Each would alternately bring the other a song he'd written for his approbation and then help him fine-tune it to a finish. Meanwhile, to pay the rent, Smith took jobs washing dishes and working in a bakery.

Their songs were coming out spikier-sounding now, jabbing like needle points. *Nevermind* blast open a path for every wannabe alternative-rock band to follow, but their way towards it was lit by Ian MacKaye's Fugazi and Urge Overkill. Between them, these two bands fired out five albums by the summer of '91. Fugazi's two records were characterised by MacKaye's furious lyrics and their almost mathematically precise songs. Urge's three by their twin lead vocalists, Nash Kato and Eddie 'King'

Roeser, particularly instructive for Smith and Gust since they both meant to sing their own songs.

With the songs flowing, they set about filling the other spots in their band. Tony Lash was the obvious choice for drummer. For bass, Smith was tipped by his Lincoln High friend Alice Vosmek to Brandt Peterson. Already by then a veteran of Sprinkler and a clutch of other local bands, Peterson grew up a West Hills kid like Lash. Smith courted him over coffee. Peterson cautioned his prickly personality tended to rub bandmates the wrong way, but Smith remained undeterred.

With the line-up complete, Smith and Gust elected to retain the Heatmiser name. For a nominal sum, a friend of Peterson's, Jason Mitchell, offered them rehearsal space at the house he was sharing with Trailer Queen's drummer Moira Doogan in northeast Portland. Nights after whatever work they were each doing to pay the rent, the four of them crammed into Mitchell's basement and ironed out their creases. Afterwards, the whole household would venture out to one of the downtown clubs, La Luna or the X-Ray Café more often than not.

'It started out being a pretty democratic band,' says Tony Lash. 'I liked Neil right away and I remember a lot of laughter and silliness between us. Brandt had a little more of a serious edge, but also he was really smart and not without a sense of humour.'

As Peterson eased into their ranks, Smith and Gust decided they should all get a house together in Portland. It was still cheap to rent in the city, much more so than up in Seattle, or down the coast in San Francisco, and with an abundance of property to choose from. There were split-level apartments, bungalows and big old wood-framed '50s houses going for less than $200 per person a month. Low enough for budding musicians and artists to subsist on coffee-shop wages and tips. Smith, Gust and Peterson picked out a rambling '20s bungalow on Division Street, a blue-collar neighbourhood south-east of the river. They took on two more lodgers to help with the rent. Lash opted out, preferring to live on his own.

It was a run-down kind of dwelling. There was a wood porch out front with a tatty couch and yet more thrift store furniture inside. They put up posters and art prints on the bare walls and a turntable player in the living room, vinyl records splaying over the worn floorboards. The basement downstairs was dank and dark, but just big enough for them to rehearse and throw the occasional party in. They shelled out for a puny PA system to go down there and soundproofed it as best they could. The place was fast christened the Heatmiser House.

As friends, Smith and Gust seemed joined at the hip, close as brothers. From now on, though, a fracture began to open up between them. It was fine-lined at first, but fragile as a spider's web and just as liable to break apart. Gust laboured at writing songs. They came to him slowly and with effort. For Smith, on the other hand, the process appeared as natural and easy as drawing breath. Whenever the mood took him, he wrote fast, inexhaustibly and one song after another in a deluge. He was hard for Gust to keep up with – fiendishly difficult for almost anyone to match – and progressing at a breathless rate.

Out in the world, it was Gust who others gravitated towards first and quickest. Smith looked uncomfortable at the best of times and getting to know him required time and effort. Theirs was an increasingly complicated relationship, just as intense and sometimes confounding for them as it was for everyone else.

Janel Jarosz played guitar and sang with Trailer Queen. She first met Smith when Gust invited her band to cut a demo tape at the Heatmiser House. 'Elliott and Neil set up to record us in the living room,' she recalls. 'I got along with Neil really well right away, because he was a bit more outgoing. I just thought Elliott was kind of shy. He was a man of few words and he had bad skin. I didn't think a whole lot about him till later on and when I got to realise he had a really dry sense of humour. His humour caught me off guard.

'That day at the house, I mentioned to him one of my favourite Heatmiser songs, which happened to be by Neil. He said, "I didn't write that song." I told him, "I know, but you play guitar on it," and he said, "Yeah . . . I guess." It was, like, "Oh, gosh, maybe I've said the wrong thing."'

The second incarnation of Heatmiser played their first show together on Valentine's Day 1992 at the X-Ray Café. They opened up for Sprinkler, who had added them on the bill as a favour to their former bass player Peterson. Tony Lash invited a bunch of his friends along to swell the audience and also remembers them going down pretty well with the X-Ray regulars. The following month, they played two more shows in town: one was at a downtown bar, Eli's, and the other at Satyricon. Between the four of them, they judged these initial shows qualified successes. They occasioned Smith slipping into character once more. He was an angry young man now, Ian MacKaye-alike, his hair cropped and bleached, a vein pulsing at his temple as he barked out his lyrics.

'It seemed like we got fairly popular in Portland pretty quickly,' says Lash. 'It felt good. Within the band, it was all pretty equal. Neither Elliott nor Neil was super outgoing onstage. The in-between song banter tended to be pretty stilted. It really was all about the music. Nobody was trying to be a showman. I didn't have any sense at the time of how out of his element Elliott felt to be playing and singing in that style.'

'I didn't know Elliott or Neil prior to the X-Ray Café show, but they were instantly my favourite band,' says Sprinkler's Chris Slusarenko. 'There was just something about Elliott and Neil taking turns with their songs and the way their music interlocked was really unusual for Portland. How Elliott's and Neil's guitar parts jutted in and out of each other, it was really mechanical. Brandt's a pretty funky bass player, too. They were just a really powerful live band and they wrote the catchiest songs.'

Their timing was fortuitous as well. Heatmiser's entry onto the Portland scene coincided with its blooming. By early 1992, there were several downtown venues putting on all-ages shows for $5 entry. La Luna, one of the bigger clubs, went a step further and launched a regular Monday night slot for local bands with a cover charge of just $1. Most Mondays, the club was filled to its 1,000 capacity. Since the three bands playing these nights also got to split the door money, one show at La Luna went a long way towards covering the monthly rent. In general, it was the same bands orbiting around the circuit and sharing bills with each other – Sprinkler, Hazel, Pond, Trailer Queen, Crackerbash and now Heatmiser.

All of their aspirations might have been modest at the outset, but Nirvana's explosion had profoundly shifted the landscape of American music. Most of all, it sparked a feeding frenzy among the country's record labels, majors and indies alike to root out 'the next Nirvana' and, by extension, the next Seattle. Sub Pop's co-founders Jonathan Poneman and Bruce Pavitt were already trekking down to Portland on scouting missions. Soon enough, all of Sprinkler, Hazel, Pond and the Spinanes were signed to the Sub Pop label. For the moment at least, Portland's relatively small, hitherto self-contained scene was a point of interest far outside the few blocks of downtown.

In late April of 1992, Heatmiser travelled 6 miles south of Portland to make their first demo tape. A local recording engineer, Dan Decker, ran a 24-track studio, Sound Impressions, from an outbuilding in his own backyard in the satellite town of Milwaukie. The band worked fast at Decker's place, putting six songs to tape in a couple of days. The songs were also quickfire and dissonant. Comprising three titles by Smith, including 'Lowlife' and 'Dirt', two by Gust and one contributed by Brandt Peterson, 'Just a Little Prick', their sound overall was a world away from any of Smith's previous Portland bands.

After their second day of recording in Milwaukie, Smith took a finished copy of their tape with him to Alice Vosmek's birthday party. The assembled partygoers, friends from Lincoln mostly, listened to it sprawled around Vosmek's upstairs apartment.

Smith's and Lash's new, and loud, incarnation caught them by surprise. Out of Smith's earshot, someone remarked, 'Oh my God, Elliott and Tony have started a speed metal band.'

'The initial consensus was, "This is *really* weird,"' says Mark Buchanan. 'It was not at all what we were expecting, but still good. Their musicianship kept getting better. We were all friends, so of course we were going to be supportive. We probably listened to the tape once, all talked about it and then we went on having our party.'

To accompany the tape, Heatmiser got a set of band pictures taken. Jason Mitchell hooked them up with a photographer. A workmate of Mitchell's at a coffee shop in town, La Patisserie, JJ Gonson hailed from the East Coast. She had grown up in Cambridge, Massachusetts, and gone on to study photography at the School of the Museum of Fine Arts in Boston. After running into the editor at a Hüsker Dü concert in the city, she had started off in music shooting punk rock bands for a local fanzine, *XXX*.

Gonson quickly made a name for herself. Nirvana stayed at her house when they passed through Boston on the Bleach tour. Alongside her photography, Gonson also took on the job of managing her then-boyfriend's band. Following university, she got a labouring job with a travelling circus, but hated it and quit. She bought a beat-up VW microbus with the money she'd made and travelled west on a whim, pitching up in Portland with a pocketbook full of music business contacts and not much else.

She was twenty-four years old, dark-haired, quick-witted and a firecracker. Smith liked her at once. Even in her earliest photographs of the band, he appears unselfconscious, with his guard down and comfortable-looking in his own skin. In one of the first shots she took of the band, Gonson caught him clowning, his hands thrown up over his head and fixing her lens with an exaggerated pout.

'That's one of my favourite-ever band photos I've taken,' she says. 'I love the playfulness of it. It wasn't a posed situation whenever I photographed him, it was candid. He's looking at me and making a face because I'm a friend and he's being goofy.'

As spring ran into summer, Gonson vanished from Portland for three months. She went off to backpack around Europe, culminating her trip in London, where she ran into Kurt Cobain wandering through Piccadilly Circus. She ended up joining Nirvana's entourage for the hour's drive west to the Reading Festival, and where they played a monumental headlining set. Smith and his bandmates evidently kept her in mind. Upon her return in September, they invited Gonson along to see their show at a riverside venue, the Melody Lane Ballroom. After their set, the four of them pressed her into becoming their manager.

'We were up in the balcony, very romantic,' she says. 'The first thing I asked them was, "What do you want?" Neil answered, "To earn a living." They all wanted to be professional musicians, they didn't want to work day jobs. None of us had to do much to survive. The rent was so cheap.'

Gonson's first significant act as their manager was to wangle them a deal to put a single out. She focused her attentions on a start-up record label in town. Cavity Search Records was the brainchild of a couple of native Portlanders, Christopher Cooper and Denny Swofford. A garrulous bear of a man, Cooper was working at a downtown record store, Music Millennium. The more diffident Swofford was recently returned from Seattle. He had headed north to work for the management company looking after Soundgarden and another band caught up in the grunge gold rush, Alice in Chains. The two of them fell into talking at Cooper's store, formed a fast friendship and hit upon the idea of Cavity Search to release 7-inch records by the new wave of local bands.

Like the Portland scene as a whole, Cavity Search was a low-key, hand-to-mouth and somewhat incestuous operation. Their first release was a 7-inch by Hazel titled 'J. Hell' after Pete Krebs' former girlfriend, Janel Jarosz, whose nickname it was. Swofford was renting an apartment above a second local record store, Ooze, which by happenstance Jarosz also owned. Cooper designed the sleeve artwork. They shifted just enough copies to be receptive to Gonson's approach and to make Heatmiser's their second release. Swofford picked out the A-side song, one of Smith's, 'Stray'. Smith was insistent a Gust composition, 'Can't Be Touched', went on the flipside.

They cut both tracks with their old Lincoln friend, Eric Hedford, producing. Musically, each was of a type and typical of the time. Driven by grinding guitars, lurching rhythms and altogether monotone. There was more of an edge to Smith's 'Stray' and the sense in his lyric of something sinister lurking in the gloom. 'Are you coming to stay?' he sings, flat-voiced, dispassionate. 'Oh, how familiar you are, coming to take my place when I wake up in the Lone Star State.' That November,

Cooper and Swofford put out 1,500 7-inch copies of the Heat-miser record. The run sold out.

Around the same time Heatmiser played a handful of Port-land shows. One at the X-Ray Café, one at Satyricon, two at Belmont's bar on 11 and 20 November, and on 21 November, one more at the Edgefield Hotel in the suburb of Troutdale. The Troutdale show was their last of the year. Officially, Smith ended 1992 a recording artist. This fact apart, his world was not so much changed and he himself no nearer to coming into focus.

'Elliott and I had got to be pals,' says Pete Krebs. 'We found we had the same sense of humour. Our friendship was predi-cated on us having a laugh more than anything else. He was pretty tight-lipped about his family. Definitely tight-lipped about Texas, although I gathered Texas was a pretty traumatic envi-ronment for him. We never really had what you would call a heart-to-heart conversation where he bared his soul.

'Like a lot of us, he enjoyed drinking. Show up at a bar at 10 p.m. and you're drinking pint after pint. It makes for a late evening and if the circumstances are there, you're feeling kind of down and someone is willing to listen . . . Then, yes, absolutely, alcohol seemed to loosen his guard a little bit. Otherwise, he didn't talk a lot about his personal life. He wasn't one of those people who would be effusive about whom he was living with at the time or anything like that.'

Marie Tak was just then passing through the same school year at Lincoln as Smith's half-sister, Rachel. Their clique shared a regular hangout with him, Dot's coffee shop on South-East Clin-ton Street. 'Elliott would be in Dot's every Monday night and we used to sit across from him,' recalls Tak. 'It was always funny to see him. He would see his teenage sister and all of her friends, and kind of wave at us and say, "Hey," but then hunker back down with his hunched-over posture. He was always polite, but never very engaged.

'His sister was smart and funny as hell, sarcastic and very witty. Rachel was always the one reading the books no one else was reading. She didn't have time for his nonsense. I mean, she was proud of him, but she would rag on him, too. She'd be like, "Oh, that loser." Elliott never knew what we were laughing at, I think he just wanted to be left alone.'

CHAPTER 7

Lift Off

Cavity Search put out a second Heatmiser 7-inch at the beginning of 1993. Smith's 'Sleeping Pill' was on the A-side and Gust's 'Temper' on the flip. Almost an equal split, but not quite as Smith's song was the prominent one once again. Around the same time, JJ Gonson sent them back into Sound Impressions to put the entirety of their repertoire to tape as fast as they could. She was plotting to have them do a full album and with a more established record company behind them than the Portland start-up. Gonson set her sights on an indie label based out west in Sun Valley, California.

Frontier Records was the preserve of a passionate entrepreneur like herself, Lisa Fancher. Starting in 1980 with the Circle Jerks' *Group Sex* album, Fancher initially launched Frontier as a showcase for the nascent Southern California punk-rock scene. Ever since, the label had gone on to embrace a more disparate collection of bands such as goth-rockers Christian Death, pop-rockers Redd Kross and the altogether more questing American Music Club, a conduit for Mark Eitzel's evocative and richly-detailed songs. While Gonson waited on Fancher's response to Heatmiser's Sound Impression tapes, the band played just six gigs during the first four months of the year. Four of these were close to home, but with a couple of sorties too up to Seattle in February and April. Fancher took the bait, agreeing a hand-shake deal with Gonson for Heatmiser to make three albums for Frontier.

Almost at once, the band was returned to the studio in Milwaukie to cut their debut album. Co-producing the sessions with Tony Lash was Steve Hanford, a fellow drummer with Poison Idea and for whom he went by the name Thee Slayer Hippy. Lash had previously engineered for Poison Idea and worked well with Hanford. With an actual budget to play with, Lash was tilting at a bigger sound for Heatmiser's record. He was inspired by the example of a New York hardcore band, Helmet, whose 1992 album *Meantime* arrived like a herald with its staccato guitars, syncopated percussion and double-tracked vocals. In the event, they were all of them over-reaching.

'There wasn't a lot of discussion within the band about how the record should sound,' says Lash. 'Overall, there wasn't a lot of vision. It was more a case of, "Okay, we're going to play the songs like we do live." We just went in and knocked out the basics and mixed the whole thing very quickly. The songs weren't done justice.'

Their egalitarian approach with the division of songwriting was also impossible for them to maintain. The fact was

Smith wrote more songs than Gust and if not as yet necessarily better ones. The fourteen included on the finished album, *Dead Air*, were weighted eight to six in Smith's favour. Two of Gust's, 'Candyland' and 'Bottle Rocket', were the more forceful. Smith's compositions, like the title track, 'Still' and 'Lowlife', piled up barre chords and angst but lacked a solid melodic framework. In this respect, they were fully of a piece with the noisy, braying and unremarkable alt-rock glut of the time. In total, *Dead Air* ran to just thirty-seven minutes, but was altogether so monochrome and stifling it seemed longer.

'It was just a combination of our shortcomings as a band at that point,' says Lash. 'I don't listen back to very much of it.'

Once they handed over *Dead Air* to Frontier, Gonson moved into action, booking Heatmiser their first proper tour. Calling up contacts she had made in cities across the country, from Minneapolis and Cleveland to Baltimore and Kalamazoo, over and again, she begged for the number of the best rock club in town. Then she got back on the phone to hustle a show for her boys. She was tireless, simply refused to take no for an answer.

'I was perpetually ignored, disregarded, brushed off and dismissed,' she says. 'I probably have stuck with the name JJ because people wouldn't know if I was a man or a woman until they actually talked to me. I worked for a circus, I was really fucking strong. I'm also classic bipolar. Maybe Heatmiser wouldn't have existed if I wasn't, because I was so manic. I booked them a national tour without thinking twice about whether I could or not. Part of the fun of manic depression is this thing called dissociation – you kind of leave your body. I'm an Energizer

Bunny who then drops into hell. This story is so much about mental health, isn't it? We were all of us navigating what it meant to live with other people and support each other.'

Gonson's efforts secured them three months of shows across the country, twenty-nine shows in total. They started off with a hometown date at the Clinton Street Theater, right over the road from Dot's coffee shop, on 5 September and finished up at the Bottom of the Hill club in San Francisco on 19 November. Six of them travelled together with all of their gear in a rental van: the four band members plus Gonson and Jason Mitchell, along for the ride as a one-man road crew. One person at a time able to stretch out on a makeshift bed built out of a plywood platform secured above the driver's seat and no air conditioning.

'It was smelly and boring,' says Gonson. 'I mean, it smelt *really* bad. I drove a lot. At one point, I had freezing migraines probably from lack of oxygen. It was super-stressful. You're always trying to get to the next place on time. There was never a moment to hug each other and say, "Good job". I feel like Elliott in particular went out of his way to say thank you – he thanked me a lot.'

Attendances and venues varied. They drew respectable turn-outs in some of the major cities on the itinerary and played to mere handfuls of folk at the more out-of-the-way stops. In Cincinnati, they performed at Sudsy Malone's Rock & Roll Laundry & Bar, an actual laundromat. On 2 November, they rolled up at Oberlin, Ohio, to discover their promoter was a sixteen-year-old schoolboy and the venue a tiny information lodge tucked in the Findley State Park. There, they set up in front of a stone fireplace and played to a bunch of delighted school kids.

Most nights, they were able to beg a floor to sleep on from some-one in the audience. Occasionally, their small guarantees stretched to a couple of rooms at a dirt-cheap roadside motel. Gonson snapped a photo of the four of them at one such stop, bouncing-on-the-bed happy just to have a room for the night. Increasingly, Smith snuck off with Gonson whenever they could grab any spare time. In Washington, DC, they visited the Lincoln Monument together. They whiled away another afternoon prowling the City Lights bookstore in San Francisco. By the end of the tour, the two of them were officially dating. Nerves already jangled from being in such proximity with each other, this latest development sent a ripple of concern running through the band.

'There was some wariness about it,' says Tony Lash. 'I remem-ber Elliott talking to the rest of us about it, knowing the situation was a little weird. For me, it was one of those things where I sort of went with the flow. I'm sure the others' experience of it was different. It *was* a little weird touring in close quarters with them as a couple, but I didn't worry about it a whole lot. Things became more difficult later on and when JJ was still managing the band.'

By the time they wound back to Portland, *Dead Air* had picked up a few positive reviews but sales were modest at best. Certainly, nowhere near enough for any of them to even consider jack-ing in their day jobs. Smith did at least land a better-paying gig working construction with Pete Krebs. It was grunt work mostly, scraping ceilings, tearing up floorboards or plastering dry wall. In the early hours of those winter mornings, Smith would pick Krebs up in his beat-up, metallic blue Ford Tempo. It was a mess of a car, the backseats lined with plastic bags full of cabling, second-hand books and assorted other oddities. Empty coffee cups littered around the footwells.

A contractor friend of Krebs' hired them for an out-of-town job, plastering on his house boat. The place was moored on a tributary of the Willamette River. Smith wrecked the suspension on his sedan driving down the potholed access road. Six weeks of work in the depths of winter, frigid cold. They kept warm with an old propane heater, the size of a jet engine, which shot flames from out of one side. It was a more technical job with all of the curves and angles of a boat, made harder by the ceaseless pitch and bob of the river swell.

'We kind of did a lousy job,' recalls Krebs. 'There were all of these exposed beams, so it was really hard to work around. A couple of weeks after we left, there were heavy rains. The house boat slipped its mooring, floated down river and crashed into the bank, so all of our hard work was for nothing.

'Elliott wasn't a slack worker. He'd show up on time. I mean, we would both of us turn up hungover, but we were still showing and working. Neither of us liked doing the job. There wasn't a lot of enthusiasm on the part of either of us, but it was a relatively easy way for a couple of guys to make money. A big reason we got hired was because people in Portland were into the local music scene and wanted to do us a solid favour by putting money in our pockets.'

Outside of these working hours, Smith and Gonson were seeing more of each other than anyone else. Gonson's parents visited from the East Coast and took the two of them up north to Vancouver on a hiking trip. In Portland, they double-dated with Chris Slusarenko and his girlfriend. One night, the four of them drove down to North Salem for the Oregon State Fair. Forty-six miles in Slusarenko's bust-up car, a blood-red Pontiac 2000 he had bought from Gonson.

The wretched vehicle gave up the ghost on the I5, a couple of miles outside of Salem. They had to hoof across squelching fields and farmland to the nearest outlying dwellings, knocking on doors until someone bid them in to call for help. There was enough room in the tow-truck for just two extra passengers, so Smith and Slusarenko got left behind roadside. For four hours the pair of them sat out there waiting for their girls to circle back around, the gloaming half-light running to dark, shivering cold and hungry.

'We finally got so tired and starved, we ran down the highway until we stumbled across a Circle K store,' says Slusarenko. 'Even between us, we didn't have enough money for any food. We scraped just enough change to leave a message for JJ from a payphone in the parking lot, telling her where to pick us up. Then we sat there for a couple more hours. Elliott came up with his own mythical language while we waited. He was babbling about imaginary creatures living in the bushes the other side of the parking lot.

'Eventually, they found us. On the way back, I remember Elliott with his head in JJ's lap and still talking in his made-up language. There was something so sweet about the moment – and about him altogether. The person I knew could be really goofy and make light of things. The two of us went to a few more county fairs together. We'd walk around eating candy apples and talking about music. He liked going on the dangerous rides, the Zipper or the Octopus. Those are strong memories, being locked in a spinning cage with him, and him laughing.'

'There's a photograph of the two us taken around the same time,' says Gonson. 'It's one of the very few of us together. We're outside of his house, playing Frisbee. He's tackling me from behind and he's laughing. We're really okay and everything is fun and good. Photographs are a little easier for me to look at. Any time I can see him being casual, his sweet face. I'm not going to lie, I don't ever watch the videos. It's very, very hard for me to see him in motion.'

As her relationship with Smith was moving forward, Gonson was also fielding an approach to Heatmiser from an executive at a major label. Andy Factor was an A&R talent scout at Virgin Records in Los Angeles. He had been with the company since 1987, when it was still owned by Richard Branson, working his way up from the mail room. Like almost every A&R scout in the country, he was a student of the finer details of Nirvana's apparent overnight success. Principally, he thought on the development deal Geffen Records initially set up with Sub Pop for the band. Between them, the two labels had agreed to Geffen contributing funds towards the marketing and promotion of *Bleach*, before officially taking on the band for *Nevermind*.

At Virgin, Factor was involved with orchestrating a similar kind of arrangement for a band out of Chicago, the Smashing Pumpkins. Virgin snapped up the Pumpkins, but effectively outsourced them to an indie label, Caroline, for the release of their debut album, 1991's *Gish*. Garnished with a vestige of indie credibility, the Pumpkins then shunted over to Virgin for their next record, *Siamese Dream*, in 1993. Factor was now on the hunt for his own Nirvana. He happened across Heatmiser while flicking through *Snowboarder* magazine and spotting a review of *Dead Air*. Picking up a copy of their CD and seeing Tony Lash listed as both Heatmiser's drummer and producer, Factor assumed Lash was the band's go-to guy and called him up. Lash passed him on to Gonson.

After a sounding-out conversation with Gonson, Factor arranged to fly up to Portland with his boss, Kaz Utsunomiya, to meet the band and make his pitch. In the meantime, Gonson went out and hired Nirvana's lawyer, Richard Grabel, to handle Heatmiser's side of any future contractual negotiations. Factor and Utsunomiya billeted themselves in one of the better hotels in the city, overlooking the river. The band and Gonson came to them. Smith had dyed his hair blue for the occasion. The meeting went ahead in the hotel bar, just as stilted and awkward as any first date.

'The guys were kind of rough-edged and I found them very difficult to crack,' Factor recalls. 'They were very insular and quiet. They had, or at least they gave off, this suspicious air of the major label guys flying in to buy them drinks. We were trying to impress them, they were not trying to impress us at all. For us, it was really all about pleasing JJ.

'JJ was fierce, super-protective and awesome. Considering she was faking it for the most part, she knew exactly what to want. She had gotten them Richard Grabel's services and ultimately, she got everything she asked for.'

Having agreed with Gonson to carry on talking, the Virgin deputation flew back to Los Angeles. What neither party could foresee was a warning light flashing red not so far down the road. In the interim between the future of the band being resolved, Smith moved out of the Heatmiser House and in with Gonson. Gonson's was one of the big old Victorian houses on Southeast Taylor Street, a few blocks north of the Heatmiser House but in the same neighbourhood. She was sharing the place with a group of other people, artists and musicians.

The routine going on in the house was familiar, easy and well-suited to Smith. Gonson did most of the cooking for everybody. There was a lot of lounging around playing video games, *Sonic the Hedgehog* mostly, and listening to music. Gonson turned Smith on to country music, George Jones and the Carter Family. For his part, Smith was honing in on singer-songwriters, Bob Dylan, Joni Mitchell and Bruce Springsteen's folksier first two albums.

His songwriting processes were kicking into gear, wheels whirring in his head even when he appeared so still and inert. Having something to occupy his eyes so his mind could wander freely, unencumbered. It might be he was parked in front of a silently flickering TV screen. Then again, halfway up the house's winding staircase, eyes fixed on the high ceiling and looking like he was lost in a daydream or in a trance. Or else out walking the city streets late at night, moonlight dancing in the puddles.

Until his head filled up with enough ideas, he took himself off to the basement of the house. Down there, he set up with his four-track machine, a Radio Shack mic and a cheap guitar belonging to Gonson, a Le Domino acoustic so tiny it might have been a child's toy. Gonson's basement was just as dark and dingy as the one over on Division Street and stuffed with detritus left behind by previous tenants. Smith eked out a space for himself over in one corner and started to record his latest batch of songs. The hiss of the tape, the scrape of his fingers on the Le Domino's nylon strings, the pop of saliva in his mouth and his singing voice, so soft and whispered, like he was telling a secret or trying to keep one.

Upstairs, Gonson was barely even aware he was making music. She didn't like to interrupt him in full flow and so didn't venture down into the basement. At any rate, she simply assumed he had squirrelled himself away to chip at the coalface of Heatmiser's next record – the very same record she was in the middle of talking to Andy Factor and Virgin about.

'I'd no idea they were solo songs he was writing,' she says. 'We were a couple of years into being friends before he said, "I want to play something for you."'

CHAPTER 8

The Basement Tape

Altogether, Smith put nine songs to four-track tape down in the basement at Southeast Taylor Street. Each of those songs came out unvarnished, muted and at times almost unbearably intimate. Listening to them is to feel as if intruding upon an act of confession, or else peep-holing someone in the act of stripping naked. In his urgency, Smith didn't even get around to giving four of the songs a title. The instrumentation is sparse. For the most part, there is nothing but the scraped Le Domino acoustic and an occasional brush of drums, like the rasp of a comb on paper. On 'Last Call', a lone electric guitar lightning bolts over the landscape as the whole of the song gathers up like a storm.

When it came to his songwriting, there weren't yet any show-stopper flourishes or solid evidence of an expert's craftsmanship for the finer details, bridges and choruses. Listening to these songs today, there is, though, an acute sense of something special coming into being, of green shoots bursting up to the sun's light and about to flower. The intricacies of Smith's finger-picking are frequently dazzling.

Deceptively, so many of the basement songs are musically lovely. Smith's melodies skip and dance. He sings them *sotto voce*, like a choirboy, the effect enhanced by his vocal double-tracking. So tenderly and spectral one must pull up close to catch his words. All the tortured secrets and lacerating Texas truths whispered in the dark. On 'Roman Candle' he sings: 'He could be cool and cruel to you and me . . . I want to hurt him, I want to give him pain.' Then again, on 'No Name #4': 'For a change she got out before he hurt her bad, took her records and clothes and pictures of her boy.'

As he progressed with the work, Smith at last cracked the door open to the basement and admitted others into his subterranean world. He invited Pete Krebs to put down a snare drum track onto a Tiki hut kind of instrumental he'd rustled up and titled 'Kiwi Maddog 20/20'. It was a piece of fluff, gallows-humoured in context. For another, folksier, but also jaunty-sounding song, 'No Name #2', he asked for Gonson's help in finishing off the music – the first and only time he ever did. When they were done, he played the song for Neil Gust: 'Neil didn't like it,' says Gonson.

Smith dug back to his college days' stash of songs to retrieve 'Condor Avenue'. Musically, his new version of the song was entirely different to the more youthful original from off the Murder of Crows' cassette, a cascade of finger-picked notes. He retained Garrick Duckler's lyrics near enough intact. In fact, Smith kept his collaboration with Duckler going almost through to the end of his life. By Duckler's estimation, Smith made use of his lyrics in around one in six of his songs up to 2000, and, by mutual agreement, mostly uncredited. 'Condor Avenue' was the exception to their general rule.

'After "Condor Avenue", the way Elliott used lyrics of mine could best be described as sprinkling,' says Duckler. 'Most often, it was just a phrase or an image, sometimes a whole line. I would never claim to have made any real contribution to his songwriting. Make no mistake about it, Elliott is the genius. I am not.'

When he was done recording, Smith approached Tony Lash to mix the tracks for him. Lash lived nearby to Gonson and their wrangling over the best way to represent Heatmiser's songs was temporarily put to one side. Smith handed his four-track tape over to Lash. They sat side by side down in the basement of Lash's house, Lash beavering away on a tiny Mackie mixer for the two days it took him to complete the task.

'Elliott asked for my help and I was always happy to oblige,' says Lash. 'There wasn't a lot for me to mix, there weren't many choices we were going to be making. At the time, I didn't really see this as a new shift for him. Elliott had a lot of ideas. He was prolific and always recording. This was one of those things that just seemed to me like normal Elliott behaviour.'

Smith ran off a couple of handfuls of cassette copies of the nine songs Lash mixed. Half a dozen of these he handed out to friends. Jason Mitchell, Chris Slusarenko, Janel Jarosz and Sean

Croghan of Crackerbash all got one. He played the tape for Pete Krebs one day at work. The two of them were clearing the ceiling of a warehouse at the time. They sat up on the edge of the scaffolding and listened to it on Krebs' boom box. Smith was fidgety and self-conscious. Krebs told him he thought the tape was pretty great.

Krebs' reaction was the general one. Janel Jarosz accosted him one night at La Luna and asked if he had any idea of just how good he was. In response, Smith stared down at the floor and mumbled something non-committal. First off, it was the sound of the tape that struck his peers. How very different it was not just to Heatmiser, but to pretty much anything else going on at the time. The only acoustic singer-songwriters anyone of their generation was listening to those days were drawn from their parents' record collections. Grizzled old guys – Dylan again, Neil Young, James Taylor, Paul Simon. Hearing music this ethereal, but also spooked and otherworldly, coming from one of their own was a shock. However, what Smith was actually singing about on the tape landed the most impactful blow. His outpouring was a revelation to some, confirmation to others.

'I was really naïve about a lot of the struggles people were having in our scene,' says Chris Slusarenko. 'People I knew quite well were battling with addiction and I had no idea. When I listened to Elliott's songs, it felt to me like he was story-telling. I knew it was personal, but not how much of it was Elliott, or him taking on the pain of someone he knew or loved. It was haunting, but everyone I knew back then was haunted and messed up for different reasons.'

'I'd had an inkling of what was going on with Elliott,' recalls Jason Mitchell. 'I knew a few things happening with him. As much of a goofball as he was capable of being, I wasn't shocked at the depth of that well. My first thought when I met him had been how similar he looked to another friend of mine, but mad. He was sort of like the more upset version of my friend. We talked about it, but he'd a lot of darkness he dealt with.'

No one was more passionate about the tape than JJ Gonson, who flat-out raved around town about it. The way she perceived it, Smith was simply opening up another avenue of expression. Gonson was sure he meant to juggle this newfound thing of his right alongside Heatmiser, and her job was to see to the smooth running of both enterprises. With Smith's consent, she pressed one of his four-track tapes onto Christopher Cooper. Or more accurately, she marched into Cooper's record store one morning and told him this was something he absolutely must hear.

On his lunch break, Cooper stepped out and listened to Smith's cassette on the tape deck of his VW bus. The instant it played out, he hurried back into the store and called Swofford, ordering him over. Once Swofford pitched up, Cooper hustled him out to the bus to hear the tape for himself. Both men agreed that Smith's four-track should be the first full-length record they released on Cavity Search. They would put it out just the way they had heard it, untouched.

'It wasn't really a big decision,' says Swofford. 'On the surface, it's a bad-sounding singer-songwriter record. Yet if you actually listened to the songs, you would laugh and cry and go, "I'm not sure I've ever heard anything like this before." Then again, only a label that almost didn't know what they were doing, with little or no money and an artist no one cared about at the time would've ever put it out.

'Also, it wasn't a difficult deal to fix up, or like there was somebody else involved in the conversation. It really was about us talking to Elliott and totally his decision. We got together with him at my place above the Ozone record store. He was honoured and excited. It was a handshake deal. To be honest, Christopher and I were hoping we would get some more Heatmiser action on the back of it. Elliott's record was important to us, but kind of just as an on-the-side thing. Our thought was we could possibly make an arrangement with Frontier to do another Heatmiser 7-inch.'

In February of 1994, Smith went back into the studio with Neil Gust, Brandt Peterson and Lash. With Lash once again producing the session, they worked out of the Center for Applied Music and Media in Portland. They put down four tracks, two each by Smith and Gust. Compared to *Dead Air*, this latest material showcased a degree more light and shade, but essentially, Smith was still operating from within tightly confined boundaries as a member of Heatmiser.

On 1 March, he struck out from the band once again, playing his first ever solo show in the upstairs bar at La Luna. It was a low-key affair. He was the middle of a three-act bill, opening up for another local band, the Worried Guys, and with Sean Croghan also appearing. Smith sat himself on a stool for his set, hunched over, white-knuckle fingers on Gonson's Le Domino, his eyes scrunched tight and as if he were imagining himself alone in the dark, his voice like a ghost in a room.

It was a short set, but the small La Luna audience listened rapt. Among them was Marie Tak, who had just recently started to play open-mic nights around town herself and billed as Maggie Motel. 'Elliott stole the show that night,' she recalls. 'As soon as he began playing, it got dead silent in the room. I immediately felt sorry for the other guys who were on before and after him. It was like he was laying his innermost feelings out there for everyone. It was absolutely heart-touching.'

The following month, Frontier put out Heatmiser's *Yellow No. 5* EP. It comprised Smith's and Gust's four new songs, plus an older track of Smith's, 'Wake', cut on Heatmiser's second visit to Sound Impressions, back in November 1992. To coincide with the release, JJ Gonson sent them back out on the road for two clutches of dates in April and May. In Portland and Seattle, Albuquerque, New Mexico, and then three in California, one in Sacramento and two in Los Angeles.

Ten days before the first show in Portland and up north in Seattle, Kurt Cobain took his own life. The Heatmiser EP went near enough unnoticed in the tumult occasioned by Cobain's suicide. The mood in the band's rented van was prickly and sour, the principal cause being Smith's and Peterson's rubbing each other the wrong way. The marked differences in their characters amplified and sparked on the long, cramped drives.

All the while, Gonson was carrying on her dance with Andy Factor and Virgin for Heatmiser. As for the band themselves, three of them at least were by now savvy to the major label game. The afternoon of their 7 May show at LA's fabled Whisky a Go Go club on Sunset Strip, they wheedled Factor into taking them all out to Disneyland. Smith, Gust and Lash delighted in going on all of the theme park's rides. Peterson sat himself out of the fun with Factor, the two of them gazing on like parents with unruly offspring.

'Elliott loved it,' recalls Factor. 'He was having the time of his life. The three of them went on Space Mountain and flipped off the camera. They were refused a copy of their photo from the park staff.'

After the Disneyland excursion, Factor secured his deal. The agreement was for Virgin to silent partner with Frontier on Heatmiser's next album, the major label stumping up for recording, marketing and touring costs. After which Heatmiser were to jump to Virgin for their third record, neat and clean as you like. Factor also had a 'leaving members' clause written into the contract. This was standard music business practice and gave Virgin first option on Smith, Gust, Lash or Peterson in the event any of them should go on to solo careers or other projects. Smith signed the Virgin contract like the others, but later reflected: 'I watched myself put my paw in the bear trap on that one.'[9]

This clause was to become a burning issue sooner than any of them, Smith included, could possibly have foreseen. Nevertheless, the ink was still drying on their contract when Andy Factor got a first inkling of the trouble ahead. Back in Portland, JJ Gonson mailed him a copy of Smith's basement tape. She wrote an accompanying note, telling him the tape was nothing for him to worry about. Smith didn't mean for this to get in any of their ways, she assured.

'I heard the tape and felt like I should call 911 or something,' says Factor. 'We were invested in Heatmiser, we had committed money to help put them up on people's radars. I called JJ up and said, "Do we need to worry, or does he need help?" It was like, what the fuck's going on with this guy? Is he going to go postal on me?

'But, you know, the music haunted me. I heard it, and needed to play it for other people. I thought it was dangerous and something I had to be super-careful with, but I loved it and probably way more than Heatmiser. The problem being, it wasn't what I had to focus on.'

For months afterwards, Smith stewed over and bemoaned the impediment of the 'leaving member clause'. Even so, it was a mere irritation next to the epic war he was waging within. He also mulled with friends on Kurt Cobain's death. Not on the whys Cobain was driven to suicide. No, these he could comprehend all too well, but on the how. On what other, cleaner ways there might be to end one's life. In his final note, Cobain wrote: 'Thank you all from the pit of my burning nauseous stomach for your letters and concern during these past years. I'm too much of an erratic, moody baby!' Smith couldn't possibly have averted his gaze, because he was regarding his mirror image.

In contrast to Denny Swofford, who maintained a professional distance from their Cavity Search artists, Christopher Cooper enjoyed being around musicians. He liked to get to know them socially and grew close to Smith. They became drinking buddies, so much so that Cooper got used to the turbulences Smith went through. Smith liked to drink and heavily, beer and Jameson's whiskey chasers. In the sweet spot of a night, the booze loosened him up, sharpened his wit. He was a joy to be around at such times, but there was also a tipping point. Two, three in the morning, back at Cooper's or another friend's place and when his light blacked out. In those wee hours, he fell into being desperately morose.

'He would turn very inward, very sad and very confessional,' Cooper told writer Keith Cameron. 'A lot of childhood memories of various sorts of abuse and confusion and neglect. I felt like if I didn't stay with him, he might kill himself. There were a number of times when he was telling me plainly, "I don't love myself, I don't love living, and I want to go." I'd hug him and tell him he was an amazing person and there were so many reasons to live.'[10]

'Elliott was a unique combination of things,' says Pete Krebs. 'He was very sensitive, but also really tough because he kind of had to be in order to protect himself. He balanced everything out with a striking intelligence. The wit I experienced was also a protective thing with him, I think. Like many sensitive people, he put a lot of energy into hiding his sensitivities and the wounds he carried around.

'Some things that happened when he was younger were really traumatising to him. This might be controversial to say, but I also felt there was always a part of Elliott which sort of liked being taken care of. I don't mean that disparagingly, I just think maybe he needed to feel a bit safer than most people. I don't think it was a conscious choice. Elliott didn't strike me as a manipulative person. He struck me as someone who found ways that worked for him to move through life and he stuck to those strongly.'

Garrick Duckler was still the friend to whom Smith would turn the most often. It was with Duckler that he shared his innermost and most desperate thoughts.

'My contribution to Elliott was not to his artistic legacy, but to his mental and emotional life,' says Garrick Duckler. 'He would only call me if he was depressed and didn't know what else to do. Up until he became more famous, he would repeatedly say there was "a very short list" of people – Neil, his dad and me, basically – who kept him alive. He said if anything was to happen to anyone on the list he would "not be around much longer". He probably said those words fifty times to me – it was like a mantra.'

'There can be a big misconception about someone who frequently discloses suicidal ideation or plans,' says Dr Leah Quinlivan. 'This idea if someone talks about suicide, they don't mean it. They're not going to do it. If they did it, then they would do it in private. This is completely and utterly untrue.

'Sometimes, someone might want help. They might be asking for help. They're speaking a direct thought of what is happening in their head. If someone says they're going to harm themselves, they need to be taken seriously. If they harm themselves once, there's a strong risk they're going to harm themselves again. If someone is in a cycle of harming themselves, the risk of suicide is just huge.'

CHAPTER 9

No Confidence Man

There was a second balance Smith was now fighting to strike, the one between the needs of his band and himself. In the spring of 1994, Heatmiser were due to go into the studio to make their next album. It would be the last one they owed to Frontier. They headed into the studio with a sore and fractious mood persisting between the four of them and the atmosphere simmering. Smith and Tony Lash continued to clash over the best ways to record the band. The basement tape had fortified Smith's point of view in regard to this, but it posed a more serious threat to the fragile songwriting dynamic going on with him and Neil Gust. Smith's imminent solo record served to harden his convictions, stood him apart and couldn't help but cast him as first among equals in their group.

He was still bound by friendship to Lash and especially Gust. Since he had nothing like the same ties or loyalties to Brandt

Peterson, it was Heatmiser's bassist who was made to suffer the most. Smith had come off the spring tour dates barely speaking to Peterson. Peterson's abrasive personality rubbed him raw. Now, he carried on a campaign of effectively ignoring him altogether in the studio. The fact was so many of their resentments and petty jealousies towards each other went unspoken. They seethed just below the surface, bottled up.

'It was complicated,' says Jason Mitchell, who had sat amid Smith's and Peterson's silent feud in the Heatmiser van. 'At some points on the tour it kind of felt like I was their confidant. Individually, they would both come to me from time to time. Maybe someone wanted to grumble about someone else in the band. I think all of their intentions were to keep things being completely equal, but that wasn't quite how it was happening.

'I've kept a photo of the band stood outside of Lisa Fancher's house. Neil and Tony are smiling, being goofy. Each of Brandt and Elliott has a very pained, serious look on their face. That picture hints at the tensions going on there.'

'Elliott had a hot head,' says Garrick Duckler. 'Once, he wanted to get into a fight with one of our high-school drummers over something he had said. This guy was very bright, but also a masculine dick and kind of like Brandt.

'This particular kind of person caused intense pain and anger in Elliott. It would be like he was going to fly off the handle and really do something brutal. I don't believe Elliott ever fought our high-school drummer or Brandt either, but it's surprising to me he didn't. I know for a fact if Jason or I weren't around, things would have been way different.'

These same tensions bubbled and festered throughout the recording of the album. Once more, Lash was co-producing the sessions with Steve Hanford. Yet again, the songwriting split was eight to six in Smith's favour over Gust. All the songs went down fast in one or two takes. From Lash's perspective, Smith was more careful over his vocals this time around and they were all united at least in their aspirations to improve upon and press ahead from the smothering sound of *Dead Air*. In each of these respects, they were only partially successful at best. The finished record, *Cop and Speeder*, was not quite so one-dimensional as its predecessor, but also just as unremarkable.

For the greater part, Smith's eight songs carried on in the same narrow vein. A barren, pancake-flat landscape of homologous alt-rock rendered in shades of grey, so formulaic and routine it's as if he were writing to order. An exception is 'Busted Lip', not a great song by any means, but one delivered with a lighter touch and the sense of someone pushing tentatively at their confines.

The most impactful of Smith's songs is 'Bastard John', but for his splenetic lyrics rather than any musical flights. To a backdrop of buzzing bee guitars and in his higher register, Smith rails: 'I'm acting dumb like you wanted, but I'm not your kid anymore. I am not your bastard John, just because I played along.' It could be he had stepped into character here, but the invocation is unmistakably of yet one more of those Texan childhood nights, baked hot and hellish.

Cop and Speeder turned out to be Brandt Peterson's last act with Heatmiser. As soon as they were done recording, he upped and quit the band, wrung out from Smith's relentless cold shouldering. Peterson was to hang around Portland for another couple of years before taking off for grad school to study anthropology. He was done with playing in bands. Ever since, he has barely spoken publicly of his tenure with Heatmiser, save for just the one time and when he tersely claimed: 'Elliott could be fucking cruel. He could be mean.'[11]

The others wasted no time in replacing him with Sam Coomes. A native Texan, Coomes had spent six years up to 1989 in San Francisco fronting an indie-pop trio, the Donner Party. When they disbanded, he moved up to Portland with his wife, Janet Weiss, where they were carrying on with their own duo, Quasi. Smith, Gust and Lash had each got to know and like both Coomes and Weiss from the Portland scene. In common with Smith, Coomes was a songwriter, multi-instrumentalist and inveterate home recorder. As well as bass, he played guitar, banjo, violin and keyboards. Crucially, Smith found him more laid-back, tolerant and altogether easier to get along with than Peterson.

Straight out of the *Cop and Speeder* sessions, Smith arranged with Coomes and Weiss to do some more recording of his own at their house off Hawthorne Boulevard, four blocks south of where he was living with JJ Gonson. Coomes had an eight-track recorder and mixer set up at his place. Smith put down an instrumental track with a honky-tonk guitar line, like something out of a Tex-Mex cantina. The sun-scorched and tequila-shot vibe of it possibly stirred up to delight Coomes as much as himself. It was the pattern he was to follow his whole life. Pressing on down the road. People and places left forgotten by the waysides and the music his only constant.

★

Christopher Cooper and Denny Swofford scheduled Smith's first solo album for a July 1994 release on Cavity Search. Smith took care over the finer details in the run-up. He handwrote a lyric sheet and credits for the liner notes, his text neat and precise. For the front cover he picked out a JJ Gonson photograph. It was a black-and-white picture snapped on tour with Heatmiser and of Gust together with another friend of theirs from Hampshire, Amy Dalsimer, walking through a street market. He asked Gust to take a couple more black-and-white portraits of him for the inner sleeve. In both these images he appears inscrutable, posed and wary. His hair, long and dark now, is brushed back from his forehead like he'd made an effort. In his liner notes, Smith also credited Gust with the sleeve design and gave a solitary thank you to Garrick Duckler.

'Afterwards, he was enormously apologetic about not thanking me,' recalls Gonson. 'He told me it didn't occur to him to put me in such a casual place, he thought I was more integral to it than that. When the record came out, he said to me, "I can't believe I didn't thank you. You made this record." There was also a very specific divide. I managed his band, not him.'

Smith titled the record *Roman Candle* after its opening track. It was a song through which his fury at his stepfather tore. The album picked up positive reviews when it came out, though in local publications for the most part. One critic posited how Smith sounded like Paul Simon. It was a spurious comparison, since either Nick Drake or Alex Chilton was so much closer to the mark, but it stuck and was to cast him as a wistful, sad-voiced folkie for years to come. Over time, it got so the mere mention of Simon's name was enough to provoke a rise out of Smith. Cavity Search's initial run on the record was small, just 2,000 CDs and half as many cassettes. Sales were slow and also local in the main.

'*Roman Candle* was a thing in Portland,' says Swofford. 'It did okay and people cared. Elliott was one of our own. Generally, the reaction in the city was: "The guy from Heatmiser put out a solo record? Wow, it's really soft and quiet!" Outside of Portland, nobody gave a shit.'

Around the album's release, Smith played a scant brace of solo shows in town. One was at a south-east coffee bar, Umbra Penumbra, with Pete Krebs opening for him, the two of them shuffling onto the tiny stage tucked away at the back of the narrow little shop. The other was an official launch night for *Roman Candle* at La Luna on 5 July. Krebs was again on the supporting bill along with Sean Croghan and a third singer-songwriter from the scene, Gilly Ann Hanner. Their friends and fellow musicians filled the small room. Smith was green-gilled nervous before both nights, but folk *really* listened to his sets.

'I tried to go every time Elliott played acoustically,' says Chris Slusarenko. 'It was amazing to see those early shows of his where everybody was leaning in and listening. No one was talking or wandering around the club. It made you proud someone you knew was so talented.'

'It was striking how different the crowd responded when I played and then when he did,' says Pete Krebs. 'As a solo artist, you kind of get used to people not paying attention. You'd hear people talking. But with Elliott, the hush would just happen. Elliott always did have an extra something. It was like the whole room locked in on him. Part of me wanted the same reaction for myself, but I also understood Elliott's abilities far exceeded my own. He was special.

'Really early on, he was at his best and brightest, I think. Not because he was our little secret for a while there. I just think he felt supported and validated and loved by his community and the people here. I don't believe he was super-confident about his stuff when he started out. I really don't think he thought of himself as a terribly attractive person. He was very self-deprecating, but he seemed to be enjoying himself at least some of the time. He laughed and joked a lot. But if you're a kind of shy, sensitive person and then all of a sudden people are telling you how great you are and you can hear a pin drop when you play, it's probably going to sit with you in an uncomfortable way. It's why he drank.'

That August, Smith cut another record, a split 7-inch single with Krebs again. They did it for the homemade label Jason Mitchell and Moira Doogan were in the process of starting up, Slo-Mo Records. Krebs pitched the idea of the pair of them collaborating on the two songs, writing, arranging and putting them to tape on the spot. Smith misunderstood the concept and wrote and recorded his own contribution one day back at Gonson's house. When Krebs corrected him, he tossed the song to the wind and right away spirited up another for Krebs to join him on.

'No Confidence Man' marked an immediate step up from the *Roman Candle* material. Delicate and paper-tissue fragile, it's a haunted house of a song, Smith's lamentation sung so soft and far-away-sounding it might as well be drifting up from a tomb. Here, at last, he gives a name to the target of his rage, placing him in the context of a crime scene: 'Charlie got a pin in his hand, a rubber loop. Says I'm the man you really want, so just act natural . . .'

With Krebs now, he returned to Sam Coomes' and Janet Weiss's house to record both 'No Confidence Man' and Krebs' song, 'Shytown'. There was just the two of them there. Smith set up the mics and ran the sound. Making use of other instruments scattered about the place, including a drum gong belonging to Weiss, they were done in a couple of hours or so. Later the same day, they went over to the Heatmiser house to have their photographs taken for the single's sleeve artwork. Smith dug out a couple of facemasks for them to wear for the occasion, one of a bear, the other a bat, picked up from some truck-stop or other on the road with Heatmiser. They stepped outside for the pictures, stood next to Krebs' old Volvo station wagon. Smith put the bear mask on and Krebs the bat. There they are frozen on film, a couple of happy-go-lucky guys clowning around in the late-afternoon sun.

'Six months later, we got a stack of maybe twenty singles from Jason and Moira and that was that,' says Krebs. 'That record is such a perfect artefact from Portland and of a time and place. It was totally low-key and before everything got all crazy and changed. We thought it was just hilarious to put on these dumb masks and make bear noises while someone was taking our picture.'

★

On 17 August, Smith joined up with a group of fellow north-west performers for his first tour as a solo artist. The opening date was at the Crocodile Café up in Seattle. Also on the bill were Sean Croghan, who had put Smith's name forward for the tour in the first place, Tammy Watson, Carrie Akre and Slim Moon, who doubled as the co-proprietor of an up-and-coming Olympia record label, Kill Rock Stars. All of the artists were to perform spoken-word sets, with the exception of Smith, who elected to speak through his songs. They were to spend the late summer travelling down the Pacific coast, finishing up with shows in Los Angeles and San Francisco.

Smith drove up to Seattle with Croghan. The first night of the tour, he opened the show. The reaction he got at the Croco-dile Café was very different from Portland. People chattered all through his set, the bar till went on ringing up. Following him out on stage, Croghan told the Seattle audience they had missed out on something completely out of the ordinary. After the show, both of them hitched a ride with the others in the tour van for the overnight drive to the next stop in Eugene, Oregon. By the time they got to Los Angeles and after six more shows, word had got around and Smith was closing the bill.

The LA date was at a poky coffeehouse on Pico Boulevard, Jabberjaw, on 26 August. Andy Factor came along to support Smith. Slim Moon, who had found himself transfixed by Smith's sets, hustled along a bunch of people. It was a sweltering hot night and the power gave out. With no air conditioning and the heat suffocating inside the small, low-ceilinged room, it was decided Smith should do his set on the patio outdoors. After setting up in a corner of the backyard, he perched like a bird on a plastic chair. He played with Gonson's Le Domino guitar on his lap, no microphone or other amplification, and nothing to light up the black night. He opened his set with a brand-new song, 'Needle in the Hay'.

'The people who were there at Jabberjaw will never forget that night,' says Factor. 'It's something I can always think on and remember Elliott by. For me, it was the complete reassurance all we were working towards was amounting to something and that it was all-time.'

Two of Slim Moon's guests at Jabberjaw were husband and wife Rob Schnapf and Margaret Mittleman. Schnapf was a record producer and Mittleman was working as a publishing executive at BMG Music. Two years earlier, they had talent-spotted another precocious young singer-songwriter playing an acoustic show just across town in Silver Lake. Mittleman went and secured a publishing deal for the then 22-year-old Beck Hansen and Schnapf recorded a 12-inch single with him for the couple's label, Bong Load Records. Five months ahead of Smith's Jabberjaw date, Geffen re-released the song, 'Loser', and with it made Beck an overnight sensation. Over the next six years, Mittleman and Schnapf were to be the single biggest influencers on Smith's career.

'Margaret was friends with Slim, so I just went along to Jabber-jaw with her and no expectations,' recalls Schnapf. 'And, yeah, Elliott killed me. I don't think we spoke too much afterwards. It was just a "hi" and then him and Margaret talked a little more, but I left thinking, "Okay, this is for real with this guy."'

'Rob and I saw the same sort of magnetism in Elliott as we had in Beck,' says Mittleman. 'It was like, "Oh my God, *what are you doing?*" But I was drawn to Elliott in a different way, the human being he was. There weren't many people there at Jabberjaw, but there was just something about him. The songs were incredible. I knew right there and then if I could work with him, it would be pretty amazing. In my head, I was thinking I could help him navigate all of this and protect him.

'Definitely, I sensed right off he needed protecting. Not like he was, "Oh, poor me," but more like he wanted to save who he was. Then again, he did have another side to him. He was sort of an innocent, but not. For me, it was like, "Elliott, you should preserve this and let's put a bubble around you to keep all of the nonsense away so it doesn't eat at you, or destroy you."'

CHAPTER 10

The Biggest Lie

After the Pop Chord tour, Smith kept up a conversation with Slim Moon. Smith told Moon he was looking beyond Cavity Search to release his next solo record. He wanted, he said, the backing of a label with better distribution and greater resources to carry his music outside of Portland. As far as he was concerned, Frontier was not an option. He meant to keep his own work entirely separate from Heatmiser's. Moon offered to act on his behalf as an intermediary. Back in Olympia, he gave Calvin Johnson a copy of *Roman Candle*. Smith was a perfect fit for K Records, Moon enthused to Johnson. Moon never did hear a word back from Johnson on Smith's account.

As they carried on talking, Smith eventually mentioned to Moon the possibility of doing a 7-inch single with Kill Rock Stars. Moon was open to the idea and countered with an offer to also release Smith's next album. He proposed a one-off deal, tailored for them both to see how it went. Kill Rock Stars was heading into its fourth year of operations. Co-founding the label in 1991 with partner Tinuviel Sampson, Moon ostensibly meant to put out records by his friends in Olympia. The first releases on Kill Rock Stars were all small-scale, 7-inch and spoken-word compilations. As things developed, the fledgling label got in on the ground floor of the Riot Grrrl movement. Kill Rock Stars had snapped up two of the local scene's trailblazers, Kathleen Hanna and her band Bikini Kill and Heavens to Betsy, featuring Corin Tucker, who was now moving on to form a second band, Sleater-Kinney.

In Portland, Smith's intensifying focus on his own career was just one of the threads tugging at his relationship with JJ Gonson. Margaret Mittleman's entry into the frame served to widen the dividing line between Smith on one side and Gonson and the rest of Heatmiser on the other. Now it was clear to Gonson just how productively Smith was writing music, but equally to his own and not the band's ends. Furthermore, his latest batch of songs were as pitch-black as the mood he'd sunk into of late and with an even more sinister edge to them.

Along with 'Needle in the Hay', Smith was delving into a junkie netherworld on titles such as 'High Times', 'The White Lady Loves You More' and 'Alphabet Town', named after New York City's notorious Lower East Side heroin haunt. His apparent fascination with heroin seriously troubled Gonson. She bore the emotional scars from a previous relationship with a heroin addict and wasn't about to put herself through the wringer twice. The seeds marking the doom of their relationship were being sown.

'My ex was a recovering addict, but someone who was genuinely abusive,' Gonson reveals. 'Like, he was really not safe when I lived with him.'

When he mustered one, Smith's defence was that he wrote like a novelist, telling fictional stories through construct characters. Doubtless, he could also lay claim to writing about what he saw in his everyday life. Portland was still suffering the after-effects of the crippling downturn in the American economy. Parts of downtown remained desperately neglected. One of Smith's favourite hangouts, Satyricon, occupied a particularly rundown neighbourhood. He couldn't have failed to register the number of desperate souls on the street outside of the club most nights. A Portland movie director, Gus Van Sant, used the city as the milieu for a junkie heist movie, *Drugstore Cowboy*, in 1989. Heroin plagued the Pacific Northwest. Already, it had claimed the lives of several prominent musicians from the region – among them, Andrew Wood of Mother Love Bone and Kristen Pfaff of Courtney Love's band, Hole.

So far as any of his friends could tell, Smith hadn't yet succumbed to heroin. Booze was still his drug of choice for the greatest part. Nevertheless, Kurt Cobain's justification for using heroin wouldn't have been lost on him. Cobain insisted he self-prescribed heroin as the most effective painkiller for his aching gut. Smith might very easily have concluded it could soothe his own bilious stomach, or else it would also serve as an excuse for his own heroin fixation.

'Elliott kept his cards pretty close to his chest most of the time,' says Pete Krebs. 'I think he was really good at presenting himself in a way people liked, but that also afforded him a lot of protection. We all have our demons, though, and Elliott's affected him deeply. And as much as he tried, the people around him saw him more clearly than maybe he would have liked.

'In a small scene, everybody kind of knows each other a little bit. There are cross-connections and cross-currents. You become sensitive to each other. People really started to see Elliott change and a lot of us got concerned. As his talent was magnified, so were his troubles. The local music family watched Elliott begin to spiral. We saw him becoming more uncomfortable. There was a growing sense of something being wrong with him. A lot of people in town really started to worry about the guy and wanted to put energy into propping him up. It wasn't done for any reason other than friendship and love.'

On 17 September 1994, Smith played a solo show back at Umbra Penumbra. He sat once more balled-up on a stool at the rear of the room next to the toilets. Neil Gust got up to join him for the tenth and last song of his set. It was another new song, 'Half Right', one Smith intended for himself but would end up using with Heatmiser. Three days after the Umbra Penumbra gig, Frontier released Heatmiser's *Cop and Speeder* album.

By then, the last bolts holding him and Gonson together as a couple were broken and irreparable on both of their accounts. He had drained her and she was exhausted with him. Their parting was bittersweet but scarring all the same. Rather than address their issues head-on, Smith put down his conflicting feelings on a cassette recording he gave to Gonson, upon which he performed for her a Cheap Trick song, 'If You Want My Love': 'I need you to need me,' he sang, soft and sad. 'I'd love you to love me. I'm begging you to beg me.'

'When we split up, he and I were tearing each other into little pieces emotionally,' Gonson revealed in 2013. 'Or at least he was tearing me – I can't speak for him. He was the love of my life in a lot of ways. I'm enormously grateful to have had that emotional experience. Everybody should be *that* in love with somebody, even if it has to come to an end.'[12]

Around the same time, Smith had a second tattoo done. This one was on his upper right arm and of a character from an old storybook he had read as a child, Ferdinand the Bull. In *The Story of Ferdinand* by Munro Leaf, Ferdinand is tempted from his pasture by the bright lights of the city to seek his fame in the bullring. As the story unfolds, Ferdinand ultimately refuses to fight a matador and retreats to the sanctuary of his grass and flowers. Smith doubtless saw his own conflicts and uncertainties with the music business reflected in Ferdinand's tale. It never stopped him, though, from entering the fray.

The same September, Smith spent a day recording at Tony Lash's house. Lash had upgraded his home studio with an eight-track machine and a couple of good-quality mics. He set Smith up in the basement and left him to his own devices, disappearing upstairs for his lunch. Smith put down three tracks in the space of the afternoon. 'Needle in the Hay' came out just as insistent-sounding as the night at Jabberjaw. His woozy, country-and-western-flecked harmonica part stood out from 'Alphabet Town'. He played the third new song, 'Whatever (Folk Song in C)', on Gonson's Le Domino. The end result was like a Gen X Woody Guthrie, his lyric a hopeless lover's entreaty: 'If you're all done like you said you'd be, what are you doing hanging out with me?'

These three were songs befitting the hypogeal environment of Lash's studio. The feel of them was shrunken-in, hollowed-out and withering in the gloom. Smith found light relief elsewhere. Chris Slusarenko and his brother, Nate, were putting together a Devo covers band to play a talent show at the X-Ray Café. They had already recruited Sam Coomes and Sean Croghan for the date and Smith wanted in. Slusarenko invited him along to practice and Smith threw himself into perfecting Devo's robotic tics and dance moves. He was there, stage-left, on lead guitar the night they played the X-Ray Café. They billed themselves the Spud Boys, all of them done up in identikit versions of the Ohio band's uniform of banana-yellow boiler suits and red flowerpot hats.

'My brother made our outfits,' recalls Slusarenko. 'We had people in monkey masks and diapers also running around the stage. All of us had to learn the choreography and be stone-faced onstage. At practice, Elliott was really quiet. He basically just wanted to know what to do. But he was one of the Portland knuckleheads, too. He was cool about acting like Devo onstage.'

Heatmiser began their tour for *Cop and Speeder* on 9 October in Fort Collins, Colorado. They played shows through to the end of the year, in the Midwest and up and down the West Coast. Coomes' presence on the tour improved the general state of the band, but Smith appeared more apart from the others than ever. He was growing ever more frustrated with how the band sounded onstage. On the spur, he agitated for them to play quieter and more restrained – in other words, more like his solo material. Matters reached a head at a band meeting a few dates into the tour. Smith set himself against the other three, Tony Lash especially.

'Elliott wanted to completely change the way we played,' says Lash. 'He got on at me to switch to playing drums with brushes, he totally put me on the spot. This was just before a show and I pushed back. I was resistant to the idea and he got frustrated with me. From what I saw later on, once you got moved into the "bad" column by Elliott there wasn't too much you could do to get out of it. It's what happened with Brandt. There were definitely times he reacted in a way I really didn't understand.

'We didn't talk about it at the moment, but then a couple of days later we had this big meeting. There was the feeling there he didn't really want to be doing the band anymore. I said to him, "You know, you don't have to carry on if you don't want to. We can go home now." I would just as soon have flown back to Portland rather than have to spend three or four more weeks in a van with that kind of tension going on.'

They slogged through to the end of the run. At the last two shows in Seattle and Portland, the rancorous mood was lifted by having the Spud Boys open for them. The Portland date was an end-of-year turn at La Luna on 30 December. On the night, the Spud Boys were preceded onstage by the Brothers E, a couple of Elvis Presley impersonators regaling with a full show band and horn section. For their set, the Spud Boys came out dolled up in wigs and voluminous hippie-chic fringed jackets and flared trousers.

'We killed it and people went nuts,' says Chris Slusarenko. 'Elliott wore a long black wig. I remember him playing his guitar behind his head, doing all this Jimi Hendrix shit. It was one of the most fun shows I've ever played.'

At the start of the New Year, Smith found another location to put the rest of his new songs to tape. Leslie Uppinghouse had run the sound at La Luna the night he launched *Roman Candle*. Like Tony Lash, she lived locally to Smith and also operated an eight-track home studio set-up. Smith worked at Uppinghouse's place through January and February of 1995, keeping up a routine of arriving early and going on deep into the night. Uppinghouse settled him in a box room with her reel-to-reel Tascam recorder and board. The room was a light, airy space with a high ceiling, bare floorboards, wood panelling and picture windows. It was an environment utterly at odds with the devastation going on in the songs Smith was tracking.

While taping at Uppinghouse's, Smith sat himself up close to the Tascam. The songs came out either brittle-sounding, as if they might break apart, or else infused with a barely contained fury and raw as grazed skin. The instrumentation was spare and uncluttered. For the most part, he stuck to an acoustic guitar, a snare drum and a ride cymbal. What shading there was came from instruments borrowed from Uppinghouse: a Fender keyboard, tambourine and, on one track, 'The White Lady Loves You More', a cello part he improvised off the cuff and in a single take.

Neil Gust dropped by one afternoon to add electric guitar to another track, 'Single File'. Rebecca Gates of the Spinanes also visited to put down a vocal on yet one more, 'St Ides Heaven'. Otherwise, Smith hunkered down by himself and with the box-room door kept shut to ward off Uppinghouse's boxer dog, Anna. His singing on these tracks is at once more assured than it was on *Roman Candle*, but more delicate and so tentative he could be tracing a fingertip line on a new lover's skin. Even so, he amassed more songs than he knew what to do with, each as wrenching and poignant as the next.

There were tender, mournful ballads such as 'Good to Go', 'Angel in the Snow' and 'Talking to Mary'. Others like 'Southern Belle', 'High Times' and 'Riot Coming' churned and surged. On one, 'Clementine', Smith re-purposed the old American folk standard 'Oh My Darling, Clementine'. Uppinghouse's mother dictated him the words to the original over the phone. Another, 'Christian Brothers', was a rare switch around, a song he had meant for Heatmiser but ended up keeping for himself. In the band's hands it was hesitant and subdued. His own rendering of it is a singular howl of anguish.

Altogether and all at once, the motherlode of material cut those weeks at Uppinghouse's place conveys a bottled-up sense of heartbreak, anger, impotence and despair. Over a blizzard of finger-picked notes and strummed chords, Smith seethes on 'Southern Belle': 'Killing a Southern belle is all you know how to do. That and give other people hell.' As well as his stepfather, he was now turning his invective in on himself and at his own perceived inadequacies. On the tumbled-out 'Big Decision', he cautions: 'You know I won't stay sober . . . You can't kick when you're down.' There was defiance, too. The opening line of 'Christian Brothers', for instance, is an arresting statement of intent: 'No bad dream fucker's gonna boss me around.' However, the most jarring lyric was dredged from the darkest depth imaginable. Amounting to seven words and one line, it was from a folksy lament titled 'Georgia, Georgia.' It ran: 'But oh man, what a plan, suicide.'

To mix the tracks, Smith returned to Tony Lash's house. By then, he had pared the material down to an intended twelve-track album. It was to open with 'Needle in the Hay' and close with one of his loveliest, but most despondent-sounding songs, 'The Biggest Lie'. The last lines he was to sing on the record seem like a lyrical sleight of hand. Depending on one's own interpretation, through them he could be seen to be either re-affirming or re-casting everything he had sung in the eleven songs preceding. 'We're so very precious you and I,' he intones. 'And everything you do makes me want to die. Oh, I just told the biggest lie . . . ' At all events and from Lash's perspective at least, Smith emerged from the whole process emboldened.

'The mixing aspect was still really simple, but Elliott felt more comfortable saying no to me,' he says. 'Definitely so if I had ideas

he didn't think would work for him. There were a few minor
impasses as a result, but we never had any kind of big conflict.'

Certainly, Smith was decisive in his dealings with Slim Moon.
He agreed to Moon's offer to release the album on Kill Rock Stars,
no strings attached. The label went ahead and put out a 7-inch
version of 'Needle in the Hay' even before Smith had finished
mixing the other tracks. Denny Swofford doesn't recall Smith
specifically telling him he was jumping ship from Cavity Search,
but remains philosophical about losing him to Moon: 'As far as
Christopher and I were concerned, it was the same thing as with
Heatmiser and Frontier,' he says. 'If a label with more resources
wants to do an Elliott Smith record, go for it. Frankly, Kill Rock
Stars had more to offer. Elliott was appreciative of Cavity Search
being there for him. Years later, he acknowledged it several times
verbally in person, which always makes me feel good. It's nice
and refreshing to have worked with appreciative artists.'

At the same time, Smith was striking up a relationship with
Joanna Bolme, who worked the bar at La Luna. Having moved
up to Portland from Florida as a child, Bolme had immersed
herself in the city's punk rock scene and spent a year playing bass
with a local all-female punk band, Calamity Jane. Their peak
was opening a 50,000-capacity stadium show for Nirvana in
Buenos Aires in June 1992. Bolme was now looking to move into
the recording and engineering side of the business. Smith got
to know her from nights hanging out at La Luna and when she
was still dating Pete Krebs. They properly hit it off over a game
of pool at the bar. Smith was timid about making an approach,
but Neil Gust successfully badgered him into asking Bolme out.

Soon enough, Smith was spending more time over at Bolme's house than at the Heatmiser House. He shared his newly recorded songs with Bolme, eager for her opinion. For her part, at the outset of their relationship Bolme found Smith to be light-hearted, easy-going and optimistic about his solo music and the future. The rhythms of their time together were never again to be so smooth. Bolme was to become his muse, his protector and perhaps the love of his life, but not so she could save him from himself. And not so he wasn't as callous towards her as he could be towards everyone else.

'One morning, Elliott went out and bought Jacques Pépin's *Simple and Healthy Cooking* book,' Bolme told Autumn de Wilde of those early, happy days of them being together. 'And he made me this amazing fancy dinner. The next night, he made another great dinner.

'He was an extremely creative person, but his left brain was functional as well. If you gave him a manual or cook-book, he could follow the instructions. He was a good driver. He was not a spaced-out guy. He was really on top of it. He didn't want to *deal* with things sometimes, but he was perfectly capable of it. He was a really well-rounded person ... Later on, when he started being surrounded by fans and peo-ple who would do *everything* for him, he lost the need to use that part of his brain.'[13]

'Things were never really awkward between Elliott and me because of Joanna,' says Pete Krebs. 'Joanna's really important to Elliott's story for a number of reasons. She's kind of central to the old school Portland rock 'n' roll scene. She dated a lot of musicians. Whenever I saw them together, they seemed like a pretty good match.

'I believe Elliott did need to be looked after. I mean, "need" and "want" are two different things, but in Elliott's case, I think both of those words would be applicable. To me, he seemed to respond to being taken care of a little bit. He was aware of the things he had done to him when he was a child and he liked the comfort especially of a companion to take care of him.

'Joanna had taken care of me. I was kind of a drunk and an asshole back then. She put up with a lot of shit from me. Maybe she was a really patient person. Maybe she was primed to be a caretaker. Increasingly, I felt Joanna became protective of Elliott, or tried to take care of him. Really, it wore her down.'

CHAPTER 11

Half Right

If anyone was harbouring lingering doubts as to where Smith's priorities lay, these would have been expelled by the spring of 1995. In her capacity as the band's manager, JJ Gonson was lining up a Heatmiser tour to run through March and April. Margaret Mittleman pressed ahead and booked Smith a solo tour for the same period. With relations between the two of them strained enough already and his second solo album scheduled for a summer release, Smith nixed Gonson's plans for the band and so as to strike out on his own.

'The band was falling apart and Elliott had someone acting on his behalf who didn't communicate with me *at all*,' says Gonson. 'It was a big part of why I ended up going through a mental health crisis, because the breakdown between us was so monstrous. I didn't know what she was doing, or what he was doing, and if he was telling the other members of the band, no one was telling me. I was watching everything crumble and feeling responsible for it. It was awful.'

'I never encouraged Elliott to move on, but only to keep on with what he had going,' says Mittleman. 'More opportunities just started to come up for him. That's management. You're trying to make the most of those opportunities and as people catch on. Elliott felt guilty about it. He loved Neil Gust. He didn't want to hurt Neil most especially, but at the same time he really wanted to pursue his own thing.'

The first show Smith played on his latest solo run was at a club in Vancouver, the Starship Room on 2 March, and the last at the Nile Theatre in Phoenix on 24 April. In between times, his black mood lifted. For the majority of the shows he was opening for a fellow singer-songwriter signed to Kill Rock Stars, Mary Lou Lord. Hailing from Salem, Massachusetts, Lord started off busking on the Boston subway. Three years earlier, she had attracted a flurry of attention when dating Kurt Cobain for a matter of weeks. She was drawn towards Smith by Slim Moon, who'd persuaded her to catch him on the Pop Chord tour. Lord was instantly bowled over. She regarded Smith as the same kind of alchemist as the triumvirate of magical songwriters she cherished the most – Dylan, Joni Mitchell and Nick Drake. Her audiences also warmed to Smith and as their coast-to-coast tour progressed, it was he who was playing to dumbstruck rooms each night.

'Elliott still had his moments on the tour, but mostly he was pretty light-hearted and a tonne of fun to hang out with,' says Jason Mitchell, who Smith took with him for company as much as anything. 'He enjoyed being able to show up and be the support act and not have make a whole lot of decisions, and to be free to have some beers afterwards.

'He could go out there and just do his thing, and of course, 99 per cent of the time he blew everybody's fucking minds. Towards the end of the tour, I felt a little bad for Mary Lou because people were consistently talking through her sets. Yet when Elliott came out, usually within half a song the room would be completely silent.'

'Early on, Elliott learned how to quiet a room,' says producer Rob Schnapf. 'If people were talking, he would start to play quieter and so he almost made them listen to him. Then it would just be like, "*Whoa!*" and everybody would be transfixed. Conversations were starting to happen, too, between groups of people going to see him play these small shows. They felt like Elliott was theirs and nobody else knew him. It was as if he was a personal discovery and belonged to them.'

Smith's mood slumped once again when the itinerary took them to Texas for four shows. On the drive down to Dallas from Denver, he seemed to become more withdrawn with each passing mile. They moved on to Houston and from there to the state capital, Austin, on Friday, 17 March, St Patrick's Day. In Austin, the annual week-long South by Southwest music festival was in full swing. SXSW was fast growing into the American music industry's leading showcase event and Kill Rock Starts had applied for slots on the bill for Lord and Smith, but been turned down. Lord schemed instead for the two of them to mount a guerrilla raid on the event.

Picking a location outside a Kinkos print shop on the festival's main drag, 6th Street, Lord organised for a makeshift stage to be put up on the pavement. As she pitched it to Smith, they would have a showcase of their own. Tempting a passing crowd right out there on the street and playing through the busking amp she kept in the back of her car just in case. For moral support, they could count on Moon and the posse of other Kill Rock Stars artists along with him in town.

As Lord recalled to *Pitchfork*, Smith was somewhat reticent about her plotting: 'Elliott was like, "I don't know about this, Mary Lou," but I kind of wore the pants on that tour,' she said. 'I said to him, "That's enough outta you." We got a bunch of booze and started playing . . . It was St Patrick's Day and Elliott was playing all kinds of Irish songs and Pogues songs. We played all night and got happily shit-faced. It was one of the best nights of my life.'[14]

Margaret Mittleman had also joined up with the tour. Her view of the night was somewhat different: 'Elliott got up there by himself and the crowd was loud,' she says. 'He left the stage several times to go use the bathroom, because he had his nervous stomach thing going on.'

Following the tour, Smith slipped back into his juggling act with Heatmiser. Five days after returning to Portland, he was onstage with the band for a show at La Luna on 1 May. They played the same venue again on 1 June, but these were isolated dates. Gonson strived to re-schedule the two months of shows originally scheduled for the spring, but without success and in large part because of Smith not making himself available. Heatmiser were to play just six more shows the rest of the year, all of them in Portland or else Seattle. When he did have to be on band business, Smith increasingly seemed sullen, distracted and more so than ever as if he were there under duress.

'A lot of the time it was us just getting on each other's nerves,' says Tony Lash. 'Elliott was really unhappy and wanting to be more off on his own. If we were away playing shows, he was missing Joanna, too. There was this dark cloud hanging over the band.'

In the immediate aftermath of a sortie up to Seattle in early June, Smith and Gust separately moved out of the Heatmiser House. Initially, Smith went to shack up with Bolme and Gust to sleep on a sofa at Gonson's house. Even so, there was something yet pulling the pair of them back together. Sean Croghan was living on the ground floor of a duplex in the neighbourhood. When Croghan's flatmate upped and left for Seattle, Smith asked Croghan if he could take on the spare room. Soon afterwards, the apartment upstairs became vacant and Gust and Jason Mitchell took it on. The four of them quickly established a routine of intermingling between the two apartments. Often as not, a stereo would be blaring out from one or other of their households, or from both at once. Each of their places soon took on the appearance of rehearsal rooms, with guitars, cables and amps cluttering the floors. Smith also purchased an eight-track reel-to-reel machine for his own use downstairs.

Smith felt at ease with Croghan and they grew to be close. As well as music, they had shared interests in literature, arthouse movies and boozing. Like Smith, Croghan was also of a downbeat disposition, but with the same sharp and mordant sense of humour to go along with it.

'Elliott had a definite darkness and depressed nature,' Croghan noted. 'And I did, too. I grew up in Portland and we called it "Doom Town". The city was grey and it rained, and it affected you. Elliott had his many moods and sides, but he was a funny son of a bitch. Because of the way his brain worked, he would grab hold of something. If I said something he thought was funny, he was like a tape loop. He would sit there and repeat it, and try to find every different way he could to set up the punchline. He could do this for two hours and until we were like, "Alright, Elliott, drop it!"

'Elliott's dad, Gary, described it best once. He said, "Elliott, you and Sean have 'Young Man's Disease'. You'll have something going on that is amazing and you'll try to sabotage it. Because you think it can't go this good." We both knew we were doing it. I think partially it was to cultivate those creative juices, but also there was a sense of security in our sadness. It was a blanket and to guard against the rest of the world, and success and all of those things.'[15]

'Elliott didn't hide the fact there were some dark things going on in his head,' says Jason Mitchell. 'And they could come out in the middle of him laughing his ass off at some stupid joke. There were times there would be a lot of drinking and discussions about how he might not be here very soon.'

Then again, Smith could turn in an instant to doing something completely unexpected and delightful. So spontaneous, it was as if he were improvising his own story and with pieces of performance art. 'There was one time we walked by a homeless guy asleep on the sidewalk,' says Mitchell. 'Elliott tucked a $100 bill into the guy's shoe. I loved the thought of this guy waking up and having no idea where it came from.'

The second of the two New York dates Smith played that summer was at a Lower Manhattan café bar, Fez, on 21 July. A subterranean venue, it was located in the basement of a café on Lafayette Street. As Smith performed, he was accompanied by the rumble of passing subway trains. The place was sparsely attended. One of the few souls who turned out to see him on the night was Mike Doughty, native of Fort Knox, Kentucky, and frontman for the alt-rock band, Soul Coughing. The band's A&R rep had talked Doughty into going.

'Our guy had this coterie of interesting, fashionable friends and he took me with him to Fez,' recalls Doughty. 'Elliott came out and he was this craggy-faced guy in a black T-shirt and with a little hat on. It was an almost-empty room and the few people there were not particularly engaged with the music happening onstage. He sat down with his acoustic guitar and straight up blew my mind. It was literally a life-changing show for me. Being in that place, not giving a fuck, and this dude walks out and changes your life. That is an image that will live in my mind for as long as I'm alive.'

On the very same Friday morning as the Fez show, Kill Rock Stars released Smith's new album. He'd elected to self-title it and as if to mark it as a fresh beginning. For the front cover artwork, he once again picked out one of JJ Gonson's photographs.

This one was an image she had snapped in Prague when she was travelling around Europe three years earlier. Gonson's picture captured a sculpture of two people made to look as if they were falling from a building. It was as stark and jarring as the subjects Smith broached on the record itself. As a piece, *Elliott Smith* impacted like a postcard sent from the edge of an abyss. Outside of Portland, it barely rated a review.

Returning to the north-west, Smith undertook a couple of back-to-back shows in Olympia and Seattle on 26 and 27 August. He was accompanied by a recently relocated singer-songwriter from California, Bill Santen. Santen had written to Smith and offered his services as driver and opening act. Smith called him up, apologising for the fact he could only afford to pay him $100 for both nights' work. The pair headed north in Santen's Toyota Camry.

'Of course, Elliott knew I'd never made $100 from playing music,' says Santen. 'It was a pretty amazing experience for me. Up until then, I'd been playing this terrible acoustic showcase at a strip club and all of a sudden, I was riding up to do this big club with Elliott. Mary Lou Lord was there and Slim Moon. After the show we went to a casino. I guess it was our bonding. There was lots of talking about music and smoking cigarettes.'

Home again in Portland, Smith cultivated a friendship with Santen, his junior by seven years. They drank together at Dot's, which was just across the street from where Santen was living. Santen got to be a frequent visitor to Smith's apartment, joining in with him on the ad-hoc recording sessions he conducted as a matter of course. Smith introduced Santen to Mittleman, who subsequently got him signed up to a publishing deal.

'I guess I always think back and wonder why Elliott wanted to hang out with me,' says Santen. 'I was nineteen years old. I'd a car and I offered to drive him, but I don't know why he let me open all those shows for him and then later on took me out on tour. I mean, his management seemed to think it was a good idea. I used to think they didn't want someone better than Elliott opening up for him. I really wasn't very good as a live performer and Elliott was incredible. He was incredible as a writer and as a guitar player, too. He would ask me to play with him on songs and I just couldn't do it.

'In Portland, I never hung out with him and his friends. It was always just the two of us, one on one. He was so completely different from anyone else I'd ever met. I used to have to wait so long outside of his house for him to get ready. He had a style of his own and was serious about it. His house was really messy. He slept really late. He could do really funny impressions of people. He had so much going for him, so many good things were happening for him, but when he drank, he'd get depressed and go to some really, *really* dark places.'

On one occasion, Santen drove Smith the 430 miles-plus from Portland to Boise, Idaho, for a show. Smith was in one of his brooding moods and the miles slipped by in an oppressive kind of silence. Then, in a flash, he brightened, regaling his young companion with a skit on the unlikely nature of carrot cake.

'This was our normal dynamic,' says Santen. 'We laughed about his carrot cake routine for two whole days. He wouldn't really talk to me about his being bummed out. I don't know if I ever even knew the same guy Tony Lash, say, knew. I was a young, extremely impressionable kid and he could be whatever he wanted around me.'

According to the terms of Heatmiser's recording contract, they owed their third album to Virgin. As their cheerleader at the major label, Andy Factor had secured them a healthy advance for the record and a good-sized recording budget. To varying degrees, all four band members needed the money. Tony Lash could at least fall back on engineering gigs and Sam Coomes was pulling in minimum wage working at a print shop. Without any income from touring, Neil Gust was living off unemployment cheques and odd jobs. Smith was in much the same boat and with his new record having done nothing to alter the fact his nascent solo career still wasn't covering the rent.

Between them, they decided to spend Virgin's money recording the album in a studio of their own making. Gonson took on the task of scouting locations around Portland and found a place for them to rent in an upscale neighbourhood east of the river on SE Ankeny Street. It was a smallish, wood-framed house painted green out front and set back from the road. Lash supervised the work of transforming the place into a studio. The open-plan living and dining rooms became their recording and control rooms. Lash sourced and leased all of their recording gear and put up big foam blocks around the downstairs walls of the house to insulate the sound. He was also going to produce the record himself.

Things started to go wrong just as soon as they began cutting tracks. The first song they tried out was one of Smith's, 'Burned Out, Still Glowing'. Lash stuck to their established routine of recording the track live to tape, ranged together in the living room, playing as a band and as if they were onstage. They took several passes at the song and Smith grew more visibly frustrated with each one.

'Elliott felt like it sounded too straightforward and like our early stuff, and to be fair, it did,' Lash concedes. 'But he wouldn't talk to me about it and it set the tone. It was fraught. I feel like it was one of the turning points in our relationship.'

'Burned Out, Still Glowing' was junked soon enough. The next song Smith brought to them was 'The Fix Is In'. He'd recorded a demo on his eight-track at home, just him and his acoustic. With its ghosting, double-tracked vocal, it was much more like one of his solo songs than anything he had done before with the band. Since he hadn't got around to putting a drum track on his demo, Smith asked Lash to start off by laying one down. Lash's drumming was tight, ordered and on the beat. Smith instructed him to loosen up.

'It was a tricky thing for me to do,' says Lash. 'There was still this whole thing going on where he felt like I always wanted things to be too perfect. We kept running into these impasses and then the mood would just go down the toilet. Afterwards, I thought my playing was on the leading edge a bit too much so I took the track and shifted the drums back. When Elliott heard what I'd done, he just kind of stormed out. And I went off some-where else to vent my frustration to Neil and Sam.'

On top of Smith's and Lash's issues, the unresolved envies and tensions going on between Smith and Gust were lacing an already toxic atmosphere with another layer of poison. Having moved to Portland together to start the band in the first place, the two friends were further apart than ever. Gust was dealing with a mix of roiling emotions. Awestruck at the extent of Smith's talent, but then again, just as threatened by it and feeling hurt, confused and angry all at the same time. For his part, Smith struggled with the impossibilities of trying to reconcile his resentments at being constricted in the band with the guilt plaguing him for leaving his best friend behind. The only common ground the two of them settled upon was to remain silent.

'It was a very weird time,' says Jason Mitchell, an observer at the sessions. 'All of us I think were missing when the lesson on communication was handed out. No, what you do is go off into the other room and you ignore, or else bitch about the person making you crazy, but you don't ever bring it up with them.'

Somehow, they managed to drudge through to finishing a record of sorts, but it wasn't one any of them liked very much. Their individual performances were flat and lifeless, the songs sounded arid and dead. Andy Factor was summoned from Los Angeles for a crisis meeting. He arrived to be told they wanted to re-do the whole thing from scratch.

'By this point, Heatmiser had taken up years of development and there were all of these other accommodations, and now

I had to go back to my bosses and ask for yet more money to start over,' says Factor. 'I did manage to get them a chance to try again, even though they had fucked it up. That's kind of what happened there. Virgin ended up spending a whole lot more money.'

Factor's additional funds paid for Rob Schnapf and his producing partner, Tom Rothrock, to be parachuted in over Lash's head. It wasn't lost on anyone how Schnapf was firmly in Smith's corner, but then again, he was their safest bet to keeping him on side. At the second time of asking, the album was completed. Under Schnapf's and Rothrock's steering, it came out sounding like an Elliott Smith solo record but with an alt-rock band happening to back him up. Or close enough at least for Smith to fully commit to the process. He stayed up all of one night with Schnapf just to nail his keening lead vocal track for one of the standout songs, 'Plainclothes Man'.

'We just kept on working at that song,' says Schnapf. 'Tom got exhausted and went back to our hotel, but Elliott and I were on a roll and we figured it out by the next morning. It's an awesome memory I have of working with him.

'The two of us were already hanging out a whole lot by then. I knew he was having difficulties in the band, but I didn't really know his communication style just yet. What I saw with the Heatmiser record were these three gentle guys not knowing how to bridge the gap between them. My role was to say to Elliott, "You can't just get frustrated and go for a walk and a smoke and not come back. That's not going to solve anything, so what are we going to do about it?" That's kind of what it came down to.'

'I don't think we'd have made it through to the end of the record if Rob and Tom hadn't been brought in,' Lash concludes plainly.

Schnapf and Rothrock also managed to strike an exact balance between Smith and Gust. Each of them was to get five songs on the finished record. The producers added polish to Gust's contributions, but there was no masking the degrees to which Smith's songs were stronger and better. His opening track, 'Get Lucky', is a jumble of ideas and possibilities, an indicator perhaps of his own restlessness. His accelerating sense of melody bursts to the fore with 'Plainclothes Man'.

When it came to putting the finishing touches to the record, the producers moved operations to Schnapf's and Rothrock's studio, the Shop, located in a verdant corner of north-west California, Humboldt County. A brace of Smith's compositions was earmarked to close the record, 'See You Later' and the song debuted with Gust at Umbra Penumbra the previous summer, 'Half Right'. 'See You Later' is shaded with Beatles' colourings, 'Half Right' is acoustic, lilting and autumnal. Equally, they are the best-crafted songs Smith ever wrote for Heatmiser, the switches turning the band from black and white to Technicolor. They were also to be his parting gifts and exit signposts.

'I hung out with them a bit more at Rob's and Tom's place,' recalls Factor. 'I mean, I had to ensure there was progress. It was such a beautiful house, out in the middle of the Redwoods and with a river running underneath it. I could instantly sense a mellower vibe. It happened because Rob and Tom turned out to be really good at keeping them positive, but also I think because they were resigned to this being their swansong and even though they hadn't told anybody yet. When they delivered the record to me, they said, "By the way, we're breaking up."'"

CHAPTER 12

Speed Trials

The New Year of 1996 opened with a significant milestone for Smith. Having arranged a publishing deal for him at BMG, Margaret Mittleman managed to persuade him to sign up to it. Up until this point, burned from his experience with Virgin and Heatmiser, when it came to his own music Smith had shied away from any kind of formal contract outside of a handshake deal. Mittleman, though, had hard-won his trust. The specifics of the deal decreed BMG was to advance Smith monies for each of his solo albums and set against future sales. The first cheque BMG wrote him was for around $25,000. By far the single biggest sum he'd ever been paid for his music, it allowed him to realise the ambition he had expressed to JJ Gonson up on the balcony of the Melody Lane Ballroom. No more slaving at odd jobs now. He could, at last, consider himself a professional musician.

Mittleman was becoming increasingly active in other areas on Smith's behalf, too. She had a good friend working at William Morris, the heavyweight Los Angeles booking agency, and cajoled her into booking Smith his first headline solo tour. The dates were to run for two months, opening in Chico, northern California, on 9 February and going on to Hoboken, New Jersey, on 31 March. In between times, Smith was to criss-cross the country. As the tour began, he travelled from San Diego, California, to Tuscon, Arizona, and on through Texas, Louisiana and Florida. Then up and around the East Coast and the Midwestern states, Ohio, New York, Massachusetts, New Hampshire, Wisconsin, North Dakota and more besides. He had an all-female indie-pop duo, the Softies, as his opening act. Bill Santen chauffeured him to some of the shows along the way. For the East Coast leg, Smith took the Amtrak train, lugging with him his acoustic guitar and a backpack.

He played at small clubs, cafés and coffee shops, just about anywhere that would have him. The *Elliott Smith* album hadn't sold very much better than *Roman Candle* and attendances for the shows generally were sparse, just a few diehards and assorted rubberneckers. Most nights, there was the low hum of people talking through his set. The scrape of shuffling feet and the ring of the cash register.

'I didn't go on the train with him, so he was pretty much on his own and he got frustrated,' says Mittleman. 'People wouldn't quiet down enough. I kept saying to him, "If you're done and you don't want to keep challenging yourself in these spaces, let's stop. But better if you could carry on and the audience will come to you." There was a lot of that kind of encouragement going on.'

In Hoboken, the last night of the tour, Smith played at a street corner tavern, Maxwell's. The Softies had a girlfriend working a bar shift at Maxwell's that night, Dorien Garry. After the show, everyone slept over on the floor of Garry's apartment. Barely out of her teens and in between full-time jobs, Garry had previously worked at a local record store and as babysitter and personal assistant to Sonic Youth's husband-and-wife couple, Thurston Moore and Kim Gordon. Serendipitously, she was soon to take a job at the very same New York PR agency, Girlie Action, Mittleman went on to hire to handle Smith's publicity. She was destined to become of one of Smith's closest confidantes.

'Bands would stay at my apartment all the time,' she says. 'I remember Elliott being there the morning after his Maxwell's show. My first impression of him was he was very sweet and kind. I thought his personality matched the type of music he was playing.

'It still bums me out how people get hung up on this identity he has as the sad guy making sad music. To me, both him and his music were sweet and sensitive, but also kind of comforting and earnest. There are plenty of musicians out there making very soft, gentle music who are total assholes. Elliott was not that type of person.'

★

Released from having to put up dry wall, Smith was now able to devote all his energies to making music whenever he was home in Portland. For the much greater part, he was his own master and most of his waking hours were filled up with writing songs. He was running just to keep up with capturing them to tape. Some he put down on the eight-track in his basement, others he demoed over at Joanna Bolme's place.

With Heatmiser in their moribund state, JJ Gonson was in the process of setting herself up in a new venture. She had taken on the rent of a warehouse space down on the east side of the river, meaning to start up her own record label. Gonson christened the place Undercover Inc. and, just as soon as she was moved in, Smith got in touch to beg to come by to record a song. He showed up with his acoustic guitar and eight-track recorder, setting up in a space adjacent to Gonson's office, raising a couple of temporary dividing walls so they were out of each other's sight. Nevertheless, Gonson could well enough hear the thump-a-clunk of his guitar, the metronomic beat of his foot on the concrete floor and the words he was singing.

'He came and went his own way, but all of the day I was sat there listening to him,' she recalls. 'We weren't interacting very much by then. Once in a while he would tell me what he was up to, but the band was falling apart and we were doing our own thing. I had my life. I had a dog. I wasn't nearly as involved in his life, but I was right there still.'

Smith meant to double-track his vocals and do his own mix of the track on his Mackie at home, but his board broke down so he turned to a big, amiable bear of man he had caught sight of along the bar at La Luna. By happenstance, Larry Crane hailed from Chico, California, where he'd served as bassist for a band named Vomit Launch. In this capacity, Crane went onstage

attired in not much more than a woman's slip. He had moved
up to Portland a couple of years earlier and opened his own
studio in the basement of his house. Laundry Rules Recording
was so-called because Crane kept a washer and drier behind
his console board. On the sheetrock of the wall above them,
there remained a past tenant's handwritten instructions for
their operation.

Having befriended Joanna Bolme at La Luna, Crane invited
her over to a barbecue party he was throwing in the back yard
of the house. Smith tagged along and she made the formal introductions. He asked his host if he could drop by another day to
wrap up a song he was working on, 'Pictures of Me', in the basement. Crane's set-up was a simple one: he had the exact same
Tascam 38 eight-track as Smith and a couple of half-decent
mics. His basement was dank and prone to flooding. But Smith
was in his element. He opened out the song working at Crane's,
layering onto it six vocal tracks and also a subtle but prodding
organ part.

'My first impression of Elliott was he was quiet, but his attention to the detail of how to make records was finely tuned,' says
Crane. 'It made the process of engineering or producing him so
much easier, because he knew where to go. You didn't have to
guide him on the basics. Straight off the bat, he had lots of little
things going on in "Pictures of Me" I thought were great.

'The two of us became friends in the studio, but it was a slow
build. One of the first things he said to me when we started off
tracking was, "This might not work. I might butt heads with you."
At the time, Tony Lash was a much more experienced engineer

than me. Tony had very strong opinions, whereas I was much more like, "You lead the way, Elliott, and I'll facilitate."

'I mean to say, Elliott had strong opinions as a musician, too, absolutely he did. But in his whole life – his personal life, his professional life, everything – to a fault he was always trying to be inoffensive, to not cause waves or be a bother to anybody. Even when he should've been speaking up and telling people what he wanted. It was a very frustrating aspect of his personality.'

All the while, the deluge of songs kept coming. It was as though Smith had made himself an open portal, hewn a gaping fissure in the wall of a dam. By Crane's estimation, he filled up six thirty-minute reels of tape with his new music. These weren't sketchy demos either, but complete takes made up of Smith's doubled lead vocals, acoustic guitar, piano and drum parts and splashes of other instrumental colouring besides. In other words, he readied three full albums. Furthermore, the depth of quality was remarkable. Within this abundance of material, there was nothing tossed off, no makeweights or filler. As a whole, the trove of material stacked up as Smith's very own, one-man version of Dylan's and the Band's *Basement Tapes*, which is to say it was a wellspring of wonder and glorious, unchecked inspiration.

In September, Smith broke off to go on tour once more. On this occasion, he was back to being the warm-up act and over the span of a bunch of shows with Sebadoh. Formed by ex-Dinosaur Jr bassist Lou Barlow, Sebadoh was just then the hot ticket in indie rock. In general, their audiences carried on talking throughout Smith's support sets, but he won small victories, too. Each night, there were a few more people gathering at the front of the stage just to be able to hear him play. It was enough to raise his spirits and make him feel as though he was out there staking a claim on new territory.

'Those were some of my favourite times to see Elliott play,' says Dorien Garry, by then managing his press for the tour. 'He seemed to genuinely enjoy performing back in those days. He would laugh so much. He would interact with the audience. He'd talk to them in this very sweet, human way. He would ask, "Do you want to hear a slow song or a fast one?" You know, they were all solo acoustic songs. He was being sincere, but also a little bit of a jokester.

'He was in a special moment of not being freaked out, or burnt out. He wasn't yet rattled by the whole machine. Sometimes he would say he felt like he'd played poorly, or messed up a song, but he hadn't got to the point he would down the road of truly doubting himself. He wasn't too unnerved by all of the things that eventually shook him down.'

'Elliott kept getting better,' says Rob Schnapf. 'I feel like this was a very sweet period of time for him. He couldn't quite believe the things that were happening for him. At the same time, he battled his own self-worth. There always was this balance of his self-worth getting lower versus what was happening in his life. The skew of it got harder as time went on, but in those days, there was a total innocence and a kind of magic to what was going on. Watching somebody who deserves something achieving it in real life is pretty great, if it doesn't chew them up and spit them out.'

★

How sapping, how conflicting it must have been for Smith to be sucked from all of this and back into Heatmiser's agonising death throes. Upon hearing of their apparent demise, Virgin had shelved the band's record, yet Andy Factor persisted in making waves on their behalf. Perhaps, also, Factor needed to justify to himself all of the time and money he had sunk into Heatmiser. At all events, he found a friend and ally in Keith Wood, proprietor of Caroline Records, the indie label through which Virgin had groomed the Smashing Pumpkins. Factor sent Wood the Heatmiser record, by now titled *Mic City Sons*. Wood liked it well enough to volunteer to put it out on Caroline.

Wood scheduled *Mic City Sons* for a late-October release and also put up the money for tour support. Through Virgin, Factor mustered additional funds for them to make a promo video for 'Plainclothes Man'. The video shoot was evidently arranged to keep Smith onside most of all. Ross Harris was hired as director, the location his north California stamping grounds. The atmosphere on set fast deteriorated, with Smith and Tony Lash picking right up where they had left off in the studio, alternately bickering with and moping at each other.

'When I got back to Portland from California, I wrote Elliott a really scathing letter,' says Lash. 'I'm not proud talking about it. If I had to do it over again, I'd have sat on it. It was unnecessarily harsh, about how much more he cared about his songs than friendships, and it was hurtful to him. I did get a reply from Elliott. It was pretty terse. I talked about it with Neil and he said he didn't know if things would ever again be okay between Elliott and me. And they weren't for at least a year and a half, or two years.'

Heatmiser's tour for *Mic City Sons* also ended up being the last rites on the band. Adding up to just nine dates, the inglorious trek ran from 17 November to 4 December with one show in each of Philadelphia, Washington, DC, Seattle and Portland, two in San Francisco and the closing three in Los Angeles. Lash opted out. His place was taken by John Moen, who was to go on to join another Portland band, the Decemberists. They played to near-empty, disinterested rooms. Alongside this, their album sank without trace.

The penultimate show of the tour was at an LA club, Spaceland, on 3 December. Backstage before the show, JJ Gonson snapped an image of Smith in the drab dressing room. The last picture she was to ever take of him, it captures him sat alone on a crumpled cream sofa, head bowed, jet-black-haired, oblivious to her camera and in the act of tuning up his guitar.

'It's the picture I print up most often and lean on hardest,' says Gonson. 'I love it as a photograph. I took it because of what I saw artistically. He could have been anybody in the picture. He's uncomfortable. He's unhappy. It was a bad time. There was a lot of not talking going on, including between him and me. Heatmiser didn't blow up, it fizzled out and we were never really reconciled.'

'The night before Spaceland, they played to literally zero people at a place called Linda's Doll Hut in Anaheim,' recalls Andy Factor. 'The whole thing was a disaster for me personally and I was pissed with Elliott. It was the saddest thing in the world. All of the love and the struggle invested, and at the imminent end only a very small set of believers to show for it.'

★

When it came to assembling his own next record, Smith went back into the Shop with Rob Schnapf and Tom Rothrock. There, the three of them endured a sometimes tortuous process of re-recording songs and editing the material on Smith's six tape reels down to a twelve-track album. Smith passed from agonising over his multiple choices to suffering a full-blown crisis of confidence about the songs themselves. As they had done for the four of them in Heatmiser, it fell to the two producers to soothe and manage Smith over the finish line.

At the Shop, Smith also recorded yet three more new songs from scratch. The first, 'Angeles', was woven with intricate, finger-picked patterns. Afterwards, he claimed to have written the other two, 'Between the Bars' and 'Say Yes', back-to-back, in a matter of minutes and as he was watching an episode of *Xena: Warrior Princess* on TV with the sound muted. 'Between the Bars' amounted to two minutes twenty seconds of bereft, but unbridled marvel. 'Say Yes' was bittersweet and ephemeral as a contrail. He wrote it for Joanna Bolme. The opening lines counted the heavy cost of his having had a head full of nothing but music for almost the whole of the time they were together: 'I'm in love with the world through the eyes of a girl, who's still around the morning after. We broke up a month ago.'

Both songs made it onto the completed record. Altogether, *Either/Or* runs to thirty-seven minutes dead. Not a second or note is wasted. Quiet, restrained for the most part, the songs are bruised and all too revealing. It stands as a mighty monument to Smith's extraordinary gift and at the very point it was fully maturing.

'That record's real,' says Schnapf. 'It's not like it's some studio construct. Those are actual performances. He's singing it. He's playing guitar. He's doing it live, in the moment, and yes, it sounds amazing and undeniable. My job was to bear witness. You bear witness, you stay out of the way and you let it happen.

'On *Either/Or* also, he didn't have outsiders blowing smoke up his ass just yet. Part of what drove him was his not knowing how good he was. That would have made him settle.'

'It didn't sound like anything else I was involved with at the time, or like anything anybody else was doing either, but I didn't care,' recalls Margaret Mittleman. 'I wasn't interested in what anybody else had to say, I felt it in my gut. Did I think it would connect with people? I wasn't sure. But I knew it was special and pure and brilliant. It was life-changing.'

To accompany *Either/Or*, Smith had organised to shoot a short film up in Portland a couple of weeks in advance of him going off on the fateful Heatmiser tour. *Lucky Three* was made over four days with a young film-maker, Jem Cohen, directing. An emigrant to the US from Kabul, Afghanistan, Cohen got his break helming a full-length documentary on Fugazi, *Instrument* (1999), shooting it on the fly on 16mm and Super 8 cameras. He used the same techniques for *Lucky Three*, framing Smith at various haunts and locations around the city. Through Cohen's lens, Smith appears slight, small and inconspicuous until he sits down to play 'Between the Bars' in a plain, white-walled room.

A second song, his version of Big Star's 'Thirteen', soundtracks a series of spectral images of the city viewed through the rain-splashed windscreen of a moving car. The third, 'Angeles', closes the film. The last shot is a close-up on Smith's face, his expression a small, tight smile. The end credits read, 'Thanks Slim, Joanna, Rebecca . . . JJ'. It was as if with this work he was settling his accounts and preparing to bid farewell to his friends, and to Portland, and to run and hide and remake himself anew once more.

CHAPTER 13

New Moon

It wasn't entirely accurate to say Smith was ploughing a lone furrow still with *Either/Or*. Across the American heartlands, there was a small band of other crusading singer-songwriters putting up beacons by the time Kill Rock Stars scheduled its release for 25 February 1997. Jeff Magnum was a Beatles nut and an inveterate home taper since his high school days in Louisiana. Launching his loosely assembled group, Neutral Milk Hotel, out of his adopted hometown of Denver, Colorado, he cut their debut album, *On Avery Island*, to four-track tape. On it, Magnum comported like a lo-fi rolling into one of Lennon, McCartney and George Harrison. Further west in Boise, Idaho, Doug Martsch was on to his third album masterminding Built to Spill, each one a mix of celestial harmonies and strafing guitar workouts.

Over in Los Angeles, multi-instrumentalist Mark 'E' Everett, son of a noted physicist, had assembled the Eels as a vehicle for his wry, literate songs. They made ripples in the summer of 1996 with their disarming debut record, *Beautiful Freak*. Then there was Beck, who the very same summer followed *Mellow Gold* with *Odelay*, his second daring, genre-hopping collection on the spin and the one cementing his status as both a genuine star and trailblazer for all of their kindred spirits. At a stroke, Smith could be seen to belong to a musical fraternity and for the first time outside of Portland and the Pacific Northwest, people were starting to sit up and take notice.

Slowly but surely, *Either/Or* began to pick up praise and then sell, much better than either of his two previous records had ever done. It was to be another year before Smith ventured outside of the US, but when he did he met with adoring notices. In the UK, the weekly music paper *Melody Maker* ventured in a glowing review of *Either/Or*: 'Is America's latest sensation the new Beck? Well, he did record this album with the team behind "Loser", but there's an emotional depth here Mr Hansen can only dream of . . . This is precious, magical stuff.'[16]

Ahead of *Either/Or* coming out, Smith was reconciled with Joanna Bolme. He moved out of the duplex with Sean Croghan and full-time into Bolme's house. He was also looking now for a new environment to go to work in, one affording him peace and privacy, but also the resources and possibilities he'd had at his disposal at the Shop. He set his sights now outside of basements and front rooms. Fortuitously, Larry Crane was thinking along the same lines. Smith offered to help Crane search for, and then build, a new studio space, in return for unlimited access once it was good and ready.

In January of 1997, they set out on their quest around Portland in Crane's beat-up Toyota pickup. Days on end, they scoured the city on the lookout for vacant buildings and 'For Rent' signs. Smith was plagued by his bilious stomach, but in good spirits otherwise and animated by the process. Eventually, they hit upon a spot in the south-east of the city. It was a drab-looking old cinder-block and stucco building on SE 50th Avenue with three rooms and storage out the back. Crane took on the lease and the pair went to work fitting it out for a studio. Smith put up dividing walls and dry-walled them. Along with Crane, he did all of the essential soldering and wiring work.

'Elliott was very focused on the task and worked hard,' recalls Crane. 'For Elliott, having the goal of a space to work out of was like the carrot. He wanted it just as much as I did. We both had partners in our lives, but we kind of abandoned them to get the studio done. For two weeks, we worked twelve-hour days. We had a crazy deadline, because I'd bands coming up from California to record with me and the place was booked out solid.

'We had started to figure each other out a little bit by then. As we worked, I would put on CDs of Petula Clark and stuff like that and Elliott would wince. We'd stop to eat together and after hours, go get a beer or a shot of whiskey. We went to see bands around town. It was fun to be hanging out with him, but real casual, too. Music was our common ground and certainly the main interest. Elliott couldn't be bothered with much else. He didn't care if his car ran or not, he wouldn't eat or take a shower sometimes. So far as Elliott was concerned, it was just about music and recording.'

Jackpot! Recording Studio officially opened its doors in the first week of February. Crane had acquired a sixteen-track mixing board for the place by then. From the outset, Smith would be at Jackpot! putting down tracks all the wee hours Crane didn't have it booked out. Crane engineered for him when he could. On occasion, Joanna Bolme also lent a hand. The nights the three of them were there, Crane and Bolme sat shoulder to shoulder at the board. Through the control room's big glass window, they looked out to Smith on the studio floor, perched at Crane's upright piano.

Smith drew measures of inspiration and joy from all kinds of musical sources. At the studio, he kept a bunch of different records to fire him up. He had a Kinks compilation, *The Kink Kronikles*, and a stockpile of recordings by the revered Spanish classical guitarist, Andrés Segovia. On a whole other tip, he retained a teenage mallrat's unashamed delight for hard rock and heavy metal. One evening, he showed up brandishing a copy of *In a Metal Mood*, an unlikely album of hard rock covers by the crooner Pat Boone. Smith proceeded to blast this outlandish collection through the studio speakers, howling with glee at Boone's ersatz rendition of Deep Purple's 'Smoke on the Water'. On another night, Smith and Bolme regaled Crane with a roaring karaoke rendition of a power ballad by German hard rockers the Scorpions, 'No One Like You'.

'We were raised around that stuff and Elliott loved the high drama of it,' says Crane. 'He saw humour in music. He'd like bits of songs and they would stay in his mind. We went to a bar one night to shoot some pool. Elliott put money in the jukebox and a Chicago song came on. At once, Elliott started enthusing, like, "This little spot, right here – I love it!" He didn't care for the song, but he liked a turnaround in it. He would be like, "Okay, *there's* something I can use." He had all of these things going on in his head.

'There was a lot of laughter, too. He could be silly. I would be in the control room, he'd be out on the floor, and he'd do that stupid thing of walking by the window and hunching, like he was going down steps. He'd do it over and again. I had a cheap little Casio guitar synthesiser with a rubber fretboard and strings like fishing line. It had a "Funky Clav" setting on it. Elliott would walk around with this thing strapped on, playing the clavinet part to Stevie Wonder's "Superstition". I mean, this guy was funny as shit.'

Then there were those nights Smith opened up Jackpot! for himself and worked alone through till dawn, cat-napping on the couch. The next morning, Crane would come in to find jumbles of cable and tape piling up on his desk. Since Smith was so habitually disorganised, it fell to Crane to sweep up after him. To clean up his actual mess, but also to rewind the recording tape to check and log whatever Smith had put down overnight so nothing was mislaid or forgotten about altogether. The other tell-tale indicator Smith had pulled an all-nighter was the reek of BO in the studio. On a roll, he was so lapse with his personal hygiene Crane christened him 'Smelliott'. The nickname stuck.

For the first year Jackpot! was up and running, Smith's drive to create seemed inexhaustible. The seam of songs he had to mine seemed infinite, too. One, with him sketching out an effervescent melody line with a sepia afterglow to it, sounded as if it could have fallen off his Kinks compilation and landed at the feet of the Beatles. Bolme referred to it as his 'Penny Lane' song, even after he had titled it 'Baby Britain'.

On 'All Cleaned Out', Smith set a strident guitar line next to his heartache vocal. 'Here come your pride and joy,' he sang. 'The comic little drunk you call your boy.' 'Sweet Adeline' ebbed and swelled like a gathering storm cloud. To have heard him excuse it, Smith's songs shouldn't necessarily be read as personal statements. He wrote in characters, he proclaimed, used metaphor and allegories, and so his words weren't always as specific as they appeared to be.

Except so often they clearly were and as much as ever in these songs. He wrote 'Pitseleh' for JJ Gonson. The title was a Yiddish word and his pet name for her, loosely translated as 'dear little one'. It was a mourning, sorrowful-sounding piece with a full disclosure lyric: 'The first time I saw you I knew it would never last. I'm not half the man I wish I was.' For the carouselling 'Waltz #2', he penned his mother, Bunny, as if she were a Tennessee Williams' creation, the ravaged Southern belle who 'shows no emotion at all', but 'stares into space like a dead China doll'.

There was one more song he picked the bones out of on Crane's upright piano. Afterwards, he put down an instrumental demo track to tape, serenading its weeping melody on acoustic guitar. He left the cassette lying around the control room for weeks before he finally got around to doing a guide vocal. His opening lines showcase a novelist's flair for detail: 'I'll fake it through the day with the help of some Johnnie Walker Red . . . But it's alright, some enchanted evening I'll be with you.'

'That song has a certain melancholy feel,' says Crane. 'Elliott would never say to me the lyrics were about this or that. I think they're way open to interpretation, but I know bits are about him and Joanna, for sure. Musically, there are always little things going on in his songs. Like in this one, there's a part where the chord changes and it does a specific thing. It's just a tiny bit, but tricky, too, and it adds so much to the whole thing. I played Elliott's demo for John Moen when he came in to do his own music. It was almost like it was painful to John to hear it. He was like, "Fuck, how come my stuff doesn't sound like that?"'

Another collection Smith and Crane were listening to heavily at Jackpot! around this same time was a new Beach Boys' box set, *Good Vibrations*. Crane detected something of the Beach Boys' man-child genius, Brian Wilson, in Smith.

'They were both of them able to keep the musical parts in their heads, like sheet music,' he says. 'I mean to say, they mentally arranged their songs. They each left a bit of wiggle room for accidents or fine tuning, but they knew precisely how their stuff was going to come out. That's an incredible amount of focus. Elliott definitely had that capacity more than I've ever seen with any other musician. And I've worked with great musicians.'

The song was titled 'Miss Misery'. Soon enough, it was to change Smith's life – and not so much for the better.

★

Smith was only stopped in his tracks at Jackpot! by having to tour *Either/Or*. At the outset, he was booked two months of coast-to-coast dates, starting at a club up in Seattle, Velvet Elvis, on 26 March. Accompanying him on the road was Bill Santen, who was opening the shows, and a tour manager, Dan Mapp, who drove them from place to place in a Ford Taurus rental car. A native of Philadelphia, Mapp made an instant, striking impression, towering at well over 6 foot and taciturn to the point of near-monastic silence.

Even on the longest drives, Mapp barely spoke a word to Smith, much less to Santen, and not one that wasn't connected to their business at hand. He banned both of them from smoking in the car and operated a strict time-keeping regime. Mapp also sold Smith's merchandise, ran his sound and cracked the whip, collecting the nightly $250 fee Smith was contractually guaranteed for each show.

'I was getting paid $50 to $100 per show, depending on the venue,' says Santen. 'And Elliott often tried to overpay me out of his fee. Whenever he did that, Dan would go and have "the talk" with Elliott.'

The earliest dates on the tour were sparsely attended, as low as a mere fifteen souls for one show and not much more than thirty for the rest. Smith's mood corresponded. Late one night,

Santen visited him in his motel room, meaning to pay him back another sum of money borrowed from him when they were back in Portland. He found Smith slumped on the edge of his bed.

'He just came out and said to me, "You know, I'm really depressed. I broke up with my girlfriend again,"' says Santen. 'I was so excited to be going on the tour and here he was, sort of telling me, "Look, sorry, this isn't going to be fun."'

In Beloit, Wisconsin, on the fifth night of the tour, the two of them were meant to be opening for a fellow singer-songwriter, Will Oldham, at a local college. Something of a renaissance man, the bald, extravagantly moustachioed Oldham doubled up on performing his rustic, lo-fi songs with acting jobs in independent movies and on TV. This scattershot approach was anathema to someone as devoted to his music as Smith. His antipathy towards Oldham ramped up another notch when they arrived at the venue to be told Santen was off the bill. Smith exploded, blaming Oldham for hijacking his friend.

'Elliott was furious and he got angrier through the day,' recalls Santen. 'The fact Will Oldham was also an actor didn't help. Elliott decided and then reported he wasn't going to do the show either. Dan Mapp and Margaret Mittleman both intervened and in the end, he agreed to play. Even though I didn't get to perform, it felt good having Elliott stick up for me for a while there.'

Steadily, the tour picked up steam. As word spread on *Either/ Or*, the shows grew fuller, the audiences more attentive. Smith's temper picked up accordingly. After a gig in Boston, he struck up an ardent conversation with a petite brunette named Amity. He never was to share Amity's surname, but he was certainly enraptured. Even though their whirlwind romance barely survived the tour, Smith was moved to write the rarest kind of his songs, which is to say one that was both exuberant-sounding and explicitly personal. He was debuting 'Amity' onstage within six months. It blazed open like a sunburst and with Smith hailing, 'Amity, Amity, Amity . . . caught stars in her arms.'

Around the same time Dan Mapp was piloting them down the East Coast, Smith was also eased into a daily routine. He slept in till noon. He liked to drink, often to excess, but after a show for the most part and not so his boozing ever affected his performance, at least not yet. After a few beers and shots of Jameson's, his mood was ever likely to drag and sink. At such low points, he was still prone to peppering his conversation with allusions to taking heroin, but for now, he didn't appear to be doing much more than popping the odd pill and hair of the dogging his hangovers.

'I spent a lot of time waiting for Elliott to wake up,' says Santen. 'We would start off his day by going and getting coffee. We had fun in the afternoons sometimes, checking out the town, but then we would also go for hours in the car without him talking. One time, Elliott read the manual for his Tascam recorder for days on end. Another time, he was totally immersed in *2001: A Space Odyssey*. He was having stomach problems, too. Dan would often have to pull over to the side of the road for him.

'For me, the tour itself didn't necessarily pan out how I thought it would. I had imagined it being like our first trip together up to Seattle, but it started to feel more professional. Something was happening for him. Things got to be intense and more of a big deal. Elliott wasn't fun to be around under the circumstances. He kept apologising for it and for his not being talkative, but I think he knew what he was doing. Nothing was being done to him. He was in charge of everything and it was what he wanted. It wasn't like I was a peer, I was just standing back, watching things happen.'

They arrived in New York on 13 April. Smith was playing a couple of consecutive nights at a club down in the East Village, Brownies, opening for Mark Eitzel. Of all the dates on the tour, these two were the ones where it was most obvious how the environment was changing for him. Almost as soon as he began his set both nights, the room fell still and silent. It was as if there was nothing so important right there and then as to be able to hear him play.

'He was sat up on the high stage at Brownies and you could have heard a pin drop,' recalls Mittleman. 'It was quite a moment. It was like, "Oh my God, you got here. They're listening. You did it." It was transformative for him.'

'The New York elite were out in force those nights and Elliott slayed,' says Rob Schnapf. 'When Margaret truly started working with Elliott, people would say to her, "Singer-songwriter? *Eeuw*!" The term "singer-songwriter" had this connotation from the 1970s, like it was old news and obsolete. Fast-forward to a year later and it was like, "*Oh my God*, have you heard of Elliott Smith? He's brilliant." Nothing changed, but for people starting to show up and listen.'

Santen was only booked for the first half of the tour. Pete Krebs took over the opening slot for the concluding run. Krebs joined up with Smith and Mapp for a date in Atlanta, Georgia, on 22 April. From there, the tour was to wind through Arizona, on into California and then back up the West Coast to Portland and Seattle. From Krebs' perspective, he found Smith in a good place. Mapp drove them in comfort. They shared beers and laughs together, just as they did back home. After the Atlanta show, they went out to a bar together and got talking to a young woman sat out on the patio. She told them she was enlisting in the army the next day. Smith spent the rest of the night trying to talk her out of it, his face pained with concern.

Driving on through New Mexico to California, Smith once again asked Mapp to pull the car over. On this occasion, he simply wanted to take some air and perhaps to grab a moment of quiet reflection. There was nothing but scorched desert surrounding them and a ribbon of blistering asphalt running clear to the horizon. Before he got back in the car, Krebs snapped a picture of him at the roadside. In Krebs' Polaroid, Smith strikes a boxer's pose. With his fists clenched up, guarding his face and one foot forward, he looks as though he's heading into battle.

They spent two days billeted in Los Angeles. There was a palpable buzz around the show at Spaceland on 7 May, a Wednesday night. The venue was sold out. It was in Beck's Echo Park neighbourhood and he came out to see the show. Afterwards, Beck dropped by the dressing room to say hello to Smith, like he was bestowing his benediction upon him. Smith and Krebs ended the evening stood out on the balcony of their Hollywood hotel, the two of them drinking beer and contemplating the twinkling lights along Sunset Strip. They were the same with each other as they always were, but never would be again.

'There was a lot of attention focused on him in LA,' says Krebs. 'Mostly, he seemed to me just then to be embarrassed by it. He was excited, like anybody would be, but also I think trying really hard to break down whatever barriers might be coming up incrementally between him and his friends, or at least me. He introduced me to Margaret Mittleman. She was really nice to me, but it was very much like my part was to be the buddy who was along for the ride.'

The tour ran full circle and ended up back in Seattle. The final show was at the Crocodile Café on 16 May. It was even more apparent by then how much more charged the air was getting to be around Smith. Reviews for *Either/Or* were gushing. Rather than having to chase them up, Dorien Garry was now beginning to field requests for interviews. Margaret Mittleman was already lining him up another tour for the summer. The demands on his time were growing almost by the day. He had more questions to answer, yet more decisions to make.

Smith brought back with him to Portland a box stuffed with fan mail and an assortment of trinkets gifted on the road. He put it into the storage room at Jackpot!, along with all of his other junk from the tour. It was as if he didn't want to appear to care too much for such flatteries. His moods also shifted again, becoming more erratic. He might seem fidgety and distracted, or else torpid and morose, but not so he was settled or balanced at any rate.

Bill Santen had a song, 'Third and South', he wanted put to tape and asked Smith for his help. Smith organised a session for Santen over at Jackpot! with Larry Crane and Joanna Bolme engineering. Smith and Bolme respectively played piano and bass on the track. The day passed in an uneasy atmosphere.

'I don't know if Elliott really wanted to do the session,' says Santen. 'He seemed a little annoyed. We didn't really hang out much. I was left feeling like I shouldn't have asked him to do it.'

Other friends in Portland noticed a more insidious change to Smith's character. He seemed to them needier and more reliant on gaining their assurances and comforts. They were well accustomed to him fretting and moping, but sometimes it was almost as if there was a method to his downward spirals now – as if he was trying on the role of the tortured artist for size to see how it fitted him. He was becoming more self-obsessed and self-absorbed, or so they surmised.

'Elliott was sort of actively involved in his own myth-making,' Sam Coomes told Autumn de Wilde in 2007. 'I kind of frowned on it and didn't want to facilitate it too much.'[17]

Also speaking with de Wilde, Sean Croghan considered: 'It was different when we started seeing people that were more or less there to take care of Elliott's ego . . . It made Elliott different. I mean, it *really* made Elliott different. He became more dependent on having that attention and on having people say, "You're okay." And it came to a point where I told him, "I'm not gonna tell you you're okay anymore because you're not telling me I'm okay. All you're saying is, 'Am I okay, Sean?'" I guess it's not a happy part of Elliott, but it's a real part . . . He had a selfishness that developed.'[18]

Some of Smith's other close friendships were fracturing, or else had broken down altogether. Following on from Heatmiser's demise, he was estranged from Neil Gust and not on speaking terms with Tony Lash. His on-off relationship with Joanna Bolme remained off. Bolme was as intolerant of his navel-gazing as Sean Croghan. Doubtless these turbulences helped pitch him towards leaving Portland. Similarly, the fact he was more acutely focusing on his career surely contributed to his wanderlust.

Whatever the clincher, Smith concluded it was high time he left Portland. Tempted towards New York City, where he had so recently triumphed, he pressed ahead with making a loose arrangement to stay with Dorien Garry at her apartment in New Jersey. For the most part, he kept quiet about his plans – there was to be no grand announcement of his departure, no going away party.

'I only heard Elliott was leaving through the grapevine,' recalls Krebs. 'I don't remember his going being a huge deal around here, it was just like he packed up a few things and split.'

'Right before he moved to New York, Elliott and I went out to a bar together,' says Jason Mitchell. 'He was super-excited to be moving to New York and to be making a solid go of things with his career. He was like, "You know, I feel like I have this opportunity to do this and I don't want to blow it or let it slide."

'Granted, we were pretty drunk, but then within the same conversation, maybe ten minutes later and after giving me this wonderful sense he was going to take off, he announced if I got a phone call telling me something had happened to him, he wanted me to know he loved me and appreciated our friendship. I went from feeling elated to crying at the bar. I didn't understand – I still don't, really – how Elliott had such a drive to make his music career happen, but also he could be so troubled, he would warn friends just in case he wasn't going to be around too much longer. And this was not an uncommon event.'

On the morning of Thursday, 22 May 1997, Smith flew to New York with as many of his clothes, books and other belongings as he could cram into a duffel bag, together with his acoustic guitar. Never to return to Portland to live among his friends and family, he was bound for new adventures, but he wouldn't ever find such safe harbour again.

PART 3

New York City, New York

CHAPTER 14

Intervention

Dorien Garry's twenty-first birthday just happened to be 22 May 1997. When Smith called Garry from Portland not much more than a week earlier and asked about coming to stay, he leapt upon it as the perfect date for his move. He had signed off telling Garry he'd be in New York in time for her party. Garry assumed he was joking, but now here he was in her office at Girlie Action, large as life and with just a duffel bag full of stuff and a guitar to tide him over.

In the relatively short time she'd been doing his publicity, Garry had formed a tight friendship with Smith. As *Either/Or* picked up traction, she was on the phone to him several times a week to arrange interviews. The two quickly fell into an easy rhythm of conversation outside of their work commitments. They shared similar tastes in music and an absurdist sense of humour. When Smith was in New York for the Mark Eitzel shows, he'd slept over at Garry's apartment. He had confided in her his break-up with Joanne Bolme had been a bad one and how they'd made a pact to both leave Portland. Bolme fled to Chicago. Garry had been careful to sound encouraging about Smith's coming to live in New York, telling him it was a great idea.

'I knew maybe it wouldn't be 100 per cent great,' she says now. 'I had a small feeling of trepidation, a tinge of worry about it. I grew up just outside of the city and up to then, it was the only place I'd ever lived. It's not an easy place to be. I didn't know anything else, but I'd watched plenty of people move there and have a hard time getting it together.

'I was also completely baffled by how somebody could move cross-country with just a duffel bag and a guitar. It seemed like a crazy thing to me, but that was Elliott. It was sort of comical, but a nice way for him to show up, too. We went out to my twenty-first party and it was a really sweet night. Right away, he got to meet a bunch of good friends of mine. Some of those people became close friends of his as well. It was a fun party.'

Garry's place was a twenty-minute commute from the city, just over the Hudson River from Manhattan in Jersey City. Her apartment was a fourth-floor walk-up, a big place with three bedrooms, a kitchen, a bathroom and a good-sized living room. Garry was sharing with two other flatmates. They were used to having bands and artists stay over with them. Smith took the same communal spot in the living room reserved for all their other guests, sleeping on the couch.

He hadn't specified how long he planned on being there and the days soon ran into weeks. Smith was forever telling Garry he didn't want to be a burden, but as far as she and her flat-mates were concerned, he was a conscientious lodger. He kept the living room tidy, hung up his wet towel in the bathroom, he made them coffee in the morning and did the dishes. When Garry and her flatmates went off to work weekdays, he was left to his own devices.

On the evenings, they most regularly headed back over the river and into Manhattan to go drinking and to see shows. There were a couple of dive bars Smith was drawn to in particular, Max Fish and the Luna Lounge, right across the road from each other on Ludlow Street in the East Village. Both places were patronised by a hipster crowd of artists and musicians – the kinds of dens the clientele spent as much time hooking up and getting fixed up in the bathrooms as stood at the bar.

'I don't know if it was New York, or just because I was young, but right then the city was this magical, exciting place and eve-rything was based in Manhattan,' recalls Garry. 'There was a group of people we would go out with a lot and a handful of bars we liked to go to. Elliott had a real thing for jukeboxes. He would immediately go to the jukebox and put in an obscene amount of money for the time, like $20. Basically, he'd organise the next two hours of music for everybody. It'd be a combination of really good songs and kind of joke songs to make people laugh.

'Elliott was truly one of the funniest people I've ever known. He'd such an amazing, contagious laugh. I can still hear the sound of him laughing in my head. He just loved stupid, funny shit. At home, we'd watch old episodes of *Saturday Night Live* or VHS tapes people had compiled of weird stuff from the TV. He loved comedy and to dress up as weird characters. He had a fascination for clowns. We talked about clowns a lot. He conjured up this whole fantasy of travelling up to Canada dressed as a clown. He'd say, "At the border, I'm going to tell them I'm a US clown trying to break into the Canadian clown scene.'"

According to Garry, Smith had an acute antenna for picking up distress signals from other people. Should anyone from their now-mutual circle be going through a tough time, he would be quick to react and often as not with the antidote of humour. The unlikely fact of Smith being the funny guy would make these interventions all the more effective.

'Those were my favourite things about his personality,' says Garry. 'It was him being a nurturing, compassionate and empathetic friend, but it was the whole deal. It was also his beautiful laugh and the expressions on his face when he was about to spring some crazy joke on you.'

Even on Smith's brightest days in New York, though, there were shadows prowling him and fathomless depths looming at the margins. He had been prescribed antidepressants on and off for years, but now he was taking them in greater amounts, more erratically and sometimes seemingly without following any instruction. It was as though he was trying to blur out the black edges, or else he believed it was possible for him to hurry up and be better. He was self-medicating more often and binge-drinking with greater frequency, too. As the amounts escalated, the combinations of booze and chemicals he was putting away became dangerously toxic.

'With a person on antidepressants, there needs to be a lot of work with a clinician to manage the right type of medication and to monitor the side effects,' says Dr Leah Quinlivan. 'The side effects can be heavy, especially during the first weeks of taking them. If you've a very chaotic person, who's struggling with a lot of things and maybe alcohol as well, then this may reduce the effects of the medication and also increase the likelihood of harm from it.'

Sunday, 8 June 1997 was one of Smith's jumbled days. Garry had a friend, Allison Wolfe, visit her over the weekend. A fast-talking livewire, Wolfe grew up in Olympia, where she had attended Evergreen State College and fronted the Riot Grrrl band, Bratmobile. Wolfe spent the day over in the city, attending the Tibetan Freedom charity concert in Randall's Island Park. She was ostensibly there to see Blur, just then transplanting their Britpop success to the US on the back of the Nirvana-like 'Song 2', and whose guitarist, Graham Coxon, she knew. After the show, Wolfe made an arrangement with Coxon to catch up with him later on at Max Fish, where she was also meeting Garry and Smith.

By the time she got to the bar, Smith was in full life-and-soul-of-the-party mode. To start off with at least, the booze would loosen him up and Wolfe found him buying rounds of drinks and feeding the jukebox. Coxon, rumpled and bespectacled, rolled up shortly afterwards, accompanied by a hulking bodyguard. This odd-looking pair took up a station at the bar. Smith was a fan of Blur since their *Parklife* album of 1994, won over by its unashamed Kink-isms, and he was goggling like an over-excited schoolboy. Wolfe offered to make introductions for him with Coxon, but he put her off. All of his insecurities wouldn't allow him to break the ice with someone he looked up to.

'Elliott was simply too afraid to come over and meet, or talk to Graham,' says Wolfe. 'For his part, I'm sure Graham didn't know who Elliott was at the time. What Elliott did instead was to go and put "Song 2" on the jukebox. Oh my God, the whole bar just exploded into the "woo-hoo!" chorus. Graham slumped over and put his head between his hands down on the bar.

'After that, Elliott kept putting the song on, over and again. Each time, he would run over to the jukebox and then come back behind Graham, snickering and giggling. I think he even had his fingers in his mouth at one point. It was kind of playful and mischievous, and also ridiculous. Finally, Graham was like, "I'm outta here," and he left.'

Following Coxon's abrupt departure, the whole temperature of the evening tilted. Smith became drunker, more raucous – as if he had slipped anchor. With the night wearing on, he announced he was hungry and Wolfe went with him to get bagels from a deli, Katz's, right around the corner from the bar. They sat down together on the pavement across from Max Fish to enjoy their food. As they ate, they amused themselves with watching another drunk lurching along the opposite side of the street. A big guy, he was pitching and rolling like a deck-hand in a Force 10.

The guy pulled up at a parked car and began to relieve himself against the vehicle. It was a beat before either of them realised the car was Garry's. As Wolfe stood up and yelled at him to stop, Smith took off at a sprint. He ran over the road and in a dead-straight line towards his quarry. The guy turned, stepped towards Smith and laid him out with a single punch before stumbling off. People brought spilling out of the bar by the commotion discovered Smith flat on his back in the middle of Ludlow Street.

'Everyone was yelling at me, "Get your friend up out of the street, there are cars coming!"' says Wolfe. 'I ran over to Elliott, thinking he was knocked out, but his eyes were wide open. He was just staring up at the sky and wouldn't move. Finally, I got him to stand up and it was like a light switch going off. In the space of a split second, he was changed from fun party guy to extremely serious and depressed. Now, I realise he'd just got punched out, but it was wild. He became a whole other person to me.'

Smith begged Wolfe to go and fetch Garry from the bar. She hurried out and, with Wolfe, piled Smith into her car. Garry and Wolfe tried to engage Smith in conversation, but he wouldn't speak. They drove home in silence, Smith sat up back and staring into the middle distance. Back at Garry's apartment, Wolfe was also bunking up in the front room.

'I tried again to talk to Elliott, but he wasn't having it at all,' she says. 'He just seemed really annoyed with me and mad in general. That kind of marked our relationship afterwards – I rarely saw him be happy again.'

'The period of time Elliott was living with me, he was starting to really struggle with all of the personal things that eventually hijacked him,' says Garry. 'Most things with Elliott were out on the table. He confided in me a lot and in a way I still feel incredibly protective about him. Then again, he would sometimes just open up to random people in a way he wouldn't totally realise. He may have sat next to some stranger in a bar and told him some really heavy story and it just ended up out there in the world.

'He had hard nights and we had hard times together. It was tough for me. I was young, I hadn't had the experience of dealing with somebody who was going through issues with addiction and having severe depressive episodes. I was always grateful for the fact we had this time together. That he wasn't alone by himself or with people he didn't feel comfortable around, but it was brutal and incredibly intense. I'd no idea what the right or wrong thing was to do. I didn't understand how to help somebody during dark times. I mean, I did the best I could and we got through it. If he was bumming out, I could always use some form of comedy to try to shake him out of it. There were a lot of nights we would just watch stupid movies, or play records. The normal things you do when you're in your twenties and living in an apartment together.'

Smith never did sever completely the umbilical cord tying him to Portland. He carried on making intermittent, but regular return trips to the city the whole time he was living in New York. Typically, he used these as opportunities to go into Jackpot! and put down tracks with Larry Crane. At Jackpot!, too, he did the occasional session for his friends. On one visit, he played guitar and helped out producing a few tracks for Sean Croghan's new band, Jr. High. Most of all, he hoped to intersect with Joanna Bolme whenever she was also back in town. The embers of their relationship were to burn for a good while yet.

Among the other Portland friends Smith kept in contact with were Garrick Duckler, Jason Mitchell, Sam Coomes and Janet Weiss. He grew distant, or else vanished altogether from other people's reach. He made himself harder to pin down. After moving to New York, he changed both his mobile phone number and email address. He was to change them again with every subsequent move. Always cautious when it came to sharing his new contact details, it was as though he was pruning friends and acquaintances just as rigorously as he had the songs from *Either/Or*. He never did explain or specify the reasons he cut people off.

'I didn't see Elliott again until I went to play a show of my own in New York,' recalls Pete Krebs. 'On that occasion, I got the chance to run around with him for an afternoon and an evening, but I felt a divide. He was now of someplace else and I was kind of coming back from his past in a way. Maybe there's something there about Elliott having issues with his past in general – he might have just really liked to reinvent himself, but he was definitely a different person.'

'People in Portland have a different sense of Elliott,' says Bill Santen. 'I think it's very painful for some of them even now how he broke off. His number still worked for me, but from what I saw and my own personal experience, Elliott would be there for you and then he'd be gone. He was always moving forward.'

Those days he was staying in Jersey City, Smith also didn't seem to be nearly so wide-eyed about the direction his career was heading. He was never happier than when he was consumed in the studio and when he'd free rein, like a painter at a blank canvas. It was the actual business surrounding the music he was most apt to bitch and moan about. Specifically, he got to resent being pressed to do so many more interviews and increasingly as well with having to travel and tour.

'Our sessions together were always productive, straightforward and easy, but things certainly changed for him,' says Larry Crane. 'It was a different kind of dynamic going on. I remember Elliott whining to me once. He was in Portland for a few days and we were doing something or other in the studio. He was like, "Oh, I've got to do this and that." He was complaining about what he was being told to do. I just said to him, "Fuck you. You've earned it and you've gotten all of the opportunities all of the rest of us wanted."

'I had the same conversation with Corin Tucker from Sleater-Kinney once, too, although Corin wasn't whining. But I said to her, "You're carrying the flag for the rest of us behind you." We all laid the groundwork for someone like Elliott or Sleater-Kinney, or whomever, to be able to go out there and do this in the indie-rock world we all lived in. I told Elliott, "I wish I had those opportunities." I understood there were things he was supposed to be doing he didn't want to, but it was also like, "Well, then, take charge. Jesus Christ, you got the chance to put a record out and have it distributed. You've someone handle your publicity. That's really terrible? Fuck you two times." It made me mad.'

Back East, Smith had the whole of June off. For the most part, he spent it idling in Garry's apartment, or else at one or other of his East Village haunts. The songs weren't coming so easily to him just then and he soon grew bored and irritable. To distract him, Garry suggested they take a trip out of town. Her former employers, Kim Gordon and Thurston Moore, had invited her to a one-off date Sonic Youth were scheduled to play in Raleigh, North Carolina, on 22 June. It was a show to mark the tenth anniversary of the band's merchandising company, Tannis Root. Also on the bill were Mudhoney and Redd Kross from LA. Garry was planning on driving down to Raleigh; Smith agreed to go along with her for the ride.

The ten-hour drive passed without incident. Following the show, the bands and their guests gathered at a bar, Sugar Ray, located in the nearby town of Chapel Hill. Sugar Ray was Smith's kind of place. It had a jukebox playing good music and mounted on the walls was a display of vintage pinball machines. Smith sat himself up at the bar, underneath one of those back-lit machines, and got on with some serious drinking. After a while he was joined by Tim Foljahn, a friend of Sonic Youth's drummer Steve Shelley and a musician with Cat Power's band. According to Foljahn, there wasn't a whole lot of conversation passed between the two of them. Smith was polite enough, but solitary.

At the end of the night, Garry offered Foljahn a lift back into town with them. Joining them in the car were Sonic Youth's former drummer, Bob Bert, and another of the band's associates, Maurice Menares. Smith sat in the back, shoulder to shoulder with Foljahn and leaning up against the passenger door. As Garry drove, the others chatted idly over the hum of the engine and the car radio. Smith was quiet to start off with, but then began to make troubled, whimpering sounds and to sob – his internal switch going off as all of the booze reacted against his medications. He worked himself up into such a state Garry had to pull the car over on a residential street. There was no street lighting and it was a pitch-black night.

What happened next is the subject of some conjecture still. For certain, Smith hauled himself out of the car and once again took off running in a straight line. At the other end of the street, there was a drop-off – a grass verge, a line of trees and nothing beyond but blackness. Afterwards, Smith described it as a cliff. Foljahn, who was almost as drunk as Smith, remembers it more as a steep embankment. At all events, Smith didn't so much as break stride, much less stop at the drop-off, but went right on running, over the edge and plummeting into the void.

Garry, Bert and Menares bolted after him. They found him sprawled about halfway down the bank. The branches of a tree had broken his fall. He had sustained a puncture wound in his back from one of the branches. After helping him back to the car, they set off again in shocked silence. Smith reached out and held Foljahn's hand. Garry drove him back to their hotel, where she cleaned and dressed the wound. Later, press reports would characterise it as a suicide attempt. From what she was told, Margaret Mittleman believed it to have been more of a cry for help.

'There was no cliff really to jump off,' she says. 'There was nothing below, but Elliott knew it wasn't so far down. But I'd never had any experience with anybody who was crying out like that. It prepped me for having children, in the sense you love them and you want to protect them and yet it can be brutal.'

'At the time, I was struggling with depression and drinking too much myself,' says Foljahn. 'So, to me, Elliott's seemed like a perfectly logical response to the world. I mean, it was super-dramatic for the other people in the car. They were really, *really* shocked by his behaviour, but me not so much.

'I remember him holding onto my hand and starting to cry again in the car. I was in my thirties and he was quite a bit younger. I said to him, "Hey, it's alright." He looked at me and said, "Can't you see that I'm crying?" I said, "Yeah. That's okay, little guy."'

Three weeks later, Smith began a second round of tour dates for *Either/Or*. Opening on 15 July with a festival show up in Olympia, the itinerary was to take him across the top of the country through Idaho, Minnesota and Illinois and from there on down the East Coast. All of the shows were now selling out and there was one other significant change in place for the tour. For the first time, he was going out with a backing band.

Accompanying him were Sam Coomes on bass and Janet Weiss on drums. Smith himself switched over to electric guitar for the greater part of their sets. Early shows caught the more regular Smith watchers by surprise. Expecting to see him play solo acoustic, they were instead met with a louder, rawer, fiercer noise. The trio onstage sped up Smith's songs, made them more abrasive. Audience responses varied. Many of the Smith die-hards were appalled. Unbowed, Smith knew his history. He was thinking of the fury Bob Dylan unleashed from going electric with the Band three decades earlier. Even on this smaller scale, he revelled in provoking anything like the same reaction.

Offstage, he was never nearly so balanced. His regime of mix-ing booze with antidepressants sent his moods surging every which way. He got into the habit of calling up Dorien Garry from payphones after each show and usually at the ungodly hours when he was wired and drunk and at his most self-absorbed. On a nightly basis, Garry found she was trying to talk him up or down until two or three in the morning and then having to get up and go to work herself. A week into the tour, Garry also received an email from Smith. He had clearly written it in another wretched state and was once more suggesting he couldn't go on in the world. Garry showed the email to her boss at Girlie Action, Felice Ecker. Ecker forwarded the email on to Slim Moon and Margaret Mittleman.

'For me, there was always a very deep worry and unsettling feeling about Elliott,' says Garry. 'There were always going to be highs and lows. It was always scary. In the span of our friendship, I never once had a period of time where I felt everything was genuinely okay, or worked out and dealt with, or like he'd gotten through the things that were so difficult for him to endure.'

Moon sprang into action, convincing Mittleman they should stage an intervention on Smith. He contacted a clinical psychol-ogist in New York, Dr Lou Cox, with a reputation for treating rock stars for alcoholism and addictions. Moon arranged for Cox to fly out to Chicago on 26 July and intersect with the tour. He also organised for Mittleman, Garry, Ecker, Joanna Bolme and Neil Gust to join them in Chicago. Like Bolme, Rebecca Gates was now living in the city and on the afternoon of Smith's show they all met up at Gates' house. Coomes and Weiss came along with Smith, who was under the impression they were going to Gates' for lunch.

The intervention proceeded in Gates' kitchen. Cox encouraged the others to share their concerns for him with Smith. Smith sat and listened to them speak in silence, but was seething inside at what he perceived as an act of betrayal. Nevertheless, he agreed to commit to the treatment programme proposed by Cox, who recommended he be booked into a residential facility in Arizona, the Sierra Tucson. His rehab was to start just as soon as he had wrapped up his current tour dates.

Together with Coomes and Weiss, Smith played sixteen more shows through August and into September. There were bright spots puncturing his gloom. On 12 August, a day off, Garry took him with her to see Neil Young and Beck play a H.O.R.D.E. Festival date at Jones Beach Amphitheatre in upstate New York. A friend of Garry's was running lighting for the show and she got the two of them crew passes. They watched Young's barnstorming set from up on the lighting gantry, teetering high above the stage.

'We were outdoors, the ocean was behind us and we were looking down through our feet, watching Neil Young play,' recalls Garry. 'It was such a beautiful moment. Elliott was freaking out with excitement the whole time.'

Smith played a brace of New York shows of his own on the nights of 5 and 7 September respectively at the Westbeth Theater in the West Village and at a Brooklyn club, the Knitting Factory. The day after the Knitting Factory show, he flew down to Arizona with Bolme keeping him company on the journey. Smith was booked into the Sierra Tucson for the minimum thirty-days stay and to undertake a twelve-step recovery programme. He left New York still burning with anger and resentment at having had to undergo the intervention and nursing a festering grievance against most everyone involved, but it was Slim Moon who bore the brunt of his wrath. Smith hadn't spoken a word to Moon since the afternoon in Gates' kitchen. Garrick Duckler visited him in Tucson and just in time. Smith checked himself out of the centre after only four days.

'Neil Gust had called to tell me about the intervention and I'd said no, thanks,' says Duckler. 'Interventions are what people do when they don't know what else to do. Elliott was not doing well when I visited, as always, but he wanted to tell me how glad he was that I wasn't a part of the intervention. He told me he never wanted to see those people again. I said to him, "Elliott, those people love you. The way they did it sucks and was coercive, but just because they don't know how to take care of you doesn't make them terrible, evil people."'

'Elliott never forgave me for participating in that first intervention,' says Mittleman. 'But I never let down my guard for that one. I felt like we were doing the right thing.'

CHAPTER 15

The Mole Man

Smith flew straight back to New York from Arizona. He caught Dorien Garry by surprise, pitching up in Jersey City almost a whole month ahead of schedule. Garry was on her way out of the apartment for the evening to meet up with Janet Weiss, who had stayed on in town after playing with Smith at the Knitting Factory. Smith invited himself along. Weiss, too, was taken aback to see him. She was still scarred from witnessing his spiralling on the all-too-recent tour. The night passed with both Garry and Weiss tense and on edge, but relatively quietly all the same.

The next few weeks were just as discombobulating. Smith was lifted by a visit from Amity. He spent a weekend showing her around New York. She slept with him in the front room of Garry's apartment. Garry remembers her being 'super-sweet' but there and gone. Smith wasn't to see her again, but he sat down and wrote 'Amity' in the immediate aftermath of her departure.

'Some friends of mine said it sounded like I was trying to get something romantic going with someone,' Smith was to reflect on 'Amity'. 'That's not what it's supposed to be about. It was supposed to be, "you're really fun to be with and I like you a lot because of that, but I am really, *really* depressed . . . When I said 'ready to go', it was supposed to mean tired of living."'[19]

'Amity' also at least re-opened Smith's creative sluices. Once again, he found himself able to fill up his days and occupy his fevering mind with the act of writing songs. Some days, he would commute into Manhattan, perch at one end of the bar at the Luna Lounge and while away hours there with drinking, chain-smoking and penning lyrics in a notebook, in solitude even during the lunchtime rush. Otherwise he laboured at Garry's apartment. Garry's bedroom was just off the living room through a set of sliding doors. She soon became used to going to sleep to the low hum sound of Smith stop-starting a song into being.

Garry kept a second-hand Hammond Organ in a small box room also adjoining the living room. A big beast of a thing, she had picked it up along with a rotating Leslie speaker from a neighbourhood thrift store a good year ahead of Smith turning up on her doorstep. Smith took to playing it now. He would warm up on it by picking out a flamboyant classical piece, a snatch of one of Rachmaninoff's piano concertos perhaps, and from there into improvising his own parts.

On the spot, he might conjure a gambolling countermelody to go along with 'Baby Britain'. The next, he would appear to channel a fully formed song. Such as was the case with 'Independence

Day', its waltzing melody tumbling all at once from his fingertips at the Hammond.

'It was wild to see his process, to watch him play,' recalls Garry. 'I'm incredibly lucky to have those memories. I don't know if Elliott even knew how it all formulated. He was not a cocky, over-confident person, there was no bravado with him. I never witnessed him be like, "I've got this awesome new song. You've got to check it out." There was none of that shit at all.

'Most often, if not always, it came from a place of him *not* being sure of it. The pureness of it was probably 80 per cent of his bewildering magic and why the songs would end up so magnificent in the end. This was in him and always in him and it had to come out, but not in a contrived way. I think also it was part of the intense protectiveness I had – and still have – for him. How kind of otherworldly it all was to me. It felt to me so monumentally special and fragile, too. No offence to all of the other musicians I was friends with at the time, but nobody else was even close to being on a par with what Elliott was doing and what he was capable of doing.'

Smith was whole studies in contrasts. There was how meticulously he crafted his songs and yet was so absent-minded about keeping them logged. How troubled and conflicted he became the more attention he had focused upon him, yet his face would light up whenever a fan told him why one of his songs meant so much. How he would very often devote time to counselling complete strangers but could be so elusive to his nearest, dearest friends. At last he was making money from his publishing and *Either/Or*. Not so he was ever extravagantly off, but enough for him to be able to pay Garry rent and be comfortable. After paying off his student loan in one lump sum, he went on shopping for his clothes at thrift stores. He was deliriously happy, or crushingly sad, so rarely on a landing ground in between these poles.

An aching tooth summed up his jumble. A molar he had once started to have root canal work on, but not got around to finishing, it was now throbbing with an infection. Smith was tortured by the troublesome tooth for weeks on end, but resisted all of Garry's urgings to go and see a dentist. He pleaded fear, or else balked at the cost. Then he got to obsessing over the tooth. The infection might spread, he speculated to Garry. It could grow inside of him like a cancer, a poison, he fretted.

'At the same he was battling with so much despair, he was expressing to me this crazy fear of having a tooth infection kill him,' says Garry. 'I went to see my parents' dentist. He was a fine dentist and I gave Elliott his number. Eventually, Elliott did go to see him. The dentist told him he would have to have his crown replaced and a couple of other things done, because the tooth had been so neglected. It was an expensive treatment, but Elliott paid for it up front. He'd the first part of the treatment done the same day, the bare minimum.

'Some time afterwards, I went in myself for a check-up. The dentist said to me, "Hey, your friend, he's got some things he still needs to have done and he's paid for them. Remind him to come in." When I asked Elliott about it, he said, "Oh, it's okay. You should just keep it as credit for yourself." He never went back.'

These foibles of Smith's were sources of amusement in the apartment, but at the same time his heavier issues were becoming more unbearably pressing and all-consuming. His slumps were getting to be longer-lasting and more intense. Then again, the arc of his upswings was steeper, shorter and less predictable. The drugs and booze temporarily numbed his pain, but then also sparked it off. As the rate of his cycles increased, Garry took the full force of them.

'Elliott kind of took over,' recalls Allison Wolfe, who visited Garry once or twice more after the weekend in June but then stopped going. 'Each time I would go down there to hang out, we'd only end up doing what Elliott wanted for the most part. I felt like his mood just kind of sucked the air out of the room.

'I was young and immature for my age, I didn't have a lot of sympathy for his situation. I didn't know anything about addiction, but I didn't like the kind of white boy genius trope Elliott had of having to have some girl take care of him and especially as a feminist. Of course, he was very smart and he could be fun and witty, but usually he was on a downer. Dorien and I didn't go out dancing or partying anymore, we would just end up in some bar where Elliott wanted to drink all night.'

'I've a tremendous amount of guilt, because it's hard to talk about this without feeling like I'm saying Elliott burdened me,' says Garry. 'It wasn't a burden. He was one of my best friends and I would've done anything to help him through hard times, as he would and did for me. But where Elliott ended up at times was in a place beyond what I was used to and what I knew I could handle. I was afraid sometimes and also very confused about how to help him.

'There were a lot of really intense times. Just like there were a lot of fun and really wonderful times. At the time, Elliott would talk about suicide regularly to me at least. It was something that was out in the open, which made it even more beyond terrifying. This was where he was at. He wasn't doing it to seek attention. It would just be the two of us talking and it was incredibly hard to be close to him during those periods. I had to make peace with the fact this person I loved was probably not going to be around forever.'

To Garry at least, the source of Smith's pain was also abundantly evident, all too frequently exposed. All routes led back to his childhood in Duncanville, all the horrors in his head were Texan born and bred. They were, she says, 'the gateway to all of his struggles. They came from all the bad things he had done to him when he was a kid.

'One hundred per cent, adults in his life stole his life from him when he was a child,' she continues. 'They took away his capability for feeling good about himself. As sad and horrible as it is to say, Elliott in his very earnest way could have been preparing people for what he sort of knew was inevitable.'

These were issues still only just starting to be openly scrutinised in 1997. Like dread secrets being carefully, fearfully uncovered, their truths almost too unbearable to confront. A scientific investigation into the impacts of childhood trauma wasn't even begun in America until 1995. Published subsequently in 1998, the 'Adverse Childhood Experiences Study' was collated out of a Kaiser Permanente clinic in San Diego and drew upon case histories from 17,000 volunteers. The final report identified ten categories of childhood trauma, including physical, verbal and sexual abuse, parental neglect and divorce, and measured their impacts in later life. It concluded: 'Persons who had experienced four or more categories of childhood exposure, compared to those who had experienced none, had four- to twelve-fold increased health risks for alcoholism, drug abuse, depression and suicide attempt.'[20]

Garry did her level best to shepherd Smith from his worst impulses. On the weekends, she might persuade him out to a movie, or else to the beach at Seaside Heights with its boardwalk and fun-fair rides. When Smith began to seriously agitate about moving out of her apartment, she encouraged him to look for somewhere quieter and away from the abundant temptations Manhattan offered up. She drove him around upstate New York to look at places in the verdant Catskills, Woodstock country. For a moment, he was taken up with the prospect of acquiring the Big Pink house in Saugerties, where Dylan and the Band had gathered to cut *The Basement Tapes*. He talked of buying the old place, doing it up and putting in his own studio, but this was a pipe dream.

In late September, he moved instead across the Hudson River to Brooklyn. His booking agent, Ellen Stewart, had friends, Shauna Slevin and her husband, Pierre Kraitsowitz, with a spare room going in their apartment in the Park Slope neighbourhood of the borough. Back in the 1890s, Park Slope had been one of the most prosperous enclaves in the whole country, a leafy bolt-hole for the city's captains of industry. The richest of them had put up the towering brownstone mansion houses on the high ground overlooking Prospect Park.

Those halcyon days were long gone. In the 1970s, the wealth had drained out of Brooklyn as the white upper classes fled upstate or out to the suburbs. By the 1990s, Park Slope was better known for its soaring crime rates and decaying real estate. One of the Prospect Park brownstones was now the local crack den. Even after he had left Jersey City, Smith retained a key to Garry's apartment – she soon became used to waking of a morning to find him crashed out again in her living room.

Out on his own in Park Slope, his behaviour appeared to take ever more treacherous turns. He was struck by the subject of a book he was reading, *The Mole People* by Jennifer Toth. A Columbia University graduate, Toth posited there were communities of homeless people living in secret in the warrens of subway and railroad tunnels beneath New York City. In her 1993 book, she purported to document her underground encounters with many of these groups.

A worldwide bestseller, *The Mole People* also proved controversial and, when a New York historian, Joseph Brennan, scorned the veracity of Toth's reporting, Smith set out to find the mole people for himself. He got into a habit of going down into the subway, alone and late at night to wander through the tunnels, but he never stumbled across another human being down there.

The miracle was he wasn't electrocuted on the rail tracks and since he was going about blind drunk in the subterranean pitch.

Around this time his levels of self-abuse ramped up, too, his drinking bouts more targeted now towards his own oblivion. He told friends he was becoming an alcoholic. He didn't share with them another of his progressions, not just yet anyway. His morbid fascination for heroin chic was developing into something more active, a step across the Rubicon. At the very least, it's likely he sampled heroin for the first time while living in Park Slope.

A professional musician himself, Aaron Embry was soon to encounter Smith for the first time in Los Angeles and would go on to play in his touring band. Embry says: 'Elliott was using heroin when he was in Brooklyn. I mean, he talked about this with me. I've struggled with addiction myself and he knew that, so there was no judgement passing between us. But Elliott's heroin use was to have a big impact on his mental health.'

In Park Slope, Smith also picked out a new drinking den. O'Connor's was a lively neighbourhood bar frequented in the daytimes by hardened boozers and with a jukebox stocked with garage rock tunes. Smith took up his usual spot, on a stool at one end of the bar, just another of O'Connor's' solitary afternoon drinkers and only distinguished by the fact he was immersed in scribbling in a notebook. Unusually for a songwriter, Smith most often wrote out his lyrics before he had any music to put them to. What set him almost entirely apart was the fact melodies and then an arrangement would so consistently pop into his head at the exact same time as he was writing the words.

'Elliott sat and wrote out songs longhand,' recalls fellow song-writer Mike Doughty. 'He was essentially writing metered verse and then translating that to a melody, which is just fucking crazy. I don't know of anybody else who did, or does that − it's *really* hard. He could write songs without a guitar or piano in front of him. That is a deep skill to possess.'

Those days, the lyrics he came up with tended to be harsh, angry and ugly. 'After that intervention, [Elliott] started writing songs about us, his friends, and getting mad at us instead of whatever he was mad at before,' Joanna Bolme observed in 2014.[21]

Out of the blue, Smith's gush of writing was interrupted by a distraction from Portland. Gus Van Sant was at home in the city, editing his new movie, *Good Will Hunting*. A native of Louisville, Kentucky, Van Sant had made his way to Portland via Los Angeles and then New York, where he had worked in advertising. He had gone on to film *Drugstore Cowboy* (1989) in his adopted city and then to make two more acclaimed indie movies, *My Own Private Idaho* (1991) with the late River Phoenix and Keanu Reeves in the lead roles, and *To Die For* (1995) starring Nicole Kidman and Phoenix's younger brother, Joaquin.

Financed by Harvey Weinstein's Miramax company, *Good Will Hunting* was to be Van Sant's first big-budget Hollywood picture. A conventional feel-good movie telling the story of a Boston school janitor who happened to be a maths genius, it starred Robin Williams, Ben Affleck, Matt Damon in the title role and an English actress, Minnie Driver, as Damon's onscreen girlfriend. Damon and Affleck had also written the script.

A keen music fan, Van Sant had once seen Heatmiser play at La Luna and kept up with Smith's solo work. He had listened to *Either/Or* in his car while scouting locations for *Good Will Hunting*. When he began the process of cutting his film, he instructed his editor, Pietro Scalia, to try out using four of Smith's songs to soundtrack key scenes – 'Between the Bars', 'No Name #3', 'Say Yes' and 'Angeles'. They fit as if written to order.

Van Sant's boyfriend knew Joanna Bolme from having worked with her at La Luna. Bolme passed on Smith's mobile number. Van Sant called Smith in New York to ask for his permission to use his songs in the film. Smith agreed at once and also to Van Sant's second request, which was for one more song, a new one they could claim was written specifically for the film and so as to qualify it for an Oscar nomination. In turn, Smith put Van Sant on to Larry Crane, who dug through Smith's reels of unreleased tracks at Jackpot! and happened across 'Miss Misery'.

Arrangements were made to have 'Miss Misery' mixed for the film by Rob Schnapf and Tom Rothrock. Van Sant also wanted Smith to record an alternative, orchestral version of 'Between the Bars' with the veteran screen composer Danny Elfman, whom he'd hired to score the movie. The session with Elfman was scheduled for November in Los Angeles, just ahead of the December release. Margaret Mittleman used the date with Elfman as an opportunity to have a series of solo acoustic shows lined up for Smith. There were nine in total, starting in Washington, DC, on 23 October and crossing over to the

West Coast for a date in San Francisco and then three nights in Los Angeles.

Smith arrived in Los Angeles on 4 November. Miramax had booked him into the swanky Mondrian Hotel on Sunset Strip. The first night he played a small, Art Deco theatre on Wilshere Boulevard, the El Rey, and the next at the Silverlake Lounge, opening for Rufus Wainwright. Mike Doughty was also in town with Soul Coughing, recording their new album. Smith paid Doughty a visit at their altogether less salubrious Hollywood hotel, the Magic Castle. They got stoned together in Doughty's room.

On the evening of 7 November, Smith played his third Los Angeles date at a tiny, 100-capacity West Hollywood club, Largo. The next day, he went back into the studio with Danny Elfman and an eighty-piece orchestra. In advance of the session, Elfman had worked up a new arrangement for 'Between the Bars', tailoring it so his score could segue seamlessly into and out of Smith's song. Elfman's version of the song was half as short as Smith's original, running to just over a minute, but it retained its aching air. Smith sang his vocal live to the orchestra, sounding just as pleading on Elfman's version as his own. The finished track had the deeply layered, finely detailed sound Smith first heard on the White Album and then on all of the miraculous Beatles' sessions run by George Martin at Abbey Road in London.

'The whole thing only took, like, five minutes,' Smith said afterwards. 'It was really easy.'[22]

When he left Los Angeles, Smith headed north to do two more shows up in Seattle on 11 November and then on the 14th, a homecoming date at La Luna in Portland. From Portland, he flew back to New York, where he played his final show of the year at Fez again on 23 November.

On this particular New York night, Fez was packed to the rafters and the crowd adoring, their whoops and cheers loud enough on this occasion to drown out the rumblings of the subway trains. The music seemed to float up and soar out from Smith, like he was its master and it bent to his will. It might very well have been one of the last times he ever felt like he was in control of his own destiny.

CHAPTER 16

The Oscars

One of Smith's half-sisters, Ashley Welch, came to stay with him in Brooklyn over the Thanksgiving holiday weekend of 1997. Just seven years old when Smith left Duncanville for Portland, Welch was now at university in California. She kept a photograph of Smith reading her a bedtime story when she was a toddler, but they hardly knew each other at all. The weekend began a tradition: Welch was to spend the next five Thanksgivings he was alive with her half-brother.

Smith took Welch out in New York, which is to say they toured his favourite bars. She couldn't help but notice how much he drank, but Smith was otherwise on his best behaviour. They ate Thanksgiving dinner together in the Park Slope apartment. Smith christened the turkey 'Tom' and carved it at the table. A happy family of just the two of them and with him playing dad. For Smith, this kind of sense of normality wasn't ever to last for long. The following Thursday night, he went into the city with Dorien Garry to see a screening of *Good Will Hunting*. On limited release to qualify it for the Oscar nominations, Gus Van Sant's film was already picking up glowing reviews. Smith sat there in the dark of the theatre, hearing songs he wrote alone in basements in Portland front and centre of a smash-hit movie. The next morning, the *New York Times'* film critic Janet Maslin cooed: '*Good Will Hunting* has fine acting, steady momentum, a sharp eye and a very warm heart.'[23]

There was change and upheaval going on in the background of Smith's career, too. He had no intention of putting another record out on Kill Rock Stars, he simply wouldn't countenance working again with Slim Moon. The sticking point was Virgin still retained its option on him from the Heatmiser contract and he was just as intransigent about the prospect of being held to those terms. *Either/Or* had opened doors for him and he wasn't short of major label suitors. One approach piqued his interest. It was from DreamWorks, a new subsidiary of Universal. The principals behind DreamWorks were David Geffen, Steven Spielberg and another powerful movie executive, Jeffrey Katzenberg. In 1996, the three of them had each put up $33.3 million of their own money, along with $2 billion raised from other investors, to launch an entertainment conglomerate. The record company operated as an adjunct to their DreamWorks movie studio.

Of the three entrepreneurs, Geffen was very much the music man. Raised in Brooklyn, the second son of Jewish immigrant parents, he was in equal measure admired, feared and reviled. In 1971, he had co-founded Asylum Records with Neil Young's and Joni Mitchell's manager, Elliot Roberts. The label enjoyed an almost unbroken four-year run of hits with the Eagles and a stable of stellar singer-songwriters, among them Mitchell, Jackson Browne, Warren Zevon and Tom Waits. Geffen and Roberts had sold up to Warner Communications in 1973, with Geffen going off to work in the movies two years later. He returned to the record business in 1980 with a second, self-aggrandising label, Geffen Records. His new label's second album, John Lennon's *Double Fantasy*, came out to damning reviews in November 1980. Three weeks later, Mark Chapman shot Lennon dead and *Double Fantasy* rocketed to the top of the *Billboard* Hot 200 chart. By the time Geffen let go of the reins once again in 1995, Geffen Records had progressed to being the most successful record company in America, having not so long ago upturned pop culture with Nirvana's *Nevermind*.

At DreamWorks, David Geffen installed two other veteran music men to run the record company side of the business for him, Mo Ostin and Lenny Waronker. At Warner Bros from the late '60s, Ostin and Waronker had between them championed such distinctive talents as Neil Young, Paul Simon, Talking Heads, Prince, Madonna and R.E.M. Waronker also had an acute regard for singer-songwriters, signing and nurturing Randy Newman, Ry Cooder and Van Dyke Parks. Already at DreamWorks, he had snapped up Rufus Wainwright and Mark 'E' Everett and the Eels.

'There was a bidding war going on for Eels, another label was offering more money and my manager wanted me to take the highest bid,' says Everett. 'But I had such respect for Mo and

Lenny because of their whole approach. Their credo was you never get hurt by making good music. They believed in letting artists grow and without them having to have hits right away.'

It was Rob Schnapf and Tom Rothrock who tipped Waronker to Smith. They brought a copy of *Either/Or* to a meeting at his office. Waronker was impressed, detecting something of George Harrison in Smith's soul-baring acoustic songs and double-tracked voice. He charged a tenacious A&R executive at Dream-Works, Luke Wood, with leading the delicate negotiations for Smith's signature with Margaret Mittleman and Smith on one hand and, by extension, Andy Factor at Virgin on the other.

'It was all about getting Elliott out of his deal with Virgin,' says Mittleman. 'Luke played a big role, because he was a fan of Elliott's music and seemed to have a deep understanding of his personality. Luke's an interesting guy. He walked a fine line of totally getting the art and then also the commerce.

'For Elliott, it was purely a business decision. He did not want to put his next record out on Virgin. Things got a little tricky because of it and it soured one relationship in the business for me.'

'Once Margaret Mittleman came into the picture it was like, "Oh, Elliott, you're going to be a star,"' says Andy Factor. 'Maybe there was something in that promise Elliott was attracted to. Then, suddenly, Lenny Waronker likes Elliott and the whole thing started to get weird. I got frustrated and defensive about what I'd invested in and supported. Virgin was already in for I don't know how many hundreds of thousand dollars. I was like, "Well, wait a minute, this isn't fair, Elliott. I can give you that here, too."'

Smith, though, wouldn't budge, and Factor's new bosses at
Virgin eventually relented. Over Factor's head, they agreed to a
deal with Waronker and Wood. DreamWorks was to buy Smith
out of his Virgin contract. On 14 January 1998, Smith returned
to Portland to play a knockabout show at La Luna. The evening
was a Kinks tribute, a chance for him to let his hair down and
catch up with old friends such as Larry Crane and Pete Krebs.
Afterwards, he sat up at the bar with Krebs like they used to do
after their shifts putting up dry wall. For a moment, they were as
easy together as they had always been, but then, just as abruptly,
the whole tone of the evening darkened. There was simply too
much distance growing between them for things to ever again
snap back to being the way they were.

'I was drunk and made a comment about "Miss Misery",
something out of jealousy,' says Krebs. 'Elliott got really upset.
He reached out to me and he was like, "Pete, I'm really sorry." I
just said to him, "Hey, no, man, I've got to go." Ever since, I've
always felt pretty awful about that night. The envy was short-
lived for me. You see someone you've spent a couple of years
hanging around with doing really well and, you know, you want
to experience the same thing. You've had too much to drink
and you say something about it. It was a pretty weird evening.
The one thing I loved was it telegraphed Elliott's discomfort. It
was him being very real. He was a guy who was under a lot of
pressure to begin with and then, when his life changed with all
of this media attention, he changed along with it. You had to
work a little harder to get hold of him. He became more protective of himself and more guarded, I think. When he came

back home, it got so he couldn't really go out anywhere in Portland and not be bothered. You would hang out with him at a bar and every five minutes or so someone would come up. He was always very gracious about it, but uncomfortable. I don't remember him laughing as much.'

The next day, Smith flew back down to Los Angeles to begin work on his first record for DreamWorks. Before going into the studio, he arranged to meet up with Factor for a parting lunch.

'We went to a place down the street from my office,' recalls Factor. 'It was quite a dramatic lunch, kind of our final shakehands. Elliott was super-polite and grateful, but direct. Once things became challenging in our dealings, I'd realised he was a bit of a businessman as well as an artist. He did have a calculation and an aspiration to being a huge star, I think. That's okay, and it's always okay, but we all went through an era where it wasn't okay to say you wanted those things.

'After it all ended so tragically for Elliott, I learned more of the truth. It wasn't until then I found out he had always appreciated my help. He was demanding and I gave him everything he asked for, because I thought it was what I was supposed to do. Somehow, I thought we'd reap greater rewards for those accommodations. Anyway, Virgin fired me. That's how it all ended for me.'

Schnapf and Rothrock booked Smith into Sound Factory's storied big brother studio, Sunset Sound. A three-room complex located next door to the more economical Sound Factory on Sunset Boulevard, Sunset Sound occupied an old car repair shop. Opened in 1962 by Walt Disney's chief recording engineer, Salvador 'Tutti' Camarata, it was used initially to record audio tracks for Disney films such as *Mary Poppins* and *101 Dalmatians*. Camarata was soon enough also welcoming the new rock and pop royalty into his flat-topped, grey-brick building. Sunset Sound was where Brian Wilson in 1966 summoned the wonders of *Pet Sounds*. Among those hot on Wilson's heels were the Doors, the Rolling Stones, Sly & the Family Stone, Led Zeppelin and Fleetwood Mac.

Along with his two producers, Smith was billeted in Sunset Sound's Studio 3. This was the same low-ceilinged, wood-panelled room inhabited by Prince during his 1980s pomp and from where he had spirited up *1999*, *Purple Rain* and *Sign o' the Times*. Smith, too, went into Sunset Sound having formed a singular vision for the record he wanted to make. He arrived at the studio with a digital audio tape containing fourteen tracks demoed at Jackpot!, arranged in his intended running order. He had also written out in black marker onto the DAT casing his proposed title for the album-to-be, *Grand Mal*.

What Smith's demos didn't begin to hint at was the full panoply of sound he imagined. This was clued by the influencer record he took to carrying around with him in LA, a box set of the Zombies' sumptuously extravagant strain of '60s Britpop-psychedelia. Smith wanted to have the same kind of cavalcade of music running rampant through his record. He wasn't thinking anymore of painting in minimalist shades of black and white, but in full, glorious, 24-track Technicolor and, like Prince again, he was set upon playing almost all of the instruments himself.

He limbered up for the sessions back at Largo, the intimate West Hollywood venue he had first played the previous November. The tiny club on Fairfax Avenue was fast becoming the epicentre of LA's new singer-songwriter scene. Largo was presided over by its garrulous northern Irish owner, Mark Flanagan. However, its ringmaster was an elfin, baby-faced multi-instrumentalist, Jon Brion, who had been performing a Friday night residency at the club since 1996. The 25-year-old Brion hailed from Glen Ridge, New Jersey, but transplanted to Boston in the late '80s, where he performed solo gigs in coffee shops and clubs. Brion also toured with a new wave band, 'Til Tuesday, fronted by his then-girlfriend, singer-songwriter Aimee Mann. When Mann moved out to LA, Brion followed and he had gone on to forge a parallel career as a session musician, playing on records by the Eels and Fiona Apple, and as a producer, starting with Mann's 1993 solo debut, *Whatever*.

Brion's Friday-night slot at Largo was a hot ticket. He conducted his weekly sets more like improv performances, or happenings, than the standard rock gig. Sat up at the piano on Largo's poky stage in his thrift-store, Carnaby Street finery and surrounded by an array of the vintage musical instruments he habitually collected, Brion would encourage his rapt audiences to shout out song requests. Any song as might leap into their heads. He would then set about re-building and re-interpreting their selections from the ground up and on the hoof. Like a mad, unruly-haired professor, he would whirl between his instruments. Here looping in a squelching synth part, there wheezing percussive breaks and thrown over the top, a flourish on his flea market Wurlitzer. He was just as liable to transform a sweet soul standard into something heavy and ominous as run a vein of gloopy break-beats through Lynyrd Skynyrd's 'Sweet Home Alabama'.

At all events, Brion was a wow and other musicians were lining up to sit in with him at Largo. Among his regular onstage collaborators were Mann, Apple, Rufus Wainwright and Mark 'E' Everett. Smith joined the procession on the evening of Friday, 30 January and having done a solo spot at the club the week before. On their first night of performing together, Brion took care of all the instrumentation, leaving Smith free to simply sing and go off into his own otherworld. The two of them hit it off offstage, too, just a couple of shy, awkward and freakishly talented souls coming together.

'We immediately got on like a house on fire,' Brion recalled. 'And we were pretty much close from that second on. You know . . . uh . . . until it officially went off the deep end.'[24]

A few days after his Largo date with Brion, Smith drove out in his rental car to pick up Larry Crane from LAX. He had invited Crane down from Portland to spend a week assisting with the early sessions at Sunset Sound. At Smith's request, Crane brought with him his toy Casio guitar from Jackpot!. Subsequently, the Casio would just about be heard on the new album, piping away in the background of a breezing track titled 'Bled White'.

Smith ferried Crane from the airport straight to the studio. As they were driving, he popped a cassette of the early Sunset Sound sessions into the tape deck of the car. One of the tracks on the tape was 'Everybody Cares, Everybody Understands'.

The song had expanded to include swooping sound effects and a filigreeing Chamberlin keyboard from Jon Brion. Crane was equally taken aback by both the fullness of the sound and also Smith's scathing, still-unedited lyric. To his ear, Smith was reaching for the same kind of dissolute, barely managed chaos as Alex Chilton grasped at on Big Star's final album of 1974, *Sister Lovers*. Chilton suffered a nervous breakdown before he could see through his grand design and *Sister Lovers* ended up coming out after the band had imploded and as a riveting but maddening patchwork piece.

'Man, I'd never heard so much anger in Elliott's music,' says Crane. 'With Jon Brion's crazy noises and weird stuff going on, it's one of the freakiest things I've ever listened to. The original song was even more biting towards Slim Moon and in a very personal way. Heatmiser was also angry and louder, but this was . . . meaner. To sit next to Elliott and listen along to it with him in his car was an intense experience. It kind of blew me away.'

The temperature of the initial Sunset Sound sessions was just as fierce. On the first day proper of recording, Smith had put down almost all of one of his finest songs, 'Waltz #2'. In a blizzard of activity, he did his lead vocal, then a double-track vocal, then the guitar, bass and drum parts, and then the piano and organ parts. He was his own one-man band, a blur of brisk, focused, manic energy. Crane sat watching him from behind the control room window with Schnapf and Rothrock, spectators to his high-wire balancing act.

'The phrase "recording artist" gets tossed around, but Elliott *was* a recording artist,' says Crane. 'I've since spoken with people

199

who worked with Prince and he sounded exactly the same. The two of them were absolutely of a mind-set and totally obsessive types. Like, "We're going to stay up for twenty-four hours – we've got to keep recording!" There are some people who just have an incredible drive to top themselves and they couldn't give a fuck about the rest of the world. I can guarantee Elliott's goal was not to become famous or to have adulation, he just wanted to know he was writing at a level as far as he could push it. Everything else was a means to an end. He told me once, "All I want to do is to write and record these songs. The interviews, the tours, the photo shoots, the videos and all the other stuff is what I've got to do to be able to do this."

'The reason Elliott's records became more expansive and crazier is because he wanted to keep on trying new stuff, writing in different ways and opening doors. There was no one telling him to do it. Towards the end of my stay in LA, I watched Elliott, Rob and Tom lay down an eight-piece string section and horns onto "Waltz #2". I was present for Elliott's meeting with the arrangers, Shelly Berg and Tom Halm. I'd never before got to see any of my friends use strings and horns. It was beautiful. Oh my God, I was crying.'

At 7 a.m. on the Tuesday morning of 10 February, Crane was also with Smith when he took a call from Margaret Mittleman. The very same early morning and just across town at the Samuel Goldwyn Theater in Beverly Hills, the year's Oscar nominations had been read out by Robert Rehme, president of the Academy of Motion Picture Arts and Sciences, and the actress Geena Davis. Mittleman was calling to pass on to Smith the news he had been nominated in the 'Best Original Song' category for 'Miss Misery' in the film *Good Will Hunting*. Smith got off the phone with Mittleman and immediately tried to reach Joanna Bolme to share his good fortune. Bolme didn't pick up. He turned to Crane instead and the two of them sat jawing in disbelief. The announcement had an instantaneous and disruptive effect upon the sessions at Sunset Sound.

'All at once, every morning there was now an hour and a half of interviews for Elliott to do at the studio before we could get to working on anything,' recalls Crane. 'Garbage interviews with garbage journalists who hadn't done any research. Time and again I would hear Elliott say, "No, Gus Van Sant did not discover me playing in a coffee shop."

'It was a terrible diversion from what he was trying to do. Up until this point, "Miss Misery" was going to be on the album. Then, Rob and Tom were like, "We think it's got too much of a life of its own." I was bummed, too, because guess what? I'd got a co-production credit from Elliott for working on the song.'

On 26 February, Smith did a further solo show back in LA at Spaceland. He was in a playful mood during his 75-minute set. Covering John Lennon's 'Jealous Guy', he snaffled a volunteer from the audience to join him up on stage and take Lennon's whistling part in the song. He played an acoustic version of 'Waltz #2' and also gave his very first public reading of 'Pitseleh'. Halfway through the set, he dropped 'Miss Misery', like it

was no particular big deal. Except just then it so obviously was and because of it the sessions at Sunset Sound carried on being fractured. Smith's temper wavered accordingly and typically governed by how many media commitments Margaret Mittleman required of him each day. Then again, the number of times he happened to be asked who and what 'Miss Misery' was about. He did press interviews in the mornings, worked in the studio in the afternoons and into the wee hours.

'That was always the battle for Elliott,' Mittleman says. 'Wanting to be left alone and wanting to live up to his obligations with whatever record label he was on, whomever he worked with or wanted to talk to him. He always wanted to give it the benefit of the doubt, but then a lot of times it came up short for him, I think. I do believe he wanted his music to be heard as widely as possible. I just think the narrative that got out there was hard for him to beat down.

'He would've loved to talk about the technique of writing songs or his guitar playing, but it would always go in the same direction: "Oh, you're sad and you've written about heroin". My focus was for him to successfully navigate all of it. "Okay, if you're crabby, we'll deal with it and can you go back now and create?" It was a wild time and he did the best he could to take it all in and eat it up. I honestly feel he wanted to try to succeed, but ultimately, he would just end up being disappointed with some part of the process. I could never put my finger on what it was, but it was hard to manage.'

The regular press interviews were testing enough for Smith, but as the Oscars' buzz heightened, he also found himself being booked onto TV shows. During the first week of March 1998, he travelled to New York to film two spots. On 4 March, he sang 'Miss Misery' on Conan O'Brien's late-night talk show. For this performance, he wore a T-shirt with a state map of Texas printed on the front and seemed not so far out of his element. The next day, he guested on *MTV Live*. This one turned out to be much more of an excruciating ordeal all round. The show's host, Carson Daly, desperately flailed around to make any kind of connection with Smith as his guest was shrinking and recoiling from him.

In LA, Margaret Mittleman increasingly found herself having to field the demands of the Oscars' producer, Gil Cates, to Smith. The year's biggest blockbuster, *Titanic*, was also up for fourteen Oscars and Cates schemed for his show to be as epically bombastic as James Cameron's film. This extended to the 'Best Original Song' category, where *Titanic* was represented by its theme tune, 'My Heart Will Go On', a surging ballad sung with a typical absence of restraint by Celine Dion.

Cates told Mittleman he wanted all of the nominees to perform their songs with the backing of a full orchestra for the live TV broadcast. When Mittleman passed this onto Smith, he dismissed Cates' idea out of hand. Cates returned with a threat to substitute Smith with someone more familiar to America's mainstream viewing public – say, hirsute pop-rocker Richard Marx – and have him sing 'Miss Misery' on the night. Smith climbed down, although Mittleman managed to extract one concession at least from Cates: Smith was allowed to do his own string arrangement.

An estimated TV audience of 55.3 million watched the Oscars ceremony unfold at Hollywood's Shrine Auditorium on the evening of Monday, 23 March. Smith invited Joanna Bolme along as his date for the night. They were on again. Miramax stumped up for him to hire an all-white suit, belt, shirt and shoes from Prada for the occasion. The night before the ceremony, Smith tried his Oscars outfit on for size and sat up at the bar at Largo, looking like a Las Vegas lounge act. It was dawn on the Monday by the time he crawled out of the club, booze-numbed, hair so greasy he could sculpt it up on end, and to go and collect Bolme.

At the Shrine, the couple walked down the red carpet hand-in-hand, trailing behind Jack Nicholson, Madonna, Dustin Hoffman, Matt Damon, Robin Williams and Minnie Driver, strobe-lit by camera flashbulbs but not so as any of the thronged media recognised or stopped them in their tracks. Backstage, Williams offered Smith a stick of chewing gum and Celine Dion fussed over him, telling him how much she admired his song. The show's host, Billy Crystal, introduced the 'Best Original Song' nominees to the stage. One after another they trooped out from the wings to sing: Dion, Michael Bolton, Aaliyah, LeAnn Rimes and Smith.

When it came to Smith's turn, he walked into the spotlight without fanfare and with his acoustic guitar strapped over his now crumpled suit. The entire stage was mocked up to look like the *Titanic*'s grand ballroom. Afterwards, he remembered seeing Nicholson sat 6 feet in front of him as he was singing, the orchestra swooning along with him, and wondering if he might be having an out-of-body experience. He had been ordered to truncate 'Miss Misery' to just over two minutes' running time. When he finished his performance, he bowed to the audience's applause and exited stage right without a word or backward glance. Madonna then entered from stage left to announce the Oscar winner. Opening up the gold-leaf envelope, she did it with biting sarcasm, sneering: 'Ha-ha, what a shocker. The Oscar goes to . . . "My Heart Will Go On".'

After the show, Smith and Bolme accompanied Mittleman, Schnapf and the *Good Will Hunting* cast to *Vanity Fair*'s traditional post-Oscars dinner, the Governors Ball. They sat at a table with Fay Wray, the original *King Kong* siren, fish out of water, interlopers to the party, but intoxicated still by the crazy-dream bizarreness of the whole evening.

'He enjoyed the surrealness of it,' Bolme told writer Keith Cameron in 2011. 'But things were changing. We had an on-off relationship by then. Drug use on his part was the main culprit; drugs and his lack of interest in his own life.'[25]

'It's really hard to say no to an opportunity like the Oscars, isn't it?' says Larry Crane. 'I remember the convolution we had going on beforehand. Elliott was like, "What do I do? What do you think I should do?" For his Oscars performance, they garbled up the input on his mic at the beginning and he looked nervous even though he probably wasn't.

'If there was a time machine he could have climbed into, Elliott would probably have gone back and done it all over again, I think. I also believe his life would've been better if he hadn't done it. It just made him out to be a caricature and it's been annoying to me ever since how people perceive him. That's not the guy I was building a studio with, or took a shot of whiskey with quietly after work. For me, the Oscars show was the beginning of the end.'

CHAPTER 17

A Question Mark

Four nights after the Oscars ceremony, Smith was back sitting in at Largo with Jon Brion. They improvised a song together on the spot about Smith's backstage at the Oscars meeting with Celine Dion and covered an old hillbilly country tune from the '40s, 'Blue Eyes Crying in the Rain', originally cut by the yodelling Elton Britt and the Skytoppers. Increasingly, Smith was frequenting Largo after hours at Sunset Sound. He found himself there in the company of kindred spirits. Aimee Mann, Ben Folds and Fiona Apple were also regulars, Benmont Tench from Tom Petty's band, too, and Mark 'E' Everett more occasionally.

Smith's closest connection at Largo remained with Brion. Friday nights, he would sit in the audience and watch Brion perform his daredevil act. Persistently, he would write out song requests on napkins and have them passed up to Brion on the stage. By the end of his sets, Brion would have accumulated a pile of napkins on his piano top, each of Smith's selections set down in neat, careful script as if they were his own handwritten liner notes. After the audience was turned out for the night, Mark Flanagan would let the two of them have the run of his place. They would sit up next to each other at the piano, talking and drinking and playing Elton John songs together until the night sky began to tinge pink. 'Goodbye Yellow Brick Road' was always Smith's favourite, the one he would sing with most conviction and as though entreating Bernie Taupin's words back to himself: 'When are you gonna come down? When are you going to land?'

'It was a little bit of a golden era when Elliott was first hanging around,' Brion told Autumn de Wilde. 'He was at the height of his creative powers. He had a certain sense of self and people were starting to notice it. He wasn't out of control yet. He was merely a very loveable alcoholic and we had a couple of years of that . . . He was an absolute delight to know.'[26]

'Elliott was just kind of always around at Largo,' says Everett. 'He was a really sweet, quiet kind of guy. I never got to know him really well, but I don't know that anyone ever knew him very well.

'Like a lot of musicians, Elliott was very different offstage and then lit up when he was performing. It was a special thing to be in a room with a hundred other people and see him. He would sort of nervously sit down, tune up his guitar and then he'd start playing, and it would be like everything else just sort of disappeared and you were transported.'

When Smith wasn't being distracted by the Oscars noise, he maintained a fierce pace of work with Rob Schnapf and Tom

Rothrock. They dipped in and out of other studios around town, Ocean Way, Sonora Recorders and next-door at Sound Factory, but for the greater part they stayed hunkered at Sunset Sound. Smith rattled through the basic tracks there like he was racing against time itself. He sang lead and harmony vocals, played electric and acoustic guitar, bass, drums, percussion, piano and electric piano, organ and mandolin. His focus was unwavering, attending to the tiniest of details like a lab-coated scientist conducting an intricate and potentially explosive experiment.

Whenever he needed to let off steam, he would join Schnapf and Rothrock in the yard out back of Sunset Sound, where there was a basketball hoop mounted on a wall. There was a 7-Eleven store just down the street selling cheap fancy-dress pirate costumes. One afternoon, Smith went in and bought three sets of these costumes and from then on, they shot hoops kitted out in plastic eye-patches and skull-and-crossbones tricorn hats.

'Elliott made what he was doing sound easy, but it was actually not easy at all,' recalls Schnapf. 'I always thought of that as his greatness. It was hard work. He was playing every single instrument and almost without a break. The other thing is, and it's true of anybody, you might have a natural proclivity towards music or writing, or whatever, but it doesn't happen unless you put the time in. And Elliott put the time in. He practised really hard and a lot.

'He had his own unique style and he was very good, very talented. He was a great piano player, clearly melodically deep. Lyrically, it was all about the word. There was one song I really liked, "Echo Park", he shit-canned because he didn't like the word "the". I was like, "Elliott, 'the' isn't even a real word." But he didn't like how he sang this particular "the" and so the song's never seen the light of day.'

Ever so occasionally, Smith would have something going around in his head he wasn't, or at least didn't feel able to channel himself. At Sunset Sound, he reached an impasse with the precise drum tracks he wanted to go on two songs, 'Bled White' and 'Bottle Up and Explode!'. Schnapf and Rothrock knew of Joey Waronker, Lenny's boy, from his drumming with Beck's band. As Smith grew more agitated over the absent drum tracks, they got a demo tape of the two songs to Waronker and arranged to have him come by the studio. Waronker arrived for his session date with drum parts for both songs worked out.

'The drums were already set up and tuned for me when I went into Studio 3,' says Waronker. 'It was very professional. Elliott instructed me, "Do your own thing. Don't just copy what I did on the demo." I did a pass and they were all like, "Wow, that's amazing." Elliott then came over to me and said, "I have just a few ideas." He proceeded to go through each little thing I'd changed and had me change it back to the way it was on his demo.

'He was an A-type personality guy. He was soft-spoken, but he was in charge. He was someone of strong opinions and very articulate with it. I mean, he was sharp. As a musician, he's probably the best I've encountered and I don't say that lightly. At first, I was totally enamoured by just how much technical skill he had, but then his music was also so soulful, and sad and intense. He had both the musical knowledge and soul, which was pretty unparalleled to me. It's insane to me how good he was. I don't know I've ever come across anyone else like him.'

★

They were done with tracking at Sunset Sound by the end of March 1998. Through to the close of the sessions, Smith used Studio 3 like his own private laboratory and to test out and experiment with different ways of encapsulating his music. The record he made there turned out to be more akin to one of the hulking, heavyweight Russian novels he read so prodigiously, since it was filled with characters, incidental colour and subplots. Rob Schnapf recalls how pumped up and excited Smith was during those weeks of recording.

'I listened to the record just recently for the first time in over a decade,' Schnapf says. 'To me, it sums up the joy of record making. When you're sending out the musical probe and it comes back with gold. As we were making it, I think maybe Elliott freed himself. When you're in a small, tight scene there are natural limitations you can subconsciously put on one another. Like what's cool and what's not. I felt like we had total freedom at Sunset Sound.'

It was a mere five years on from *Roman Candle*, but artistically Smith had travelled a span of light years. The spare, hushed, flat-earth terrain of his debut gave way here to a universe of symphonic sound. He'd ultimately decided to title the record *XO*, after a lyric from 'Waltz #2'. *XO*'s canvas is filled up with fourteen songs and a dizzying, heady array of bold colours and daring. The strongest sense they convey is of a grand master operating at the height of his powers and towards the farthest reaches of his imagination. The sheer wonder of it all countered and starkly contrasted by the many indicators he also gave to the depths he was dredging here. The final lines of the closing song read off the page like a last will and testament: 'You once talked to me about love and you painted pictures of a never-never land. And I could've gone to that place, but I didn't understand.'

As *XO* was being mastered, Smith undertook a short tour beginning on 4 April in Orlando, Florida, and finishing back in LA with a brace of dates at the famous Troubadour club on Sunset Strip on 19 and 20 May. He performed the first clutch of dates solo and acoustic. After the Orlando gig and one in Atlanta, Georgia, he returned to LA to headline a Saturday night at Largo on 11 April. He played a 75-minute set, opening with 'Tomorrow Tomorrow' from the barely completed new album. Jon Brion joined him onstage for 'Almaeda' and a cover of a Quasi song, 'Clouds'. Basking in the adoration of the small Largo crowd, Smith also served up a typically wry Hank Williams' tune, 'All My Rowdy Friends (Have Settled Down)' and rounded off his set with Big Star's 'Thirteen', the room so reverent by then one could hear the hum of the air-conditioner unit.

Four nights later, he resumed over on the East Coast at the Middle East club in Cambridge, Massachusetts. He played a shorter set in Cambridge, fifty-five minutes, and with no songs off *XO*. Also on the bill were a band out of Portland, Modest Mouse, and Bill Santen and his Birddog band, opening for Smith on this leg of the tour. Both Margaret Mittleman and Joanna Bolme were travelling with the touring party, too, each as protective of Smith as the other. Like all of the shows on the run, this one was a sell-out. Right off the bat, Santen saw first-hand the transformation in Smith's circumstances following the Oscars.

'I went into Elliott's dressing room at the Middle East and there was a line of people going out the door,' Santen recalls. 'It was such a weird thing to see people queued up to speak with him. Elliott was sat there, like he was receiving them. And some people in the line were crying.

'When I walked in, he happened to be talking to one of his sisters from Portland. She was giving him his birthday present and she had also waited in line to see him. Things changed. He stopped communicating with people. It got so if you wanted to see him, you had to go to one of his shows.'

When the tour got going again in mid-May, Sam Coomes and Janet Weiss joined up to play an opening slot as Quasi and then to back Smith for the latter part of his sets. The three of them were evidently still processing the harrowing experiences of their last tour together from the previous year. Quasi had very recently put out a new album, *Featuring 'Birds'*, on which Smith was credited as 'executive producer'. His uncredited contribution very likely extended to ghost-writing the lyrics of its third track, 'The Poisoned Well'. A sweet-sounding pop confection, it nonetheless reads like an apology and a confession wrapped into

one and as Coomes mouthpieces: 'We went through hell, just to
get to hell . . . At least I never lied, I'm not trying to document
my suicide.'

The following year, Smith cut an answer song of his own,
'From a Poison Well'. He lifted its drifting downstream melody
from another of his studio outtakes, 'First Timer', a track put
down at Jackpot! in 1997 and during the fledgling sessions for
XO. His lyrics playfully suggest his role in the Quasi original, the
declarative opening line announcing: 'I'm a ghost writer for an
ocean in a shell, from the poison well.'

Smith and Quasi played the Showbox in Seattle on 14 May
and then the Western Washington University in Bellingham on
the night of the 15th. At both these shows, Smith made a visible
effort to keep the atmosphere between them light and upbeat.
Backstage, he clowned around with a rubber chicken glove
puppet he had picked up from a truck stop. Meanwhile Bolme
and Mittleman strived to keep a watchful, caring eye on him – it
was a full-time job.

CHAPTER 18

The Long and Winding Road

For the duration of the next year, Smith was hardly ever at home in Brooklyn. Even when he was, most often it was for no more than a couple of days or so at a time. He spent months on end touring *XO*, a rootless tree blown along by a whirlwind. At the end of May 1998, he travelled with Margaret Mittleman to Europe to play his first ever shows outside of North America. Their itinerary was relentless: Paris on 29 May, Amsterdam on the 30th and Stockholm on 2 June. He was back to performing solo with an acoustic guitar, interviews by day and a show at night. Not a spare minute to take in the sights outside of his hotel rooms.

On 3 June, Smith and Mittleman arrived in London. Smith had a show booked the same evening at a north London club, the Highbury Garage. His new UK promoter, Russell Warby, picked them up from Heathrow Airport. As Warby drove them into town, he ventured to make small talk with Smith, sat next to him with his arms wrapped around his guitar case as if it was a life raft. Warby managed to extract a few cursory responses from Smith, but then Smith shut up. The car journey continued in an uncomfortable silence, Smith hunched over in the passenger seat as if he were being rained on.

Smith's debut London performance proved to be just as charged and intense. Warby had booked him into the Garage's smaller upstairs room. The place was packed, hot and stifling. As the set unfolded, the audience stood still and silent, like they were hanging on each note, scrutinising his every inflection. The exceptions were a couple stood front and centre of the low stage, who kept up a loud and running conversation. Eventually, a guy stood nearby to the two talkers snapped. 'Will you shut the fuck up!' he exhorted, finger-jabbing at them. An argument broke out between the three of them and then a scuffle, drawing in other folk in their immediate vicinity. A security guard finally interceded to break the melee apart. Meanwhile, a matter of feet apart from the ruckus, sat up on stage, Smith carried on playing. He seemed oblivious to the disturbance, or else so attuned to such strange currents they no longer registered.

'I spoke to Elliott about it afterwards,' says Warby. 'About how he was up there performing this very heartfelt and quiet music and how incongruous it was to have the audience kick off like that. He just said, "Oh yeah, it often provokes that kind of a response."'

On his return to the US, Smith undertook four East Coast shows on a bill opening up for Beck and along with his Largo running mate, Ben Folds. The last of these was on 11 June at Jones Beach amphitheatre, where the previous summer he had stood on the lighting gantry and watched Neil Young play, looking down from the gods and through his feet, a distant spectator to the action.

After the Beck dates, Smith was given a brief respite from touring. He was able to visit Portland and then go home to Brooklyn, but his need to create was so insatiable he wasn't able to let up. He had a young music video-maker from California, Steve Hanft, trail him from Portland to Brooklyn. Hanft had got his break shooting the freewheeling clip for Beck's 'Loser' single. Smith hired him to make a short film to go along with the release of *XO*, repeating the blueprint he had set out with *Lucky Three* and *Either/Or*.

Like Hanft's Beck video, the result of their labours, *Strange Parallel* (1998), amounted to a series of scattershot, elliptical images. They conceived it as a *faux* documentary and in Portland, Hanft shot a series of interviews with Smith's friends. He filmed Larry Crane and Joanna Bolme in the control room at Jackpot!, Sam Coomes and Janet Weiss – the latter inexplicably attired as an ancient Egyptian queen – in their back garden, and Sean Croghan, reprising a barking drill sergeant role he had adopted back when he and Smith were housemates. Over a couple of steamy July days in Brooklyn, Hanft shot Smith idling in a bland-looking hotel room and also a collection of satirical TV ads. These fake TV spots poked at the rampant commercialism of the music business, represented by the clunking metaphor of a giant robot hand.

The whole came out an indulgent mess, an in-joke lacking a punchline. Its subject remained elusive even when present and in plain sight onscreen – apart, that is, for the briefest moment when Smith bares himself. Off camera, Hanft asks what he thinks the future holds for him. Smith smiles as he replies, but his answer is too knowing and fearful to be taken as glib. 'I think the music business will eventually crush me,' he tells Hanft. 'But I'm ready. I like it better than spreading gravel for a living, you know?'

DreamWorks released *XO* on 25 August. The cover photograph was taken at Jackpot!, a black-and-white picture of a beaming Larry Crane watching Smith at work out on the studio floor. One could read it as an embodiment of Smith in his element. Or else his nostalgia for a recent past, one already now fading away. 'Miss Misery' and the Oscars had made him enough of a talking point for the album to be reviewed in *Rolling Stone*. 'Elliott Smith is the very model of a modern troubadour,' appraised the august magazine's critic, Rob Sheffield. 'He writes intimate café ballads . . . filling his songs with emotional wreckage; the man who knows how to give bad love a good name.'[27]

The whirlwind swept Smith up once more. On 28 August, he flew back to London. The next day he performed at the Reading Festival on a bill also featuring the Beastie Boys, the Prodigy and the Foo Fighters. He had a second festival date in Belgium on the 30th and on the 31st a solo acoustic show at a club in Camden, north London – Dingwalls. After this, four solo acoustic shows opening up for the Scottish indie-pop band Belle and Sebastian, a brace in Leeds and two more at the Shepherd's Bush Empire in London again. Belle and Sebastian attracted their own reverential audience. Their fans were disinclined to listen to the mere support act and gave Smith short shrift.

'I had convinced Elliott to do the Belle and Sebastian shows,' recalls Russell Warby. 'I knew they had a partisan audience, but they were also enlightened musically or so I'd liked to have thought. But I went to one of the London shows and it was absolutely appalling. Elliott came on and they talked all the way through his set.

'Anyway, Elliott responded. It was the first time I'd seen him be like this. At one point, he reached into his back pocket and said to the audience, "I've got a gift for you. I've brought something with me from New York." Then he pulled his hand out and gave them the middle finger. Fair enough, they deserved it, but Elliott also wasn't a person to suffer fools gladly. Just because he was a gentle person didn't mean he was in any way weak, there was a real strength at the centre of him.'

Even so, the relentlessness of Smith's schedule was beginning to take its toll. Being in constant motion, the lack of sleep, too much access to free booze and other temptations all conspired to run him down, to weaken his will. It left him vulnerable. In mid-September, he was allowed three more days at home in New York. Not time enough for him to decompress, but plenty to get into trouble. Smith spent the daytime of Saturday, 12 September drinking at O'Connor's. In the evening, he moved on to Manhattan, where Bill Santen's band Birddog were opening a show for British post-punk vets the Mekons at the Mercury Lounge on the Lower East Side.

Smith caught Birddog's set and met up with Santen afterwards. It was Santen's birthday and together with Birddog's drummer, Glenn Kotche, their party headed out into the New York night to celebrate. Smith was drinking beers and chasing them with shots of Jameson's whiskey. Inevitably, they eventually wound their way to Max Fish, where Smith had also arranged to hook up with Dorien Garry. As ever at Max Fish, Smith fed money into the jukebox and chalked up his name on the blackboard to shoot pool. When it came around to his turn to play, a group of rowdy frat-boy types were gathered around the pool table.

'It had been such a perfect night, we were having a great time and then all hell broke loose,' says Santen. 'Basically, Elliott hit one of these guys. It was over something so stupid, a drunken verbal thing. It was absurd. Glenn and I pulled the guy up off the floor. We were literally holding him up by his arms. And Elliott hit him again. Then, God, it turned to mayhem and with all the craziness, Elliott ended up slipping and falling on a beer glass, gauging his back. Glenn and I managed to get him out of there. One of the Max Fish bouncers escorted us out through a back door. The people in the bar thought these frat boys were trying to beat up on Elliott Smith, when it was Elliott who'd started the fight.

'I talked to Dorien about it later on and she told me Elliott had got into this habit of trying to get his ass kicked. It was a new side of him to me. Elliott had gashed his back on the bottle. He was all bloody. I tied his sweatshirt around his waist to try to stem the bleeding, but there was blood everywhere. We got him in a cab with Dorien. Altogether, it was a depressing experience.'

Garry cleaned and dressed Smith's wound back at her apartment. The cut was deep and needed stitches, but Smith wouldn't let her take him to a hospital. His lower back was left with a permanent web of scarring. Four days later, he returned to the road for a month of coast-to-coast dates in the US. He started out at the Showbox in Seattle, before playing a couple of shows in Portland at EJ's and then La Luna. He left 'Miss Misery' off the setlists all three nights and for the whole rest of the tour.

Smith played three shows in LA, the first at Spaceland and the next two at the Roxy Theatre on Sunset Strip on 22 and 23 September. The Roxy show brought out Tinseltown's gawkers and rubberneckers, the Hollywood 'in' crowd. The first night, Michael Stipe of R.E.M. and Courtney Love dropped by together. 'Oh, Elliott,' Love cooed as she entered the packed room. 'Where's the genius boy?' Without acknowledging her, Smith slipped quietly away from the scene.

By the middle of October, Smith was home in New York and booked to perform on *Saturday Night Live* on the evening of 17 October. He had adored *SNL* from being a kid in Duncanville. To become a part of its institution was to live out a schoolboy fantasy. Adding to his dream state, *SNL*'s guest host for the night was Lucy Lawless, the New Zealand actress who starred in *Xena: Warrior Princess*, the TV show he fixated on when writing songs for *Either/Or*. Lawless introduced Smith to the watching TV audience. He struck up 'Waltz #2' with his three-piece band,

Jon Brion sitting in with Sam Coomes and Janet Weiss. Temporarily once more, he was restored.

Into November and he was off to Europe again, Joanna Bolme accompanying him. There were shows in Belgium, France, Norway, Sweden and then London and Sheffield in the UK in December. Smith had begun sifting through the scraps of ideas he had already got down on tape and filling up his notebooks. Back in LA in September, he'd floated an idea to Luke Wood at DreamWorks to do some recording at Abbey Road. Wood followed through on the suggestion and made the arrangements for a four-day session at the legendary studio.

Together with Coomes and Bolme, Smith stepped into Abbey Road's Studio 2, the Beatles' room, at noon on Friday, 4 December. Rob Schnapf and Tom Rothrock had flown in from LA to run the Neve VR Legend board made famous by the Fab Four's producer, arranger and mentor, George Martin. Joey Waronker, who happened to be in town playing with R.E.M., joined the group later on the same afternoon. The first of Smith's new songs they started to work on was 'Stupidity Tries', the sound rising to the 24-foot-high ceiling and resounding around the room. Their last day at Abbey Road, Smith brought in a piece he had worked up around a waltzing piano part and therefore titled 'Honky Bach'. He played it sat at the upright piano in Studio 2.

'That upright piano just sounded so familiar,' recalls Rob Schnapf. 'I constantly bothered our assistant at Abbey Road, Paul Hicks, about it and until he finally told me it was the very piano Paul McCartney had used to record "Penny Lane".

'As Elliott was playing, I said to him over the talk-back mic in the control room, "Hey, the piano . . . you know what it is? 'Penny Lane'." Elliott carried on playing for a moment and then, all of a sudden, what I'd told him settled in. His playing got slower and slower and then he stopped altogether. It totally freaked him out and it was really funny. He was like, "*God!*" I told him, "Well, dude, everything in here is from *them*."'

On the other side of Christmas, the tour kept rolling into the New Year. Through January 1999, Smith played his first shows in Australia and Japan, a clutch of dates in Melbourne, Sydney, Osaka and Tokyo. On 22 February, he started up yet another North American tour.

Two nights later, they pulled into Portland to play at La Luna. That night, Smith performed three songs solo acoustic, 'Say Yes', 'Everything Reminds Me of Her' and 'Between the Bars'. After his set, he played host to a small gathering of friends and family in the upstairs bar. He made an effort to get around the room, to be attentive, to be his old self. Nevertheless, to everyone there it was apparent how something was very wrong with him.

'Seeing Elliott that night at La Luna was when I realised he'd gone off the rails,' says Pete Krebs. 'I mean, he really looked like shit. He seemed pretty out of it, very detached. He was carrying around all of his stuff in a plastic shopping bag – his wallet, pens and a notebook. I don't know if he was doing drugs, or just really drunk. He was just not there.'

'I went to the after-party with my friend Christine and it was pretty tragic actually,' says Janel Jarosz. 'Elliott didn't look so great. Both Christine and I got to give him a hug and tell him we loved him. He told us he loved us, too. Then I told him I was worried about him and to hang in there. After he left, Christine looked at me and said, "I think that's the last time we're going to see Elliott." And she was right.'

'Elliott's persona got to be weirder and more selfish,' Sean Croghan, who was opening the shows, was to recall. 'It wasn't like he was in control. He was just totally out of it, because he was popping all these different medications. It was like he was carrying a shoebox of medications he had to take – fifteen, twenty, thirty different pills a day. There was still this amazing talent, but when I talked to him it was like it was a cardboard cut-out. It was like, "You're not there, you're vacant."'

PART 4

Los Angeles, California

CHAPTER 19

Go West

There wasn't time for the dust to settle from after the long tour, which had seen Smith rapturously received in the UK as well as France and Belgium, before he was on the move once again. *XO* had been his most commercially successful record yet, selling over 150,000 copies and climbing. This was a healthy return, but not enough to afford him the time to pause and take stock. There were the reins of the next record to be picked back up and carried on from the Abbey Road session, momentum to be maintained. Even while he was still on the road, arrangements were being made for him to continue with it and now, once again, he was bound for Los Angeles.

Margaret Mittleman took care of the advance planning. She found him a place to rent for the duration, a home rather than a hotel room. It was a neat, white, stuccoed cottage in a small, gated complex on Sutherland Street in the artsy neighbourhood of Echo Park. The location was picture-perfect, halfway up a hillside and overlooking the Pacific Ocean. There were three other identical bungalows on the development, each one dating from the 1910s, ancient by the city's standards. They were arranged around a bigger, two-storey house framed on one side by a huge rubber tree and with a Bougainvillea plant climbing up the opposite wall on a trellis, its violet flowers brilliant against the white stucco.

Mittleman chose the location very deliberately. A photographer friend of hers, Autumn de Wilde, was living in the big house with her partner, Aaron Sperske, a drummer and full-time musician. De Wilde had not long shot some portraits of Smith commissioned by Mittleman and she had established an instant rapport with him. Mittleman's young assistant, Alyssa Siegel, was also occupying one of the other cottages. As far as Mittleman was concerned, it was the safest kind of spot for Smith to be put, surrounded by folk who would look out for him and have his back.

Sperske's band, Beachwood Sparks, were on a hiatus and he took on the task of getting Smith's cottage fixed up for him to move into, painting and redecorating the place. Siegel hired a car for him to get around the sprawling city. In June 1999, Smith packed up his Brooklyn apartment and left for the West Coast once more. It was to be a temporary arrangement again, nothing but a work trip, or so he told Dorien Garry and his other New York friends. In reality, he was never to return to live in New York, or anywhere else but LA.

'My thinking on Elliott was, "In the middle of all this activity and insanity, how do we make things better moving forward and what could we change or do differently?"' says Mittleman. 'Elliott had done his Portland thing and I felt like he'd done his Brooklyn thing now, too. LA was sunny and Rob and I were there. He could be around Rob whenever he wanted to write. We'd got great friends and I knew he would love some of the same people we did.

'For Elliott, it was always about getting away from whatever it was he thought was doing him wrong. Or else from how he was doing it wrong. Looking back, what he needed was to just stop and not lose the support of people around him.'

'At the same point Elliot was leaving for LA, I was moving out of my apartment and into an identical one next-door with my boyfriend,' says Dorien Garry. 'We had an extra bedroom in the new place and Elliott asked if he could rent it off us, so he would have a place when he came back. He and I moved all of his stuff out from Brooklyn and into my new apartment.

'But he so very rarely came back, after a while I said to him, "This is stupid. You shouldn't be paying me rent, you can just stay here whenever you need to. It's a guest room and it's yours." Even then, he never really ever moved his stuff out. Most of it was books and CDs, piles of stuff he'd accumulated. For a year or two, he kept on telling me he didn't live in LA, that he was just out there because other people needed him to be. Eventually, he kind of gave into it. By then, I don't think there was anywhere that felt to him like a permanent home.'

As a scholar of such things, Smith was drawn to LA as much as anything else by its musical lore. LA was America's dream factory. For four decades now, sounds of sun-kissed fantasy and golden-hued wonder had drifted in from its beaches and rolled down from its canyons. All of them neatly packaged up and then sold on to the rest of the world like the tantalising promise of something better just over the horizon.

LA was where magic happened and myths were made. Somewhere to escape to, get lost in and to reinvent one's self, it was a city of intoxicating apparitions and miraculous tricks of the light. Only in LA could an awkward army brat such as James Douglas Morrison become mighty Jim Morrison, the leather-clad Lizard King. Then there was the flipside, the dark underbelly lurking beneath the city's gleaming surfaces. LA was also cruel, treacherous and sinful, a contemporary Babylon by the Pacific. A vast, sprawling tract of land, at once lush and fertile and then again barren and inhospitable, the beautiful people and the damned co-existing side by side.

Initially, Smith eased into the rhythm of his new city. As Margaret Mittleman had anticipated, he quickly grew close to his immediate neighbours, Siegel, de Wilde and Sperske. On the Friday night of 6 August, de Wilde and Siegel threw him a thirtieth birthday party at a local hotspot, a Chinatown dive bar-cum-restaurant, Hop Louie. De Wilde baked him a cake for the occasion. Hop Louie's vintage jukebox pumped out old-school 45s the whole night and Smith, de Wilde, Siegel and all of their other guests got up and danced along on the tiny, 6-foot-square dancefloor.

The party went on into the early hours of the next day, but Smith kept a Saturday recording date at Capitol Studios. There in the bowels of the famous old Capitol building on Hollywood and Vine, he put down a cover of a Beatles' song, 'Because', for the soundtrack to another movie destined to go on and win Oscars, *American Beauty* (1999).

He turned up for the session clutching his skateboard and in the same clothes he had worn the night before, an orange T-shirt, thrift-store jeans, scuffed sneakers and a trucker's cap. Bleary-eyed and hungover, he nonetheless soared. The movie's musical director, Bill Bernstein, had intended to use the Beatles' own *Abbey Road* track to play over the closing credits, but was unable to secure the rights. It hardly mattered, since Smith's substitute version was every bit a match for the original. His multi-tracked vocals were as heavenly as those of Lennon, McCartney and Harrison, his take on their song altogether as bewitchingly lovely.

Most other nights, Smith was out and about on the town. He became a regular at Hop Louie, ticking the jukebox over, and at a second local diver bar, Little Joy, which had both a jukebox *and* pool tables. At Spaceland in Echo Park, too, where he got to be good friends with Aaron Embry, sat up at the bar to catch whoever happened to be playing the club on any given night. The nights at Largo also carried on, but also now he hung out at the club all hours, enjoying the chance to be in the company of other musicians. Even there, among his peers, Smith would so often seem separate and different somehow. One afternoon at Largo, he was killing time before a show, small talking in the upstairs office with Mark Flanagan, Mark 'E' Everett and Lisa Germano, who was then playing fiddle in Everett's band, the Eels. Flanagan's dog, a big, white, fluffy Husky named Seumas, was also padding around the place.

'Lisa and Elliott were sat on the couch,' says Everett. 'Lisa started to tell Elliott a long, involved story and Elliott got very engaged with listening to Lisa. As Lisa went on, Seumas also got up on the couch, straddled Lisa and began humping her back. Lisa seemed oblivious. Flanagan and I were beside ourselves with laughter. We were laughing so hard, we were crying. Elliott, though, never broke concentration and gave Lisa the respect of listening to her whole story.

'I was also living in the same neighbourhood as Elliott. I would bump into him on the street. On another occasion, I happened to be in the local video store with my girlfriend at the same time as Elliott. He had a big bag of videos he was taking home to watch. I said to him, "Oh, what'd you get?" He pulled out these tapes, one by one. They were all documentaries on art, architecture and nature, really smart stuff. Then he goes, "What did you guys get?" We had one video and it was a shitty rom-com. Stuff like that happened often and you always felt as if Elliott was on a pedestal. Same as up in Flanagan's office, you would walk away going, "Ah, Elliott's so great."'

At the same time as he was navigating his new life in LA, Smith was putting even greater distance between himself and his circle of friends back in Portland. To them, he became still more elusive. Upon moving to LA, he changed his contact details yet again and didn't readily give them out. He was hardly in touch with either of Sean Croghan or Pete Krebs. On one isolated occasion, he called JJ Gonson. It was the first time they had spoken in a couple of years, but to Gonson, he sounded a mess on the phone, rambling and incoherent. Also once more estranged from Joanna Bolme, he was pulling back from them all. Burning bridges and breaking ties, whether to start himself over again or else to keep secret from them what he was doing with and to himself – one or the other, or both.

Smith remained in touch with Larry Crane up to the end of 1999. Until then, he continued to drop into Jackpot! during intermittent visits back to Portland to see family. He still used Crane's place to demo tracks and as a storage place. Crane went on capturing him at the height of his powers and right to the point Smith simply stopped dropping by anymore, one more bridge burnt. Crane was left holding a bunch of Smith's gear for him and the songs he just upped and left behind.

'There's a song we ran down called "Taking a Fall" that was so good and it never got released,' says Crane. 'Another, "A Silver Chain", was left as an instrumental and needing words and a top-line melody. I've always wondered where it might have gone, what it could've been. Whatever we tracked, all the way to the last thing, I would always be pretty amazed by him and sat there marvelling. It's kind of sick as a recording engineer how easy it was to make things sound good with him, compared to how hard it could be with someone else. It was just because of his internal focus and work ethic, and also because it's great writing and playing.

'For a while, a bunch of Elliott's touring gear stayed at Jackpot! – all of his pink road cases. Different people would come up to grab them for him and to take them on tour. Eventually, they ended up somewhere else. Elliott and I had our little misunderstandings. At one point, I was storing a recording console he'd bought at another place in Portland. I wasn't making any money at the time, but I was paying rent on the storage. It wasn't intentional on Elliott's part, but he'd forget about such things. Eventually, he would turn around and say, "Give me the modules out of that console." And I'd be like, "I sold them to pay the rent on storing them." I was working my ass off and I kind of got left holding the bag on certain things.'

There was one other new acquaintance Smith made in LA that summer. They met one night at Spaceland. Smith had gone along to the club with Steve Hanft, who happened to know the band playing that night, an all-female group called the Warlocks. After their set, Hanft introduced him to the band's bass player, Jennifer Chiba. Tokyo-born to a Japanese father and an American mother, but raised in Houston, Texas, Chiba was, like Smith, a study in contrasts. They shared common, troubled ground. Four years his senior, Chiba appeared insouciant and self-assured, but she, too, suffered with depression, had self-harmed and was battling through her own drug issues.

Chiba was also striking, she made a strong first impression. For three years, she had dated another musician, Rivers Cuomo from the band Weezer. After they split, Cuomo devoted a chunk of Weezer's second album, 1996's *Pinkerton*, to songs detailing his heartbreak. At the end of the night at Spaceland, Smith and Chiba exchanged phone numbers. Smith couldn't recall his new number, so gave Chiba the number to Alyssa Siegel's mobile phone instead. They were to date on and off for the next nine months and until Smith went away on tour again.

According to Chiba, she and Smith swore a mutual pact not to self-harm. In this respect, they were like two survivors of a shipwreck, flung together and clinging to each other for support. Yet on the rebound from Bolme, Smith didn't want to be entangled in another serious relationship, at least not just then, so in all other aspects he kept things with Chiba on a more casual basis.

Work also gave Smith his point of focus, a safe harbour to settle the fevering storms in his head. By the time he was ready to go back into the studio in LA, he had amassed more than twenty new songs. Many of them were the products of all those long, late nights at Largo when he was sat up at the piano after hours, the club emptied and still.

'Honky Bach' and 'Happiness' were two songs begun at the Largo piano. The latter was yet another song Smith wrote thinking about Joanna Bolme. Its plangent coda surged forth with both a promise and a plea: 'What I used to be will pass away and then you'll see, that all I want now is happiness for you and me.' There was another he channelled in the wee hours of a night when he couldn't stop his brain from whirring and racing. Later on, he told friends he had got into such a frenzied state he'd carved a cut into his own arm just to snap himself out of it. Then he had sat at the piano and picked out a tumble of minor chords. Over the top of them he sang a mournful mantra: 'Everything means nothing to me.'

At the very same point, Smith was obsessing over an album from 1968, Nico's notoriously spooked *The Marble Index*. Made in the immediate aftermath of her torrid tenure with the Velvet Underground, Nico put down *The Marble Index* battling heroin addiction and in the midst of a deep psychic pain. The sessions went ahead over four days in LA and with her onetime bandmate, John Cale, co-producing. The result of their labours was a body of harrowing, glacial music, so unremittingly bleak-sounding that Cale's fellow producer, Frazier Mohawk, cut the finished record to just thirty minutes – the absolute longest he was able to listen to it without feeling despondent.

After the high, relentless intensity of the *XO* sessions, Rob Schnapf suggested they try a different tack for this new record. Schnapf pitched a more leisurely schedule, one designed to release the pressure valve on Smith. His approach called for them to record in two-week blocks, whenever Smith had a batch of songs he wanted to put down and at whatever studio around town took their fancy. In between times, Smith would be granted the headspace to relax and breathe, or so Schnapf theorised. Smith started out again with Schnapf and Tom Rothrock at the end of the summer of 1999. They demoed tracks at Schnapf's home studio, before going back into Sunset Sound. Over the months ahead, they also visited Capitol Studios and Sonora Recorders on Los Feliz Boulevard.

To begin with at least, Schnapf's plan appeared to pay off. Smith entered into the LA sessions appearing focused, settled and in the mood to stretch out. Whatever darkness he had extracted from the Nico record, it was nevertheless suffused with the brighter light of his own melodic sensibilities. In his mind, he foresaw his next album as being made up of many shifting and interlocking parts. The songs were to fit together like Russian Matryoshka dolls, simpler, smaler-scale acoustic pieces set inside of more grandiose adventures in sound. He was just as attentive to his lyrics, re-editing each line four or five times over.

'It was a very different record to make than *XO*,' says Rob Schnapf. 'Elliott was keen to experiment more, but also, *XO* had got us to a certain point. I know DreamWorks felt like they almost broke *XO* over into the mainstream. People at the label were like, "Man, we were just a city or two short on radio and then we would've had it." That also brought with it some expectation.'

In the autumn of 1999, there was a natural break-off point from the sessions. Margaret Mittleman was heavily pregnant with her and Schnapf's first child, a son. She went into labour on the evening of Thursday, 21 October. Smith rang Schnapf at the hospital to ask if he could come over to keep him company. The two of them passed the night wandering the hospital corridors, falling asleep sat side by side on a couch outside Mittleman's room – as close as they ever were, or ever would be.

'Elliott was there when our son was born,' recalls Mittleman. 'I mean, he was in the room with Rob and my parents. When I was actually giving birth, Elliott and my father stepped out for a smoke. That meant the world to me. The fact he came, that it was so important for him to come, was beautiful.

'We had this deep thing going on and it was there, something solid. I still have pictures of him holding my son. He would come over to our house on a Sunday to watch the football. One year, we had a wig party for Rob's birthday and Elliott came as Elvis. He wore a black Elvis wig. Those things are my favourite moments with him.'

'It was just easy to hang out with Elliott,' says Schnapf. 'It was, like, low investment. We shared an interest in books and movies, and there was also a competitive side. We played a lot of games together – basketball, pool and also croquet out on our lawn. We both of us had long skateboards, so we would take those out, too. He wasn't like some nerd muso guy, he was actually competitive and coordinated.

'These are the thoughts of a 58-year-old guy reflecting back on something that ended more than twenty years ago, but I always felt like Elliott was different with different people. My relationship with him was never dark and for a good period of time, our house was a safe place for him. Margaret was here and she was, in a way, his central protector and his interface with the music business. Maybe I provided the entertainment. But who really knows? Elliott was a complex person and sometimes complex people give you what they want you to have, which makes your relationship with them unique. I don't mean unique necessarily in a special way. My point is it's unique because it isn't up to you what you get, it's up to him. So your relationship is ultimately on his terms. Which brings us back to he was different things to different people.'

The labour on Smith's record carried on over the course of another three or four sessions and through to the end of the year.

Jon Brion joined them to sing back-ups on 'Happiness' and Elvis Costello's Attractions' drummer, Pete Thomas, came in to play on a further three tracks, 'Junk Bond Trader', 'Wouldn't Mama be Proud' and 'Can't Make a Sound'. 'Junk Bond Trader', with its rolling piano and jabbing electric guitar, was a re-write of 'Fast Food' from the third and final Stranger Than Fiction cassette, *Waiting on the Second Hand*. On the liner notes accompanying his album, Smith gave 'special thanks' to Garrick Duckler for his original lyrics. The melody remained essentially intact and unchanged from the one Smith himself had written as a seventeen-year-old high-schooler.

Smith took the title of his new record from a cover song he had put down in the studio, but didn't end up using. 'Figure Eight' was a plaintive piano piece recorded by the American jazz pianist Blossom Dearie in 1973 for a Saturday morning kids' TV show on ABC, *Schoolhouse Rock*. An ornate, self-contained '8', he considered, best represented the album he had made. *Figure 8*, as he rendered it, was certainly decorative and singular. Its musical backdrops were intricate and showy, the arrangements detailed and complex. A dancing piano here, curlicues of guitar there, swooping strings one moment and drums like exclamation points the next.

His lyrics, too, were wry, clever and arch. A rich, bitter vocabulary, outside of 'Happiness' and 'Everything Means Nothing to Me', their meanings were more generally obtuse and obscured behind the cast of characters populating the songs. Among them was a wartime nurse, 'Pretty Mary K', the 'drunk conquistador conquering the governor's ball' in 'Stupidity Tries', and in

'Color Bars', the tragic figure of German actor-painter-musician Bruno Schleinstein, who attained a short-lived fame starring in a couple of Werner Herzog films, but who also suffered lifelong with mental health issues from an abusive childhood.

As involved as it was, *Figure 8* was also by Smith's standards a long record. Sixteen tracks with a running time of over fifty minutes. It was as if he was compelled to put everything out there, driven by a premonition this was to be the last record he would ever get to complete and so nothing could be left to waste.

Smith seemed incapable by this point of writing anything approaching a bad song and the whole of *Figure 8* is so carefully and artfully crafted. There is, however, an overarching sense of emotional distance to the record. Not so much raw feeling as calculated artifice, the nuts and bolts of the mechanics over messy, bloody instinct. All show and relatively little tell. The distinctions were so clear, for the first time some of his oldest friends also now found themselves being left out in the cold by his music. Sam Coomes recoiled from the bigger-budget production and the more lavish arrangements. Tony Lash was to listen to *Figure 8* once and then never again.

'I hadn't seen Elliott for a while by then,' recalls Lash. 'I felt like it was an overwhelming record, too much going on. It also struck me as much more detached and I didn't ever go back to try to kind of fight my way through it.'

Towards the end of the actual recording sessions, a more troubling aspect came into play. Smith got to be more highly strung in the studio, not so much on the level or focused as he had been at the start of the process. These shifts in his demeanour were a new thing to Rob Schnapf, who was used to Smith's drinking but not this kind of skittishness. The plain fact of the matter was, Smith had stuck to his regular medicines of booze and prescription pills whenever previously he had been in the studio with Schnapf and Rothrock. Now that he was living in LA full-time, there were once again other and more dangerous temptations on offer to him.

'At some point into the making of that record, I believe drugs entered into Elliott's life,' says Schnapf. 'On reflection, I think he was dabbling at least, which led to some difficulties from time to time. I mean, we had fun, but there were also hints of what was to come.'

CHAPTER 20

Ground Control to Major Tom

Easing himself back out of the studio, Smith joined Jon Brion for a Friday night show at Largo on 10 December 1999. It was to be his last appearance on the Largo stage. He got up to play six songs, opening with two from the record he had only just then completed, 'Happiness' and 'Son of Sam'. Then he let his hair down doing four covers, Led Zeppelin's 'Livin' Lovin' Maid', two Beatles' songs, 'I'll Be Back' and 'Dear Prudence', and finally David Bowie's 'Space Oddity'. Just like Bowie's Major Tom, Smith was also in peril of becoming adrift in a space all his own, cut-off and 'floating in a most peculiar way'.

For Christmas, Smith went back up to Portland to be with family. He stepped out to see Pete Krebs play a show at a local bar, the Laurel Thirst. Afterwards, they stayed on at the bar and shot a few games of pool together. It was just the two of them, like old times. Krebs wouldn't ever be so close to him again. Smith also went out drinking downtown on Christmas Eve, revisiting his old stomping grounds. He happened across a couple of faces from the LA musicians' scene playing a bar date at a place on SE Hawthorne Boulevard. Aaron Espinoza was in the process of putting together a band of his own, Earlimart, and had lined up Scott McPherson to be their drummer. Both of them had also travelled north to be with their respective families over the holiday and taken the bar gig for beer money. They each knew of Smith, but neither had met him before then.

'It was the first time Scotty and I had even played music together,' recalls Espinoza. 'There was next to nobody in the place, but for our parents and three or four other people stood at the bar. We had just started playing and in walked Elliott. My stomach did a roll. After we finished, I got up the nerve to go over to him and say hi. He was super-sweet, said how much he liked our set. We chatted for a bit and then he bailed.

'Back in LA, there was a really tight community of artists around Echo Park and Silver Lake and everybody talked about the fact Elliott was now living there. All of us musicians, we had insane respect for this guy. He was special.'

The last thing Smith was feeling by this point was special. He was seeing in the new millennium playing a solo show at the Knitting Factory, back in New York. Arriving in the city on the afternoon of 31 December, he at once called up Dorien Garry, needling and fretting about the imminent gig. The Knitting Factory was sold out, but Smith told Garry he couldn't understand why people had paid over the odds to see him perform on such a momentous evening. In his racing, paranoid mind, he could only ever let his public down. He begged Garry for her help in propping him up for what he had convinced himself would be an excruciating ordeal.

'Elliott had a fair amount of self-doubt sitting within him at this point,' says Garry. 'It was such a bizarre New Year's anyway. I mean, there were people thinking the world was going to end. Elliott said to me, "I feel like I need to do something for all of these people who're coming out to see me." I was like, "Yeah, you're going to play a show for them. That's what they're there for!"

'He wanted me to bring along something wacky for him to wear. He said, "Maybe I could go off in the middle of the show and change into a weird outfit." I was constantly collecting vintage clothes, so I had closets full of bizarre crap. I brought him a full-length, red, fluffy robe and a red knit hat. He was immediately so into this ridiculous red costume. He put it on after soundcheck and then walked around backstage in it for an hour. He must have got it out of his system, because he didn't end up wearing it onstage.'

As it transpired, it was enough for Smith to simply be himself. No matter the encroaching new century, the room stood still, silent and reverential as he played, unadorned and unaccompanied but for his acoustic guitar and in spite of the fact he started off his set with a number of songs unfamiliar to his audience: 'Happiness', 'Son of Sam', 'Easy Way Out', 'Everything Means Nothing to Me' and 'Stupidity Tries'. Up onstage, Smith visibly relaxed. He got into the spirit of the occasion, counting the room down to midnight. The club's management had provided him with fifteen bottles of champagne and, one by one, he handed them out into the audience.

He led the Brooklyn audience into the new millennium singing along with a George Harrison song, 'Give Me Love (Give Me Peace on Earth)'. He played on for another forty minutes, smiling in between songs. Anyone watching on would have surely thought him happy and yet, he finished off the night with the bereft 'Last Call' and singing his own deeper, darker truth. 'I guess it must be some kind of holiday,' he intoned. A club full of exultant, upturned faces to hear him confess, 'I can't seem to join the celebration.'

Altogether, 2000 was mapped out to be Smith's busiest professional year to date. It was also meant to be the biggest and best of his career. DreamWorks was set upon giving *Figure 8* a concerted promotional push. Enough, the label schemed, to lift Smith up from the level he had got to with *XO* and tip him over to a much broader audience. For his part, Smith was committed to playing more than 120 shows before the next New Year rolled around. Along with all the touring, he submitted to hawking himself, more brazenly than ever before. To answering more facile questions, to schmoozing more radio DJs, to gripping and grinning, yacking and yawing.

However well-intentioned these ambitions, from the outset the whole enterprise was bound to end in failure. *Figure 8* was simply too thorny and too cerebral for a mainstream audience. In 2000, Middle America was destined to fall hard for a couple of all-singing, all-dancing graduates of Disney's *Mickey Mouse Club*: Britney Spears and, in the boy band NSYNC, Justin Timberlake.

The flipside to Spears' and Timberlake's fresh-faced appeal were the doses of teenage angst and rebellion being ladled out by Eminem and such nu-metal bands as Limp Bizkit and Creed, each as route-one blunt and unsubtle as the other.

★

When he got home to LA, Smith went to work with Autumn de Wilde on both the cover artwork for the new album and also a promo video for its lead-off song, 'Son of Sam'. Smith turned up for the video shoot with a new haircut acquired over the Christmas holiday from Joanna Bolme. She had sheared his mop into a dreadful, pudding bowl shape, forcing de Wilde to Photoshop him more of a Beatles' cut for the *Figure 8* cover. For the video, de Wilde dressed him up differently, too, in a charcoal-coloured, '30s-style suit. Smith didn't enjoy being in front of a camera any better than usual – he was in a morose, crabby mood all of the day they filmed the video.

De Wilde lifted the concept for her clip from a French short from 1956, *The Red Balloon* by Albert Lamorisse. Set in Paris, Lamorisse's engaging piece of magic realism charts the adventures of a cherubic young lad who happens across a red balloon with a mind of its own. In de Wilde's video, Smith trails his own bobbing red balloon along an unremarkable section of Sunset Boulevard running between Silver Lake and Los Feliz, the expression on his face blank and unreadable.

For the album cover shoot, de Wilde picked out a location on the same stretch of Sunset Boulevard and outside of an electronics repair shop, Sound Solutions. Causing the store to stand out from all of the other drab, flat-roofed retail units on the block was a mural painted over its diesel-grimed white wall, a swirl of bold black and red lines. On the front and back cover of *Figure 8*, de Wilde pictured Smith leaning up against it and returned to his more typical thrift-store uniform. For the back-cover photograph, she had her make-up assistant, Jorjee Douglas, turn a cartwheel in front of Smith.

Smith sct himself to the task of assembling a new touring band. He could always count on the ever-dependable Sam Coomes, but no longer on Janet Weiss; he also wanted to expand the line-up with a piano player and called up Aaron Embry. It turned out Embry was acquainted with Scott McPherson, whose drumming Smith had previously admired. Smith instructed him to invite McPherson along to their rehearsals.

Coomes was bunking up at Smith's cottage and at first the four of them got together there to rehearse, squeezing into the already cluttered front room. They soon moved on to a bigger and bespoke space on Sunset Boulevard, Studio Instrument Rentals (SIR).

'Elliott was the kind of guy who liked to learn the songs based on the recordings,' recalls Scott McPherson. 'We didn't really go off the map, but by the script. If you didn't know Elliott, you might have thought he'd be shy and awkward, but he was very welcoming and funny. It wasn't a real, full-time band as such, but it felt like one. If we took a break, we did it together.'

'We had some wonderful evenings at SIR, playing, talking, hanging out and cooking food together,' adds Aaron Embry.

'Elliott was really in very high spirits just then. I know he wasn't using heroin at the time. Sam Coomes was staying with him. They were always very close and Sam's never done drugs. He's pretty much teetotal, too. Elliott being clean was one of the reasons Sam agreed to doing the tour.'

Smith made his public debut with his new band at that year's SXSW festival. On this occasion, he didn't have to busk his way onto the bill. He had a personal invite down to Austin from the organisers and as one of the week's top-drawer acts. They played a downtown venue, La Zona Rosa, on the closing Friday evening of the festival, 17 March 2000. Larry Crane was in town with another band he was working with and watched their set from the side of the stage. It was to be the last time Crane saw Smith play. Smith's new PR from his UK record company, Polydor, Andy Prevezer, was also in the audience. Prevezer had brought with him from London a journalist and photographer from the *NME* and by then had spent four fruitless days trying to get Smith to sit for an interview and photo session with the iconic British weekly music paper.

'We really had to chase Elliott down,' says Prevezer. 'There was no management representative with him, we were dealing with a tour manager only, and Elliott simply didn't fit the corporate record company world at all. He wasn't grumpy. He was never deliberately awkward, he just didn't give a shit. You would be sat downstairs in the lobby of his hotel for two hours at a time, waiting for him to get out of bed.

'Even though, I think, he did want to be successful. He certainly wanted to be loved and he was loved. The people that loved Elliott and his music, they *really* loved him. There was just this disconnect in his head, I think, and you couldn't account for it, or do anything about it. Above all and more than anybody I've ever met, before or since, Elliott's music was his thing. That was it, the whole deal with him. It's what I found so intriguing about him. You wanted to put your arms around him and say to him, "It's going to be alright, Elliott. You're going to get through this." And tragically, ultimately, it's what did for him.'

CHAPTER 21

Crash Landing

Figure 8 was released on 18 April 2000. By then, Smith had been making records long enough for the critical tide to begin turning back on him. The reviews this time around were widespread, but mixed. A general consensus was he was treading water. Writing in *Rolling Stone*, Jon Pareles concluded: 'Smith stays alone in a musical niche where he's unwilling to budge.'[28] On the music website *Pitchfork*, meanwhile, Ryan Schreiber picked at the same thread. 'Oh, Elliott, are things really that bad?' Schreiber asked rhetorically, adding tartly, 'In the grand scheme of things, you only need to hear so much Elliott Smith before you get the point.'[29]

Three days after the album came out, Smith and his band performed an early-evening set at the New York Virgin Megastore on Union Square. Surrounded by racks of CDs, the audience pressed up to the small, makeshift stage, they played for over an hour and above the ceaseless rumble of the Manhattan traffic. On 4 May, they left LA to begin the marathon tour for *Figure 8*.

'It was my first experience of a hired gun gig, but it didn't feel like it was one,' says Scott McPherson. 'Elliott acted like he was just the singer in the band, he didn't have an ego.

'He was a real clown, too. He would have this smirk on his face the whole time. Sometimes he couldn't restrain from bursting out laughing. He cracked himself up. I remember him wearing a black cowboy hat one time, striking a ridiculous pose and then moonwalking like Michael Jackson. He was a funny motherfucker. He actually could moonwalk, but it was just so weird seeing him doing it. Not what you would expect.'

On 9 May, the fourth night of the tour, fate intervened at the 328 Performance Hall in Nashville, Tennessee. It was a damp, humid night. A spring storm raged outside the venue, rain cascading down, tornado warnings on the local radio station. It was ten degrees hotter inside the hall than outside, steam rising off the sodden audience. As Smith and his band were preparing to take the stage, the power went out across the city, plunging the venue into darkness.

Backstage, Smith convened an emergency meeting with his band and crew. He decided to start the show regardless, just him and Aaron Embry, playing without amplification. Candles were fetched from storage cupboards and used to light the stage. Fifteen minutes after the power cut, Smith went out and spoke to the audience, pitching his voice about as loud as he ever did to be heard. He asked them to shuffle forward, as close to the stage as they could get, and then to sit. He also took a seat, his chair pulled up to the lip of the stage, Embry joining him on piano. The pair started off playing 'Son of Sam' to the hushed hall. Introducing 'Waltz #2', Smith told his audience, 'This is a song I'm sick of playing.' After he and Embry had played it, he reflected, 'That time that song was actually for me. I might've actually banished it.'

After Nashville there were shows in Raleigh, North Carolina, Washington, DC, Philadelphia and then in Boston on 15 May. They arrived in Boston on the 14th. Nine o'clock the same morning, Smith took the band into a local recording studio, Fort Apache, where they spent the day putting 'Pretty (Ugly Before)' to tape. It came out sounding more intimate, much less polished than anything on *Figure 8*, all the better for being unvarnished and left unguarded.

'We just showed up that morning at the studio and played the parts we'd been doing live,' says Aaron Embry. 'We tracked our parts live and then Elliott did a couple of acoustic doubles. Scotty, Sam and I went to get lunch while Elliott did his vocals. We were done by early afternoon. Elliott had very precise ideas about what he wanted us to play, but then he also gave us freedom to improvise and to relax into the music. It was a wonderful time.'

It was also ephemeral. The tour ran down the East Coast to New York, about-turned into Canada and then dog-legged over to the West Coast. Smith, their bellwether, set the tone overall and the longer they were out there, the heavier the air got to be on the tour bus and in the corridors backstage. On 7 June, they pulled back into LA for the last two dates of this latest run around North America. They were playing consecutive nights at an old Hollywood theatre, the Palace. Friends, associates and well-wishers turned out to greet them: Autumn de Wilde with Aaron Sperske, Margaret Mittleman and Rob Schnapf. Sperske at least was alarmed by what he saw.

'Elliott and the band got off the bus outside of the Palace and I immediately noticed how no one was making eye contact,' Sperske recalls. 'When I got to talk to Elliott, he had this little bucket hat pulled down right to his eyeline, so he didn't have to look at me or at anyone else. We chatted just for a moment, but I still got a good enough look at him.

'After he walked away from me, I turned around to Autumn and said, "Elliott's definitely using again." She was, like, "No, no." But he was, he was loaded. Autumn didn't believe me. She mentioned it to Margaret and Margaret had the same reaction as her – Margaret thought they were all just tired. Later on, second-hand, I heard they were partying on the bus. I have a spider's sense to discern when people are high, and especially on opiates, and I could tell.'

Less than two weeks after the shows at the Palace, the tour started up again in Europe. In the UK, Smith and his band performed at the Meltdown Festival at London's Royal Festival Hall and two days later, at the Glastonbury Festival on the same bill as David Bowie. At Meltdown, they opened the show for the head-lining Scott Walker, the festival's curator that year and Smith's diffident equal. Right after Smith had played his set with the band and at the famously reclusive Walker's instigation, the two men met for twenty minutes in Walker's palatial dressing room. They sat on opposite sides of a coffee table, concentrating on each other like chess players, the teetotal Walker sipping bottled water and Smith with a glass of Jameson's. Kindred spirits, but flashing by each other in very different directions.

'I went with my wife, Sophie, to see Elliott at Meltdown,' says Andy Prevezer. 'Elliott had said to me to come backstage afterwards and say hello. Sophie had quite an intense chat with Elliott for about ten minutes. On our way home in the car, Sophie turned to me and said, "I really liked him, but I'm also really worried about that guy. I don't think he's going to make it, he's so in his own head."

'That conversation has stuck with me for twenty-three years now. You felt there was something so deeply uncomfortable about Elliott. Physically, he was awkward-looking. He was gangly and hunched up. He deported himself in such a kind of troubled way. I'm not being wise after the event, you could actually see he wasn't right.'

'As the tour progressed, Elliott started using again,' says Aaron Embry. 'Jackie Farry, our tour manager, was an old friend of Elliott's. She said to the rest of us, "Okay, he's back on it, so now we just have to try to keep things functional." Jackie was already dealing with all the tasks of a tour manager, but on top of those she had to now make sure we could actually play a show each night.

'There was a sea change in Elliott's personality. There was a lot of emotional abuse. Elliott started getting really depressed and frustrated and he projected a lot of those frustrations onto us as a band. Tensions started to seep into the relations of everyone on the tour, it got pretty dark pretty quickly.'

Following the trip to Europe, there was another lay-off of almost two weeks. By the time they re-grouped in New York on 17 May, no one's state of mind was improved. They were there to make an appearance on the *Late Show with David Letterman* and Smith was in a foul mood from the start of the day. His guitar had got broken in transit from Los Angeles. A good portion of the afternoon was tied up with getting a replica instrument delivered to the Ed Sullivan Theater in midtown Manhattan, where the Letterman show was filmed. The atmosphere deteriorated even further when Aaron Embry told Smith of his intention to quit the tour after their appearance at the Mount Fuji Festival in Japan on 28 July and before they started up again in earnest in late August. Smith hit the roof.

'That was such a horrible day,' says Embry. 'I had already told Elliott I wasn't happy, but he got so angry at me for wanting to leave the band. We were riding together in a cab to the Ed Sullivan Theater. Elliott was totally silent next to me on the back seat until "Goodbye Yellow Brick Road" came on the radio. Right at the point in the song where Elton John sings, "Maybe you'll get a replacement," Elliott turned to me and sang, "Maybe I'll get a replacement." Then he told me I wouldn't be going to Japan.

'It was so difficult, because I was with someone I didn't know anymore. Even in the short time I was home again with my then-wife, it got to be really difficult to justify my place in that kind of environment. I know Sam Coomes was also struggling with whether he should stick around or not, because Sam really cared for Elliott.'

Smith replaced Embry with Shon Sullivan, another musician jobbing on the LA circuit. Sullivan made his debut with the band at the Reading Festival in the UK, on 27 August. From there, they flew back over the Atlantic to play at the Bumbershoot Festival in Seattle on the Saturday of the Labour Day weekend, 2 September. Just seven months since Smith had stepped out solo at New York Town Hall, clear-eyed and boyish, an altogether different person walked out onto the stage in Seattle. Wearing the same brown bucket hat he had worn for the Palace shows and pulled down just as low to cover his eyes, he was rail-thin, greasy-haired, the wisp of a beard growing on his chin, his skin bad and with a sickly sheen.

After the Seattle date, they crossed back again to Europe, starting off with a show in Hamburg, Germany, on 20 September, then a string of UK shows in early October and finishing up with a handful of Scandinavian dates opening up for Oklahoma psych-rockers the Flaming Lips. Most of the time now, Smith maintained a nocturnal regime.

He found a co-conspirator with the Lips' drummer, Steve Drozd. Struggling with a heroin addiction of his own, Drozd rode with Smith and his band on their tour bus. When they couldn't score, the pair went through the agonies of withdrawal huddled together at the back of the bus. An ex-girlfriend of Drozd's, a bubbly young Scot named Valerie Deerin, had also joined up with the tour to look after the merchandise. By the time the run around Europe ended, Smith was seeing Deerin. In the absence of Joanna Bolme or Margaret Mittleman, it fell to Deerin to worry and fuss over him.

'Valerie was such a lovely, sweet person,' recalls Scott McPherson. 'She was a really nice, positive presence to have around. She was a bit of sunshine.'

'Up until then I'd always gone on tour with Elliott, but I decided not to go to Europe,' says Mittleman. 'I just got weird vibes. Plus, my life and career were changing. I had my son, I had other things going on. It was easier to have other people do things on my behalf.

'Your priorities change in your head. It was like, "I've a child, I have to separate this and I can't let it consume me". There were things happening I just could not accept, although I didn't know how bad things had got. There was shit going on and no one wanted me to know, and maybe I was okay with that.'

There was one more run around the US left for Smith and the band to do. Five weeks of cross-country shows sponsored by *Rolling Stone*. Smith took Valerie Deerin with him for this leg of the tour, too, and handpicked Grandaddy as their opening act. The two groups hit it off at once. A week into the tour, they had a rare day off in Asheville, North Carolina. They were being billeted at the same motel just outside of the town. As the sun was setting, members of both bands began to trickle out, sitting and drinking beers on a small patch of grass next to the motel pool. Grandaddy's bass player, Kevin Garcia, went and strung a bunch of extension cords to their rooms, so they could bring out their lamps and play music from a boom box.

After a while, Smith came out with Deerin to join them. The whole party sang along to Blue Oyster Cult's 'Don't Fear the Reaper', their voices raised up from the bald lawn, laughter filling the air.

'Elliott seemed super-comfortable around everyone,' recalls Grandaddy's frontman Jason Lytle. 'He was joking, light-hearted. He had an awesome sense of humour. He and I, though, shared the same characteristic of both being kind of loners. We each spent an exorbitant amount of time alone and being on tour, your liberties are forever getting stripped away. We played shows with no days off and to the point where it started to become a grind. My way of dealing with that was just to get drunker. I would remain in this fog, so the edges were dulled.

'Rumours started to circulate around Elliott's camp of drugs coming in and out. People would say, "It's not as bad as it used to be and getting better now." There's so much secrecy involved in that kind of stuff, but it became more of a prominent thing. It was very erratic. There were good days and bad days. It kind of turned into, like, "Alright, what's today going to be?" There would be all this tension going on backstage. Elliott would have shown up late. He'd had a bad night and you would be thinking, "Oh God, this is going to be a disaster." And then, once again, he'd go out there and blow everyone's mind.'

The penultimate show of the tour was in San Francisco. At one point in the set, Smith asked the mystified audience if 'Garrick is here.' Garrick Duckler wasn't there. Like so many more of Smith's friends, Duckler had also been given the cold shoulder. He had repeat messaged Smith, but not had a word back, so he steered clear.

'At the time, I was way too hurt to reach out to him,' Duckler says. 'I hated being in this subservient position, so I just refused to bother him during this phase. I was in contact with him through-out his life, but there were long stretches that were extremely painful to me. I remember walking around Berkeley where I was teaching as if my heart had been pulled out of my body. I felt rejected, abandoned, thrown out. When Elliott became more famous and more drug-addicted, he stopped doing a lot of the things I was familiar with – like read books, or have conversa-tions about anything other than his anguish.

'I wrote him a long letter, basically saying I couldn't stay friends because I was in a painful place of wondering how he was, what was happening in his life and so on. I always tried to remain available to him whenever he did call. Once, he called to ask me about my father, who was dying. Elliott was totally on drugs and he said all of these hurtful things, asking me why my father wasn't dead yet. He kind of became a monster who didn't care about anyone other than himself, which is obviously incred-ibly common for anyone under the same kind of scrutiny and pressure. Beneath it all, I still think he held onto our friendship to some degree.'

On Smith and the band rolled, back down to LA for the clos-ing night of the tour at the Wiltern theatre on 14 November. Joey Waronker, off the road with Beck, came along to check out the show. Waronker was just as shocked by what he saw as Aaron

Sperske had been five months previously. Smith appeared to Waronker altogether changed from the last time he'd been with him at Sunset Sound.

'I went backstage and Elliott seemed weird,' recalls Waronker. 'He was just being slow. Everybody seemed different. It was like seeing *Invasion of the Bodysnatchers*. It finally occurred to me, "Oh my God, they're all strung out." My next thought was, "Oh shit. It's good I didn't go on the tour."'

Smith still had five more shows of his own to play, solo dates in Japan. Starting with two in Tokyo on 3 and 4 December and wrapping up in Osaka on the 8th. Deerin went with him. The long flight to Tokyo from LA was a draining, nightmarish experience for both of them. Once again going through the agonies of a heroin withdrawal, Smith snapped at and argued with Deerin the whole time – he had broken up with her before their plane had even landed in Japan. Nevertheless, Deerin flew home with him to LA. Each of them was worn out from their ordeal in Japan.

For Christmas, Smith escaped on his own up to Portland. Tony Lash ran into him in EJ's one night, the last occasion he ever would: 'I had heard about the drugs and stuff, but I hadn't gone out of my way to stay connected with him during this time,' says Lash. 'I noticed he was wearing much fancier clothes than he had before. For a standard Portland rock club, he seemed a bit dressed up. We just shot the shit, hung out and had a beer. It felt pretty relaxed. I wish I had known more about what Elliott was wrestling with, the trauma. I mean, it was sort of hinted at, but we didn't have any deep discussion about what he had experienced. I wish I'd had more wisdom about how it factored into the way he dealt with relationships, too.

'For people who've experienced trauma especially, music can be an attachment. It's a way to find a place outside of yourself to connect the things you're wrestling with. But then again, it can also trigger a lot of the same deep stuff, especially when there are other people involved and in a tight space like a studio or tour bus. It's like you can feel your vision being interfered with. If I would have understood that back then, if I'd known more about what Elliott went through growing up, I would have been more compassionate. I'd still have been frustrated at his refusal to communicate, but I'm sure he'd have gotten better at that, too. And if he would have gotten to be older.'

CHAPTER 22

LA Noir

After spending the Christmas of 2000 up in Portland, Smith returned to LA and retreated to his bungalow on the hill. With the willing Valerie Deerin's help, he planned to ween himself off heroin. He moved Deerin in with him and she fast became his full-time carer, fixing his food, cleaning the house and fetching his prescriptions for him. Infinitely tolerant of him, she was entirely selfless in her devotion. A guardian angel. For his part, Smith had no qualms about being so completely demanding of Deerin's good graces – he was to take far more from her than he ever gave back.

Smith also had his extended support network. Autumn de Wilde, Aaron Sperske and Alyssa Siegel were all still just next-door, while Margaret Mittleman and Rob Schnapf were nearby. Schnapf could always tempt him out for a game of croquet, but Smith otherwise spent his daytimes holed up indoors and with the sun shut out. His idea of cleaning up was soon reduced to rubble.

'There was no air conditioning in the little bungalows and indoors, they were blisteringly hot,' recalls Aaron Sperske. 'Elliott put blankets up all over his windows and never opened the door. I did manage to step in there one day and it felt like a sauna. Elliott had moved a 24-track machine and a big console into the tiny front room. You walked in and there was just studio equipment everywhere. It was pretty wild. Elliott was in the bathroom. Valerie told me he never came out of there. "He needs help," she told me.'

Margaret Mittleman bore the brunt of Smith's growing frustration with how his career was going. For all the touring he had done, all of the promotional work he had given himself up to, *Figure 8* had sold nowhere near as well as its predecessor, *XO*. On the one hand, he blamed DreamWorks for the relative failure of the record. Yet on the other, he fretted about being dropped from the label. Whichever way Smith happened to swing, he couldn't get past the issue.

'To some degree, he felt like a failure,' says Rob Schnapf. 'He'd tried to play the game, made all of these radio appearances and done all of the bullshit you had to do at the time to get radio play and the record had done worse. He was out of his wheelhouse. He was a shy guy. He didn't want to have to show up at a radio station at 8 a.m. and get the "*Heeey*, Elliott Smith!" kind of guy as a DJ.

'The label didn't actually care the record hadn't sold as well as *XO*, but there was no convincing him. The label was like,

"Make another record." They were so supportive, but a negative feedback loop started to develop. Elliott began to have different people in his life. He was not hearing things from the right people. He had people who were telling him, "Yeah, major labels are bullshit, *blah-blah-blah*." They can be, but in this case, he had support from the top. DreamWorks loved him. Combine that with all of the other shit he had going on and it made a bad situation worse.'

For her part, Mittleman tried to distract Smith with other opportunities. Briefly, there was talk of him doing a song for a Gap commercial. A film director, Brad Siberling, also approached Mittleman with the suggestion Smith score the music for his next movie, *Moonlight Mile* (2002). Smith, though, simply wasn't in a fit state to do any kind of heavy creative lifting and neither project was to get off the ground. One day, Mittleman took a call from Smith's business manager, who told her of his alarm at the rate Smith was draining his bank account.

'He asked me, "Why is Elliott taking out money every day?"' says Mittleman. 'I had no idea, but I said I would try to get to the bottom of it. I didn't know at the time Elliott was buying drugs.'

Smith did attempt to go back to work with Schnapf. The two of them had discussed making a rawer, more stripped-down sounding record using the garage studio Schnapf ran from out of his home. They managed to get the bare bones of two songs down to tape there, but Smith was drinking heavily and his heroin use wasn't abating either. His physical condition generally was poor and Schnapf couldn't get him to focus his mind on the sessions for any appreciable span of time. Schnapf was intolerant of his self-destructive side.

'Elliott was sketchy with me about the words he'd written for both of the songs we did manage to do and because he was singing about heroin,' says Schnapf. 'I don't think he really wanted to reveal that side of his life to me. We maybe weren't hanging out as much as we used to. But, yes, I knew what he was doing and I wasn't okay with it. It wasn't cool and I made it clear to him I wasn't down with it in any way. Elliott played the choice card. You know, "This is what I want to do and you've just got to support me if you're my friend." I was like, "Nah, that's not how it works. That's not how it works at all. It's not only your choice and this is not a hostage situation. I won't stand by and watch you do this to yourself."

'Absolutely, 100 per cent, I feared for him. I mean, that's why I said those things to him. That's where I was coming from. It was like, "You are throwing yourself into harm's way." He was way too smart for it. This was a smart guy, but smart people are also great at rationalising. I knew what he was subjecting himself to. It's like, if you have to go and score drugs, you're right *there*. That's not a safe place to be.'

Superbowl Sunday was 28 January, 2001. The Baltimore Ravens against the New York Giants down in Tampa, Florida. In LA, Smith had begun a tradition of going over to Schnapf and Mittleman's house to watch the game. On this particular Sunday, he arrived at their place with Valerie Deerin in tow. He had let his hair grow out and had braided it into pigtails. He appeared to have just rolled out of bed, or not to have slept at all. Schnapf and Mittleman were in the kitchen, mixing a pasta sauce for dinner. Smith bowled in and straight off informed Schnapf he didn't want to work with him anymore: he would be making his next record with Jon Brion, he announced.

'I just didn't like how Elliott handled it,' says Mittleman. 'I knew I had to keep the Rob and me side of it separate from Elliott's career, yet also it was like, "Okay, go work with Jon, but could you be in a better place when you're deciding this?" It was the beginning of all the "*Ooh*, what's going on?" with Elliott, it just took on a whole other thing.'

'I'd always said to Elliott, "You don't have to work with me. If it's not weird, don't make it weird,"' says Schnapf. 'And then he made it very weird. But that was also because of all the shit he had going on in his life.

'Margaret did carry on working with him, at least for a time, and I didn't want to be negative with him. Who wants to carry that around? For Margaret, it was heading to the point where there was nothing left for her to manage anymore.'

On Smith's behalf, Mittleman reached out to another, independent record label, ANTI- Records, a subsidiary of Epitaph Records and well-regarded for its stable of West Coast punk rock acts. She was beginning to think Smith might be better off away from DreamWorks and taken off the major label treadmill. ANTI- was forging a reputation for working with iconoclastic singer-songwriters, too, having signed already both Tom Waits and the country music veteran, Merle Haggard. Mittleman opened up a line of communication with the label's chief executive, Andy Kaulkin.

At the same time, Smith started up sessions with Jon Brion. When he rolled up at Brion's studio, he was in no better shape than he had been for Rob Schnapf. He was able, though, to cut a handful of songs with Brion. These included a version of 'A Fond Farewell' and two brand-new songs, both of them lovely, lullabying acoustic ballads, 'Twilight' and 'True Love'. Smith unveiled 'True Love' alongside six other new songs at his first show of the year, a truncated solo acoustic spot he performed at the Silverlake Lounge on Tuesday, 6 February. It didn't take any great leap to read it as a love song to heroin, or to comprehend from it the extent of his psychic torture. 'I feel cold, useless and old,' he sang. 'Take me up, my Lord, take me out of this place.'

If Smith expected Jon Brion to be any more tolerant than Rob Schnapf of his escalating drug use, he was to be very much mistaken. Brion stuck at recording with him through into March, then called him out just the same as Schnapf had done. Nor did Smith respond any better to Brion's entreaties than he had to Schnapf's. The sessions came to an abrupt and terminal end, Smith's and Brion's friendship also over. Speaking about their conclusive showdown, Brion told Autumn de Wilde in 2007: 'I remember the conversation. I remember his inability to speak coherently. I remember realising he had gone too far. He had consumed too much.

'It felt like the person I loved wasn't home anymore. And the filter that normally exists between the soul and the rest of the world was so mangled . . . I knew it, and it hit me hard. That was the day when I cried and cried and cried and was inconsolable . . . The last few years he was alive, thinking about him was too painful.'[30]

Word on Smith's debilitating state had spread fast around the tight-knit, incestuous LA musicians' scene. The rupturing of his relationships with both Schnapf and Brion was more fuel to the fire, adding heat and credence to the gossiping already going on about his bedraggled appearance and erratic behaviour. Smith was beginning to withdraw from his other LA friends, too. He didn't drop by Autumn de Wilde's house nearly so often. Alyssa Siegel found it was getting harder to rouse him even for their regular game of Scrabble. To his friends up in Portland, he might as well have been living in another galaxy.

'We didn't have much contact,' recalls Larry Crane. 'I got a few phone calls from Elliott when he was in whatever sort of drug haze. The last call I had from him, it got sort of nastier. That one went kind of unresolved between us.'

'One afternoon, Autumn answered our door to Elliott and he immediately went into this rant, telling her I had never given him his house key back after I'd decorated the place for him to move into,' says Aaron Sperske. 'I hadn't had his key except for the two weeks I worked on the bungalow to clean it up and then I'd handed it over to Margaret.

'Elliott was in this really confrontational, argumentative state. Autumn was going, "Elliott, we don't have your house key." I came down to the door and I was like, "Dude, what's the matter?" He said to me, "My stuff is not where it should be, my stuff is getting moved around." It was insane. That was a moment where the good times, the golden era of having Elliott live up on the hill with us, went into decline.'

As he went on sinking, Smith followed his own strongest inclination: he ran, and hid. With Valerie Deerin, he upped and left the Sutherland Street bungalow, placing distance between himself and de Wilde, Sperske and Siegel. He moved instead across town and to the next-door neighbourhood of Los Feliz. There, he and Deerin took up the rental on one of a cluster of storied properties on Griffith Park Boulevard. The Disney Cottages were a collection of eight low-roofed, black timber-framed dwellings, set back from the road and huddled in the shade of a towering line of trees. The cottages were built in 1931 to look like storybook creations and so-called because Walt Disney used them to house the team of animators working on *Snow White and the Seven Dwarfs*.

One of the couple's near-neighbours was Aaron Espinoza, who was living a couple of blocks over from the Disney Cottages. Like Smith, Espinoza had also got to be good friends with the guys in Grandaddy. When, in April, Grandaddy came to town to play the Troubadour, Espinoza threw a party for them over at his house. He invited Smith along. From that night on, Smith and Espinoza were to be running mates. Their friendship followed the same undulating rhythm as all of Smith's relationships: he would be close and intimate with Espinoza one minute, distant and unknowable to him the next.

'Yeah, Elliott was complex, for sure,' says Espinoza. 'There was obviously the darkness, that almost goes without saying.

But he was also incredibly intelligent, super well-read and really funny. In the right setting, Elliott could be really goofy and basically take over the room.

'At one point, he went through this phase where he was really into these Japanese silk pants. It was the whole Jimmy Page look – big, bell-bottomed silk pants with dragons embroidered down the legs. We were at some other house party, one of those nights when Elliott was in charge of the room, and he had these goddamned Jimmy Page pants on. I couldn't tell if it was a joke or if he actually really loved wearing them.'

The same April, two of Smith's songs, 'Snowbunny's Serenade' and 'Splitsville', popped up on the soundtrack to a feature film directed by Steve Hanft and written by Ross Harris. Smith also made a cameo appearance in *Southlander* (2001), a wholly surreal and uneven work, as a tour-bus driver for a hapless, fictitious pop band. On the whole, the movie was populated with moonlighting musicians. Also appearing were Beck, Hank Williams III, Beth Orton and Jennifer Herrema from the band Royal Trux. Jennifer Chiba popped up in a blink-and-you'd-miss-it role as a pool girl at a party. *Southlander* came and went, hardly making a ripple.

But then, the lifestyle Smith was pursuing was far and away from the fantasy bright lights of a Hollywood fairy story. He was blowing through several thousand dollars a week on both heroin and crack-cocaine now, too. In addition, he was taking ever greater doses of prescription pills and in all kinds of concoctions. Daily, he was consuming twelve, thirteen and up to fourteen different types of medicinal drugs, variously prescribed for him by the retinue of doctors he was seeing. It had reached the point where he was living his life in an entirely altered state, numbed, disconnected and removed from everyone else around him and oblivious to the world at large.

'Taken from various sources, such medications as antidepressants and opioids are potentially highly toxic,' says Dr Leah Quinlivan. 'Historically, Benzodiazepines for depression and anxiety were prescribed for longer than necessary and leading to substantial dependency and withdrawal issues. The risk of overdose is also substantially increased when they are taken with other drugs, especially opioids. Taking those amounts of medication, he must have been really struggling.'

'I was able to follow what was going on with Elliott just a little bit,' says Tim Foljahn, who had sat beside Smith the fateful night in North Carolina when he jumped and ran from Dorien Garry's car and then leapt out into the void. 'I heard stories from Dorien, I gathered from her he wasn't doing so well in LA. He'd kind of turned into one of those guys who walked around with a doctor's bag is what I heard. I knew a lot of people like that in New Mexico when I'd lived there. It wasn't good and it never ended well.'

CHAPTER 23

A Basement on the Hill

Smith's third attempt to make his next record was initiated by Shon Sullivan. After coming off the road with Smith's band, Sullivan had begun work on his own record with a guy who ran a recording studio, Satellite Park, out of his home in Malibu. David McConnell had started off in the music business as a songwriter-for-hire before moving into production, where he got his break running sessions for Lou Barlow. The Malibu property belonged to McConnell's then-partner of seven years, Josie Cotton. A singer herself, Cotton had scored a minor hit in 1982 with a song originally recorded by the Go-Go's, 'Johnny Are You Queer?'.

Sullivan had spent several weeks recording with McConnell out at Satellite Park and recommended him to Smith. In particular, he enthused to Smith about McConnell's capacity for capturing a vibrant, live sound to tape and also his collection of vintage recording gear. Smith was piqued and took McConnell's number from Sullivan. With the scarring still fresh from his breakup with Rob Schnapf, he got Valerie Deerin to call McConnell on his behalf rather than Margaret Mittleman. It was Deerin who played the role of match-maker between the two men and established McConnell was interested in working with Smith as his co-producer. The very next day, Smith was emboldened enough to call McConnell for himself.

'Elliott and I talked for a couple of hours,' says McConnell. 'He said he wanted to be a little more involved in the production element. He wanted his co-producer to be somebody who had experience of engineering with vintage equipment and also was going to experiment. It sounded like fun. I was already down with Elliott's music, I knew he was special. The way his music was composed was very unique. He had created his own voice. Most pop singers copy each other. Elliott sounded like Elliott, he sang without affectations.

'Even on that first call, I could tell I was dealing with someone who was pretty complicated. He was talking about his issues with DreamWorks and Jon Brion. He was clearly frustrated with where his career was at. I could tell he was struggling in general so I knew I was getting into something heavy. I couldn't tell if he had been drinking or was a little high, but I could hear the emotional strain and distress in his voice.'

By the end of their call, Smith had hired McConnell. Not that any formal contract was ever drawn up between them: Smith simply promised McConnell he would pay him a lump sum of $50,000 once the completed record had come out. McConnell assumed they would spend the next few weeks thrashing out the arrangements for the sessions, but Smith told him he wanted to start work just as soon as the following night.

McConnell's and Cotton's place was set at a remove from the Pacific Coast Highway, high up in the Malibu Hills. A sprawling, gate-fronted estate, it nestled among a canopy of trees at the end of a snaking track road and overlooked the deep blue waters of the Pacific. There was the main house and a separate guest house on the property. The Satellite Park studio, a big, airy space, occupied the basement of the main house. In the upstairs bedroom he shared with Cotton, McConnell also kept a smaller studio facility reserved for working on his own music. In fact, McConnell often used the whole of the main house for recording. Smith was to put down all of his drum tracks in the high-ceilinged living room.

The evening after their phone call, McConnell sat in the living room and waited on Smith's arrival, expecting him for around 9 p.m. In the event, Smith and his two-strong party didn't appear until 3 a.m. the next morning. They pulled up in two cars. Smith and Deerin were together in Smith's Volkswagen, a friend of theirs drove the other vehicle. The three of them were coming back from a weekend trip down to a mountain resort to the south of the state, Big Bear Lake. Both cars were otherwise full of Smith's stuff – his guitars, a keyboard and drum kit, the tape reels he had run off at Jon Brion's studio, his clothes and books. The Disney Cottages were a 45-minute drive away from Malibu, but Smith didn't mean to go home. For the duration of the sessions, he moved himself and Deerin into McConnell's and

Cotton's spare bedroom, right across the hall from his hosts. He also wanted to make a start in the studio right there and then. Racking out two gigantic lines of cocaine on a coffee table, he told McConnell, 'And this is how we're going to do it.'

'I had been napping while I was waiting on him, so I said to Elliott I could probably manage a couple of hours' work,' recalls McConnell. 'He had me do a mix of a song he had been working on already. Then he just wanted to stay up and keep going. I ended up having to take little cat naps to get through the whole of our first day of working together.

'I was also still trying to get a grasp on what was up with this guy. He was obviously struggling with a chemical addiction. Besides the stimulants, it was only later on I found out he was taking other drugs, too, like as a cocktail of chemicals. I realised I was going to have to totally change my schedule to fit with his, sleep during the day and stay up all night. This was all going in within the first twenty-four hours of him arriving, it was just crazy.'

'Elliott's arrival was like a whirlwind,' says Cotton. 'He moved so quickly. He ended up taking his relationship with David to an odd place, too, or at least so David thought. He told David he thought the two of them were identical, one and the same person.

'This bothered David, really upset him. The longer it went on, they started to fight about it. Elliott would say to David, "We're the same." And David would shout back at him, "We're not the same!" It became a recurring argument between them. They were both of them completely bull-headed about their views on life. That's one thing they definitely did share. From the beginning to the end, the experience of having Elliott at our house was all pretty surreal.'

★

Indeed, both McConnell and Cotton found Smith's tenure with them so bewildering they can't agree on how long he remained at their house. McConnell believes Smith was resident with them for six weeks. Cotton insists the period was closer to three months. McConnell's recollection is likely the more accurate and with Smith remaining in Malibu until the middle of June. For Cotton, the duration very possibly only seemed so much longer. What's for certain is the reality of Smith's living with them left an indelible impression on them both. More than twenty years later, Cotton says she has still not fully come to terms with what she went through from having Smith as a house guest.

'Honestly, I was shy around Elliott,' she recalls. 'I was intimidated by his talent. In the early evenings, Elliott would start telling stories and play piano for us so beautifully. He would play Tchaikovsky and Rachmaninoff pieces and tell us how different songs of his came to be written. This would be before David and Elliott went into their night-time sessions, right at sunset. Those would be my favourite times of the day.

'Elliott would get terribly sad as well. He would really open up to us. He had a lot of anger towards his stepfather, who was so cruel to him. The horrible irony was his real father was an eminent psychiatrist. His life could have been so different if his parents had stayed together, but would he have been so great an artist? That's the ultimate question about Elliott, isn't it? Was it worth it? Those short times in the evenings, he would also play us songs. One night, he cut his finger. He wiped his blood on the piano keys. David and I held on to that piano for a long time. It was an old, wooden thing. Eventually, it just fell apart.'

On occasions, the house would be bustling with other guests. Smith soon decided he preferred the ambience of McConnell's private studio in the bedroom upstairs to the big basement studio. He and Deerin decamped to McConnell's and Cotton's room. A couple of punk rock producers, Paul Roessler and Geza X, took over the basement studio. Roessler's wife, Helen, also lodged at the house for a time. Another regular visitor was pioneering recording engineer John Stephens, a friend of McConnell's. With Smith, McConnell was using one of the reel-to-reel tape machines Stephens designed in the 1970s. Smith enjoyed the older man's company. Stephens had worked as a scientist with NASA and was a fount of UFO conspiracy theories, which Smith listened to rapt.

For the greater part, though, Smith worked alone with McConnell. He would rise late in the afternoon and they would head up to McConnell's studio when the sun went down. Normally, they would go on taping up there until sunrise the next day. They stuck to this nocturnal regime throughout the sessions. Valerie Deerin often as not stayed shut up in the guest room. Desperate for some peace and uninterrupted sleep, Josie Cotton moved out of the main house and into the guest house with her two dogs.

'Josie thought the whole thing was insane – the craziest, most dramatic type of soap opera situation,' recalls McConnell. 'Elliott actually felt very uncomfortable whenever Josie was there. He didn't want her around. He preferred it to be just him and me working and nobody else in the room. He didn't trust Josie, but he didn't trust anybody. He had a lot of paranoia.

'Typically, I would go to bed at sun up but Elliott would often want to carry on working. I would set him up with something automated he was able to manage, so he could record by himself. I'd wake up five, six hours later and he would be asleep by then. He'd get up a couple of hours later, but he was like a zombie when he woke up. He had a ritual where he would sit and eat his breakfast cereal, very slowly, and have his coffee. Then he would probably be off doing drugs in the bathroom. Eventually, he'd begin to come round and we'd start work again for another twelve hours. I would have to crash every three days. Elliott worked pretty much round the clock and then he would crash every five days.'

'I felt like a refugee in my own house,' says Cotton, 'but I was happy for David. He thought it was insane, too, but he was excited at the same time. I hardly ever saw him after I went to the guest house. David and Elliott worked for days without stopping. Once in a while, David would sneak out to the guest house to give me a big hug. He'd say to me, "I don't know what's happening."

'After his breakfast, Elliott would usually go off in his car to score drugs. Valerie was desperate to stop him. Sometimes she would throw herself in front of the car and then have to jump out of the way. Or else, she would be sprawled on the hood of the car and Elliott would still be driving. That was a typical day, it was high drama at all times.'

McConnell thought Deerin a sweetheart. On the occasions Smith was upstairs sleeping or absent from the house altogether and he was able to strike up a conversation with her, he enjoyed quizzing her about her native Scotland. McConnell's ancestry was Scottish and they might spend a couple of hours talking together about the old land. For Deerin, these were blessed distractions.

'Valerie was just so frustrated with Elliott and his drugs,' says McConnell. 'She really wanted him to clean up and so they could have a life together. I know they had discussed trying to have a more normal relationship and even having children together, but I don't believe Elliott felt he was up to the task of being a father at the time.

'With Valerie, I guess he had what you would class as a codependent situation and where she was the mother figure. Unfortunately, those situations usually don't work out very well when somebody is really struggling with addiction. You can't babysit it out of them. They fought a lot. Valerie seemed like a good, solid person to me, but she was in tears quite a bit.'

In the midst of all this mayhem, Smith retained a clear, razor-sharp focus on the kind of music he meant to make. Tired of the slicker, glossy sound of his two records for DreamWorks, he was intent upon stirring an altogether harsher brew. Thinking on his totem, the White Album, he was reaching for something just as instinctively in-the-moment, as densely layered and wildly unbound.

'Elliott would sit on the end of my bed and play songs for me on his acoustic guitar,' says McConnell. 'He was productive, but he also made things a lot harder on himself with the drugs. He was a workhorse even when he was high, but he was not efficient, he would make more mistakes. The other side of the coin is he did some creative stuff with me he probably wouldn't have done had he been sober. He ended up creating a new sound for himself, too. Elliott wanted the record to be unique and totally experimental. The John Stephens tape machine was one of the first things I started messing around with for him. I would drag my hands on the reels to change the speed as we were recording. I'd hit the stop-start button so you would get this whirring sound on the tape.

'Because he was looking for those happy accidents, Elliott encouraged me to experiment as much as possible with sounds and to keep all of the mistakes. If anything ever sounded too polished, he would tell me to mess it up. We would re-do the part, even to the extent of de-tuning the guitars slightly, or the drums. We detuned Elliott's guitars and drums in all of these weird ways. Elliott would say to me, "Whatever happens to me, you can't let anybody clean this up."'

The work Smith was doing with McConnell frequently touched upon sheer brilliance, yet the glory was all too often overshadowed by his own strangeness at this point in his life. McConnell and Cotton might find themselves awed by their house guest one moment, but then bamboozled by, or else terrified for him the next. For just one thing, there were the vagaries of his diet.

'His nutrition was terrible,' recalls McConnell. 'He didn't eat food much, he would only eat his breakfast cereal and ice cream. Sometimes he would have a protein-type drink, the kind of thing made for people who can't have solid food. It's no wonder he felt like shit with his drug problem and bad sleep patterns on top. Nobody living like Elliott was could possibly be happy.

'It was rare we had a happy, good day. Occasionally, we would go off on little road trips. Spend a day driving around in his Volkswagen, listening to our mixes. Some of his quirks were kind of funny. Like going to the grocery store with Elliott, I would be getting actual food – meat, vegetables and eggs – and he would fill a shopping cart up with ice cream – he would spend $300 a throw just on ice cream.'

'I never saw Elliott even eat a meal,' says Cotton. 'But he would buy fifty cartons of ice cream at a time, every different flavour imaginable. He would go fetch it from the grocery store late at night and the security guards would follow him around the store. They thought he was a homeless person. There was never a time we went out for dinner together, or watched a movie. Elliott didn't do normal things. He just worked. And worked and worked.'

A pall settled over the whole house. McConnell and Cotton grew accustomed to living in a perpetual state of fear for Smith.

'Elliott talked constantly,' says McConnell. 'He talked a lot about things from his childhood and his past. He talked about his ex-girlfriends and how he felt he was treated like shit. He was a true sweetheart. He had a huge heart, but also, he had a lot of remorse and frustration and sadness about his life. I was always scared for him. There were crazy amounts of drugs going on. I knew he was doing heroin, I knew he was doing cocaine, I knew he was doing crack cocaine. Then there were all of the psych meds. He was always very explicit about it. He said to me, "David, don't try to stop me doing drugs. If you do, I'm going to do them anyway, but not at your house."

'He would go on these insane drug runs. He'd go and buy large amounts of heroin and cocaine from these gang guys in the ghetto. He was putting himself in situations where he could be killed. There was one particular night Elliott told me about, he went over to some guy's house and they made him pull his car into the garage. All of these guys had guns and they shut the garage door down on him. Elliott thought he was going to get robbed, or killed. All I asked of him was to please do the drugs at our house, so I could supervise him. If I ever needed to, I could give him CPR or get him to a hospital right away. Elliott was, like, "Cool, fine, as long as you don't give me shit for doing drugs, I'll do them here and we can keep recording."'

'The atmosphere was dark,' says Cotton. 'Elliott talked about suicide, mainly as a way to get back at certain people. It was generally assumed he was going to overdose one day. He took a lot of prescribed drugs, for sure – antipsychotic, antiseizure and all kinds of psycho-tropic drugs. But the amount and variety of drugs he took recreationally was astounding: coke, speed, Valium, Seconal, pot and lots of alcohol.

'Crack was his favourite. He usually procured his crack from a dealer in Venice Beach and often he would come back with a new crack pipe he had picked up. He had a huge collection of crack pipes, he lined the bathroom shelf in our room with them. Like a little kid, he made David and I come and look at them. They were kind of extraordinary, like little works of art, and Elliott was delighted by them. What could I say? I wasn't judging him, but then I had never seen or experienced anything like this before.'

Always, too, there was Smith's obsessive musing on Dream-Works. How he gnawed over the ways he thought the label had wronged or slighted him. Time and again, Smith moaned to McConnell about the pressure he was being put under by Lenny Waronker and Luke Wood, and of his urgency to get out from DreamWorks' clutches.

'Lenny and Luke came out to the house a lot,' says McConnell. 'They came just to hear what we were working on and they were blown away. They loved the record, they couldn't stop complimenting us. I mean, Lenny Waronker literally sat and cried in my studio listening to the record. He was a grown-ass man and that there was the power Elliott had with his music.

'Elliott invented a lot of the conflict with DreamWorks, I think. From what I saw, Lenny and Luke wanted to help him any way they could. They showed sincere effort to help him with his personal problems, with money. I heard all of these conversations, I was present in all of their meetings, but Elliott just wouldn't stop from talking shit about DreamWorks.'

All the while, Smith carried on recording tracks with McConnell. Hours of tape filling up with music and as the California summer began to bake. One night, McConnell and Cotton invited a friend of theirs over to the house to meet Smith, someone who was a huge fan of his music. The four of them spent the evening gathered around the piano, Smith playing for the others. Until he upped and retired to the bedroom studio with McConnell, ready to go to work once more, as if just then it was the only thing that mattered to him in the world.

'Elliott was looking pretty dishevelled and he was very, very thin by then,' says Cotton. 'When our friend left, I happened to look out of the window and I saw him sat there in his car, sobbing. I went out and asked him what was going on. He answered me, "Elliott's going to die, he's going to die."'

CHAPTER 24

The Weight

Smith left Malibu in the early summer of 2001 meaning to continue working with David McConnell. However, their progress on his new songs slowed to a crawl and soon enough stalled altogether. Smith was living back at the Disney cottage with Valerie Deerin, but theirs was never to be a fairy-tale romance. For all Deerin's well-intentioned efforts to clean up after him and clean him up, Smith was too far gone into his own private hell for her ever to be able to reach him. The whole Hollywood scene he was embroiled in was heavy and druggy, so dark it was hard to see a way back towards the light.

The film director Wes Anderson reached out to him, wanting another Beatles' cover song from him for his upcoming third movie, *The Royal Tenenbaums* (2001). Anderson was a kindred spirit of Smith's. He, too, had grown up in Texas and they were the same age. Like Smith, he was a true artist, his films highly stylised and uniquely his own. As such, Smith wanted to do his best for Anderson, but he simply wasn't fit to be of service. He tried cutting a version of 'Hey Jude' for Anderson's film, but the session turned out to be a mess and he scrapped the tapes. When *The Royal Tenenbaums* came out four months later, Anderson had instead resorted to using one of Smith's own, older songs in the scene in question. Tellingly, it was 'Needle in the Hay'.

'Elliott had clearly entered a very dark phase and it was talked about a lot between those of us who worked with him,' recalls Russell Warby. 'People were saying to me, "The Elliott you knew is not the Elliott of now, he's not there." There was a very real concern. You would very often think the people you'd most worry about are the ones who don't talk about things. Well, Elliott *did* talk about it. He carried a very big burden, a lot of pain, and he didn't hide the fact.

'Valerie was a very dear, old friend of mine. She was absolutely in love with him, but it was terribly painful for her. Valerie was the happiest person in Glasgow and she became the saddest in Los Angeles. You could actually see she was going through something really awful.'

'I was afraid to be around Elliott,' says Joey Waronker. 'I didn't want to deal with what he had going on. Occasionally, we would be at the same party. Elliott would be over in a corner, the place you would go sit if you were into hard drugs. If not, meaning nine-tenths of everybody else at the party, you would avoid it. It was all too sad and depressing to me.

'There was one time I tried to see him, but it was like he was totally gone. There was nothing I could do. It was too dangerous for me to handle at that point in my life.'

Already way past the boundary of having any notional kind of self-control, Smith's spending on drugs had escalated to truly frightening levels. He shared with Aaron Sperske the fact he was blowing through as much as $10,000 a day; he was also still buying his drugs directly from off the street. Sperske claims he was moved to make an enabling intervention purely out of fear for Smith's well-being.

'I was familiar with the place he went to buy his drugs,' Sperske says. 'It was by a taco truck in West Hollywood. I went down there myself in the '80s, on the back of a motorcycle with Courtney Love and when I was young, naïve and not really aware of what was going on. It was a place normally reserved for low-level crackheads, not guys like Elliott. I didn't think Elliott's sense of mortality, or of his own personal safety, was correct. He was going down there at night, putting his trust in these characters on the street corner − I thought he was in real physical danger.

'He was doing a mixture of heroin and cocaine and I knew a private dealer. I gave him a phone number, so he wouldn't have to go down to the taco truck and risk getting killed every time he wanted to get drugs. It was just a matter of time before something tragic would have happened. I viewed it as harm reduction, because Elliott was going to do what he was going to do. Neither I, nor anyone else, was going to talk him out of it.'

Along with Smith's drug abuse, there was another growing menace: the amount of crack he was smoking was making him more paranoid and delusional. Smith's perspective on his fraying relationship with his record company was becoming ever more distorted and warped. He became insistent representatives from DreamWorks were mounting a guerrilla campaign against him, meaning to steal the record he was making with McConnell out from under his nose. Railing about it to friends, he was adamant his home was being broken into, songs hacked from his PC.

He had some grounds for these fears at least, albeit they were shaky and tenuous at best. In the preceding year, unreleased music from two high-profile acts, Madonna and Radiohead, had been pirated onto an online file-sharing platform launched in 1999, Napster. Yet, by 2001, Napster was drowning in legal actions as the music business fought a rear-guard action against its operations. In recent months, Dr Dre and Metallica independently, and collectively a raft of major labels, including Warner Bros, Sony and Universal, DreamWorks' parent company, had all filed suits against Napster, seeking to impose restrictions on the company or else shut it down altogether. By the following year, Napster was to have filed for bankruptcy.

The further it advanced, though, the more Smith's conflict with DreamWorks became a war waged entirely in his own head. He convinced himself the label was spying on him, had gone so far as to hire teams of agents to follow him around. He shared with David McConnell, Aaron Sperske and others his conviction he was being watched. DreamWorks' agents, he maintained, were trailing him around town in fleets of white vans, or else from helicopters hovering overhead. On the odd occasions he visited McConnell in Malibu, Smith would have Deerin drop him off at the bottom of the hill road leading up to

McConnell's property. From there, he would make his way to McConnell's house on foot, sneaking through the undergrowth so as to throw off his tails.

'That summer, I wound up going down to LA to see Elliott,' recalls Garrick Duckler. 'He told me about the white vans following him around. He pointed one out to me, parked across the street from the cottage. I said to him, "Okay, let's go and check it out." Elliott looked panicked, but after we had gone outside and seen who was in the driver's seat of the van, he clearly felt better. I had taken him seriously and we were together investigating whether there was some merit to what he thought.'

'In the end, Elliott hired this odd bodyguard guy because he was so sure he was being tailed,' says Aaron Espinoza. 'This guy worked as a bouncer on a kind of Mexican-language TV version of *The Jerry Springer Show*, keeping members of the audience from getting into fights with each other. Whenever Elliott went out, the bodyguard would follow behind him on a motorcycle. One day, I drove over to Elliott's cottage and the guy was stood guard outside. We had seen each other a few times by then. He said to me, "Hey, man, I just wanted to let you know your friend is really sweet, but he's not doing so well. There is no one following him." I was, like, "I know, thanks."

'Elliott's mood swings were often and broad. When he was on the high end of things, he was really fun and engaged and interested but then there were the dark times and a lot of paranoia, too. Elliott didn't take me into too many situations with the drug stuff. There were times he would be doing drugs in the bathroom.

I would knock on the door and he'd tell me to go away and leave him alone. Those occasions were scary and weird.'

★

There was serious concern about Smith's well-being over at DreamWorks, too. Enough so as one day that summer Lenny Waronker made a personal visit to the Disney Cottage. Waronker came under the pretence of speaking with Smith about his new record. In reality, he wanted to assess for himself his artist's condition. Smith required urgent treatment, he concluded. Aaron Sperske says he recommended the Pasadena Recovery Center to Waronker and Margaret Mittleman. Sperske had been treated there for his own drug addiction and the facility was just a fifteen-minute drive from Smith's home.

The Pasadena Recovery Center first opened its doors in the 1920s. During the so-called Golden Age of Hollywood, it was where the major film studios sent their contracted stars to dry out before they commenced to shoot a movie. The comedian W. C. Fields spent the last two years of his life being treated for his alcoholism at the centre, dying there as an in-patient on Christmas Day, 1946. When the time came, Sperske drove Smith out to Pasadena. He was checked into the care of Dr Drew Pinsky, something of a celebrity himself as the host of a nationally syndicated radio talk show, *Loveline*.

'That's when I finally realised, "Wait a second, I don't know how bad this has got – I'm disconnected,"' says Margaret Mittleman. 'Once I knew, my approach with Elliott was "Don't do this to yourself, don't let your body take the toll. It shouldn't carry the burden of what's happening." I told him we should change direction. Nothing was worth him having to be high just to get by, or feel good about himself.'

'I told Elliott this rehab wouldn't be anything like what he had previously undergone,' says Sperske. 'The grounds of the centre were beautiful, there were all of these manicured green lawns and a little putting green. We were taken on a tour of the grounds and then Elliott met with Dr Drew. He was reassured it wasn't going to be like a penal colony. Taylor Hawkins of the Foo Fighters was checked in at the same time. He and Elliott became fast friends. Elliott had a really positive experience and he went for it, he got clean.'

A matter of days after Smith returned home from his rehab, Sperske took a call from Mitchell Frank, the owner of Spaceland. Frank was in the process of organising a local music festival, the Sunset Junction Street Fair, for the last weekend in August 2001. He had already booked Sperske's band, Beachwood Sparks, to play his show and was now looking to secure Smith as his Saturday night headliner. Like so many others, Frank wasn't able to get hold of Smith himself, he was calling to ask Sperske if he would pass on his offer. Sperske was wary, knowing how Smith was still in a fragile condition and vulnerable.

'But I did tell Mitchell I would ask Elliott,' says Sperske. 'Even though Mitchell didn't give me a budget number, I went and put his offer to Elliott. He thought it over and said, "Tell Mitchell I'll do it for $20,000." It was basically Elliott's way of saying no, pricing himself out of the game. I relayed Elliott's response back to Mitchell and he just went, "Okay." When I told Elliott how Mitchell had agreed, he said, "Oh, crap." Elliott wasn't yet fully recovered. He was sober, but he hadn't given himself enough time. In retrospect, he shouldn't have said yes to Mitchell for any amount.'

None of the portents for the Street Fair show were good. Smith hadn't played a gig in six months and even then, it was a quick spot at the Silverlake Lounge, back in February. The festival went ahead at the Silver Lake end of Sunset Boulevard, at the junction with Hoover Street. The stage spanned the cross-section of the road, a crowd of several thousand turning out on the balmy evening of Saturday, 18 August. It was just going dark when Smith stepped out under the hot stage lights. His hair was braided again like Willie Nelson's. He had on the same clothes he had worn at the Bumbershoot Festival in Seattle eleven months earlier, his bucket hat and a pair of violet pants.

He managed to get through three songs, 'Shooting Star', 'Let's Get Lost' and 'Twilight', before unravelling. He lost the threads of the next three songs he started out, 'Say Yes', 'Alameda' and 'Son of Sam', abandoning each of them. His singing voice cracked and drifted out of tune. He didn't seem able to correctly navigate his left hand along the fretboard of his acoustic guitar. Altogether, Smith gave up on nine songs during this tortuous set, coming apart in front of his audience's eyes. The big crowd on Sunset Boulevard fell silent. Smith took two stabs at the last song of his set, 'Needle in the Hay', the first hopeless, the second faltering but intact. As a performance, overall it was a train wreck and as a spectacle, it was desperately upsetting, tawdry even – a sick man flailing and drowning in public.

'I didn't even see Elliott's whole set,' recalls Aaron Sperske. 'Autumn looked at me and said, "Oh, this is so hard to watch, let's go." So we left. The next day all I heard about was how hard Elliott had bombed. People were going, "He was so horrible, what's happened to him?" Having so recently gone through a treatment programme, Elliott just didn't have control of his motor skills.'

'Elliott couldn't remember any of his own songs,' says Aaron Espinoza, who was also watching on, shocked. 'He stopped in the middle of the choruses and even during the intros. Oh God, there were thousands of people there and so many of them our mutual friends. A group of us went to a gathering at someone's house afterwards and the mood was bleak. We were all of us just stunned our local hero was in such a really, *really* bad way. We'd had some fun times hanging out, but Elliott was doing down . . . down . . . down.'

Once more, Smith retreated. He shut himself up in the cottage with Valerie Deerin to nurse him. David McConnell tried to tease him out again, appealing again to Smith's interest in vintage recording gear. He suggested he begin investing in a collection of his own, stockpiling to also be able to kit out his own studio one day. Smith took the bait and metamorphosed. He grew excited and animated, brought back to life again. McConnell knew of a guy living just over in the Valley who was shuttering his studio and selling off a horde of equipment. McConnell drove Smith out there for a viewing. On the spot, Smith dropped $30,000 on buying up gear.

'This guy had got amazing pieces,' recalls McConnell. 'One of the things Elliott picked up was an original LA2A leveller, which would be worth a small fortune these days. He gave it to me as a thank-you present. For me, the whole idea was for this to be a way for Elliott to hold on to his money – he was having financial troubles and because he was spending so much on drugs.

'Of course, Elliott got totally into collecting gear. He even bought a few pieces off eBay. He would hit me up, like, "The bids right now are at $1,300. How high should I go?" A lot of that was happening. I felt good I'd encouraged him to invest in something, to save his money for the future. The downside was it delayed our recording process. He had so many technical issues with all of the gear, because it was so old. It also takes a while to accumulate enough for a great studio, you can't do it overnight. The upside was everything he bought appreciated in value. He built up quite a bit of wealth in equipment alone.'

Months drifted by with Smith invested in his hunt for recording equipment, but otherwise inert and disengaged. Towards the end of the year, he re-emerged at last to play a smattering of solo acoustic shows. The first brace of gigs was home in LA in November 2001. He did a Monday night spot at Spaceland on 5 November and four nights later made an appearance at a benefit concert organised by local radio station KCRW at the Wiltern theatre. At both, he again played truncated sets of ten and nine songs respectively, most of them his new ones. He appeared as if he were coming out of a long hibernation, nowhere near fully up to speed. His hair was unwashed and grown past his shoulders, his face a mask of hard concentration. Listening to him each night was to hear back his journal of the hard, desperate near two years just past. The songs told their own harrowing story – 'True Love', 'Strung Out Again', 'A Fond Farewell'.

In December, he did four more dates, beginning with two nights at the Great American Music Hall in San Francisco on Monday 17th and Tuesday 18th. Each of these was a longer show. Smith still lent both of his sets towards the newer songs, but also aired such familiar selections as 'Needle in the Hay' and 'Between the Bars'. The first night in San Francisco, he played a Led Zeppelin song, 'Friends'. On the second, he sang George Harrison's 'Give Me Love (Give Me Peace on Earth)' and also Willie Nelson's maudlin 'Blue Eyes Crying in the Rain'. Garrick Duckler came out to catch him on the Tuesday night, visiting him backstage.

'Elliott showed me all of the drugs he was taking just to get off all of the drugs he had been taking,' recalls Duckler. 'It was definitely an invitation to see what I would do, to put me in an impossible kind of situation. Would I say something to make him stop, be alarmed, do nothing, judge or dismiss it? "Any way I go," I thought, "he will use the response to feel persecuted." So I just said, "Wow, that is a lot. What's worse, all this or the stuff you were on?" He was a little wooden and told me about this doctor he was seeing, who was obviously a complete quack. Elliott had found him in a shopping mall.

'We wound up leaving the venue in separate cars. I was glad to see he was getting off whatever he was on. I wondered if we would be friends again. I doubted it, but maybe. I was driving my own car and Elliott was in a cab in front. The strangest thing was, he turned around in his seat and made this funny monster gesture at me through the window. It was a reference to a pinball game we had used to play at a diner we went to, back in Portland. That game always made us laugh. I didn't laugh on this occasion. I don't even know why I got the impression, but I knew Elliott was saying goodbye.'

The next day, Smith made the familiar journey up the Pacific Coast road to Portland. There he played two more back-to-back shows at the Crystal Ballroom. Those among the old gang who came out to see him were taken aback. Up on stage, Smith looked broken. After the show, he accompanied Sean Croghan to a mini reunion over at Neil Gust's house. Joanna Bolme was there, too. Croghan and the others present tried their best to talk him into moving back to Portland, to come and be looked after and made well. All of their entreaties fell on deaf ears.

Leaving Portland for Seattle, Smith performed his last show of the year at the Showbox on 21 December. The Portland gig was bad enough, but this was even worse. Onstage, Smith appeared to have run out of juice completely. He crashed and burned just as he had at the Sunset Junction Street Fair, experiencing the same muddle and struggle to remember one after another of his own songs. One he did manage to complete was a destitute ballad he would never get around to properly recording. Wryly, he titled it 'I'm Doing Okay, Pretty Good'. It contained perhaps the most wrenchingly sad lines he was ever to write: 'And I hate people A through Z. And everything . . . everything.'

Smith began the New Year of 2002 shuttered at home in Los Angeles. To renew her visa, Valerie Deerin had to fly back to the UK and leave him untended, unguarded for a couple of weeks. His half-sister, Ashley Welch, moved to the city to be nearer to him. She slept on his couch until she found an apartment of her own in the same neighbourhood. The two of them soon eased into a routine. Most weeks, Welch would go over to the Disney cottage to have Smith cut her hair. He would sit her on a stool in the bathroom, address her in a comically exaggerated French accent, spend hours snipping at her hair with his scissors and as the Beatles boomed from his record player.

This ritual aside, Smith continued to secrete himself. He didn't hang out anymore at Largo or Spaceland, he had stopped seeing Alyssa Siegel altogether. His relationship with Autumn de Wilde and Aaron Sperske never really recovered from the house key incident and was getting to be ever more strained and intermittent. In New York, Dorien Garry hadn't seen or spoken with him for going on a year.

Margaret Mittleman had carried on liaising on Smith's behalf between Lenny Waronker and Luke Wood at DreamWorks and Andy Kaulkin at ANTI- Records. Smith attended the occasional business meeting at Mittleman and Rob Schnapf's house, things between them kept as formal as possible. Until Smith pushed Mittleman, too, to her breaking point. One winter's afternoon, he turned up at her house in a belligerent, bellicose mood.

'I had moved my office into the basement of our house,' recalls Mittleman. 'My son was upstairs, running around with our nanny. Elliott and I were down in the basement and he was yelling at me about some kind of nonsense. He didn't believe I'd done this, or that. It was all a matter of distrust. He had been coming over and being in a weird place for a while, but I'd got to where I couldn't take it anymore. I just thought, "Right, I'm done." I didn't know how to help him.

'Looking back, I feel lucky. We did something right together. I feel sad also with how it ended between us. I wish our communication hadn't of broken down. After I quit that day in the basement, I didn't go to another show of Elliott's, or have anything to do with him. I never saw him again.'

CHAPTER 25

Strung Out

Margaret Mittleman's departure at the beginning of 2002 left Smith with a gaping void to fill, but he put off attending to it for the time being. The whole pace of his career, of his life in general, had slowed to a torpid crawl but for intermittent spells of action. On a graph, it would show up as a symmetrical pattern of long, flat lines interrupted by occasional eruptions of thin, jagged peaks. Those peaks were the spells where there was something sharp enough to have penetrated the fog in Smith's brain.

Producer David McConnell's notion of Smith having a place of his own to work was just such a lance. As much as anything, it carried with it the promise of a way back, to the same kind of set-up and control he had exercised at Jackpot! with Larry Crane, to the glory days. Out of the darkness and into the light. Smith enlisted McConnell to help him find the perfect spot to build a studio. Their search led them to a miles-long stretch of car dealerships on Van Nuys Boulevard and in their midst, an equally unremarkable-looking lump of real estate, Valley Center Studios. A subdivision going for sale inside of the small Valley Center complex looked promising, with room just enough to fit in a studio. It was a narrow space with a low ceiling, too, as intimate and cloistered as a womb.

Smith took on the lease and in so doing, opened up another money pit for himself. With McConnell, he set to work on putting in his studio. He shelled out for yet more gear to fill the place up, a litany of vintage tube microphones and archaic amplifiers. He was most occupied with finding a particular sound board. The type he craved, a Triad Trident A-Range recording console, was a giant and near-mythical beast. So rare, just seventeen of them were ever made. The Beatles had put down 'Across the Universe' through a Triad. One was housed at Abbey Road's Studio 3 in London, where Pink Floyd had employed it recording *Dark Side of the Moon*. It was a long shot, but McConnell persisted and found Smith a Trident going for sale in Nashville. This particular model dated from 1972 and had once occupied a recording facility called Le Studio up in Morin-Heights, Montreal. Rush had cut a bunch of albums with it there. It had also been employed on a Cat Stevens record from 1975, *Numbers*, and Chicago's 1979 album, *13*. Smith bought it sight unseen, meaning he failed to establish how the board's jungle of wiring and circuitry was so frayed and faulty. From the minute he took delivery from Tennessee, the Trident was nothing but trouble.

His burst of activity with the studio also shifted Smith up into gear creatively. He made a guest appearance playing guitar on a track for a band out of New York, the Jon Spencer Blues Explosion. A barnstorming garage-blues number, 'Tore Up & Broke', it was slated for their new album, *Plastic Fang*. More pressingly, he got back down to his own record. The sessions were intermittent and Smith called upon a revolving cast of supporting characters. Sometimes McConnell ran the sound for him, otherwise a second engineer, Fritz Michaud. He had Scott McPherson and Shon Sullivan in his studio to lay down parts and also Aaron Espinoza and Jim Fairchild from Grandaddy to help out. Over a period of two to three months, an assortment of tracks were worked up. The new sound Smith was reaching for was proving to be ever more feral and unhinged, the resolve gained from his Pasadena rehab stint untenable.

'The work was erratic,' recalls Aaron Espinoza. 'In my experience at least, it certainly wasn't a case of going into the studio every day. It wasn't like a job. Elliott wasn't paying me to come by and record with him. Some of his mood swings were pretty wild. Some days he would just not return your call and you might feel like, "Oh, shit, am I out of the loop now?" He would just kind of veer off into other worlds. I imagine he was going downtown and buying drugs.

'There were other times I felt like it was a great opportunity to get him up and going. If he was strung out or high on some fucked-up meds, I'd be the guy that would come over and be like, "Let's go to the studio." Until I was actually in the studio with him, I didn't realise how insanely talented Elliott was musically. He was so special and I just loved him so much, I considered I had a duty to get him up and moving. When he was *on* it was like

Disneyland, but he would also just go, like, flat. I would go down the 7-Eleven and grab us a six-pack of beer. I would play guitar with him. I'd tell him, "Let's get some lunch. Ice cream is not food, buddy." I would even clean his house for him.'

'I was with Elliott a handful of times,' says Jim Fairchild. 'There was usually drinking involved and a lot of talking about music and relationships. We were like teenagers together in a way, he was easy to hang with.

'The music Elliott was making was definitely reflective of where he was at in his life. There was one track I get chills thinking about even now. It was called "See You in Heaven". He never got around to cutting vocals for it, but it was a monumental piece of music. The two of us would drive around LA, listening to it in his car. It's a testament to his crazy intellect how he was able to make music of such quality during that time. There are aspects of Elliott's music where I know exactly what's happening, but then again, I *don't know*. The word "genius" is tossed around too much, but Elliott's the closest I've seen to it in a lifetime of playing music.'

Trouble was they never did manage to get a smooth run at things. Serially, the sessions were pulled up by the poor condition both Smith and his nascent studio were mired in. Even at the best of times, the studio was in a state of disarray. Half of the gear Smith had bought seemed in need of repair, or else broken altogether. He never threw anything out either and so the room got to be as shambolic as a junkyard. The Triad board was his biggest and most consistent bugbear. He got hold of an old manual for the console by mail order and spent hours taking the board apart and putting it back together, soldering its bits and parts. Yet try as he might, he couldn't ever get it to fully function.

'What Elliott was trying to do there was another demonstration of his personality – a very assiduous attention to detail,' recalls Jim Fairchild. 'He basically rewired the Triad, or parts of it, all on his own. He did his best and had to dig really deep with his research, but it's a weird board and for a lot of the last year or so of his life, he was working on that thing.'

There were other aspects of the Triad's inner workings too fiendish for Smith to work out by himself. He began summoning a steady stream of recording technicians to the studio to help him fix the infernal thing, but without their having any appreciable success. More money was frittered away to no ends.

'Elliott got really angry with the technicians,' says McConnell. 'He thought all of them were scamming him, because they would come in for five hours and nothing would be working still. They would be like, "Well, I've found this other problem with the board." Elliott started to think that they were taking advantage of him. That could have been a little paranoia on Elliott's part, but some of the techs he was using weren't very good. Altogether, we basically had many months of simply not being able to record.'

Eventually, the ongoing technical issues with the studio beached the sessions entirely. At the same time, Smith was still agitating to free himself from his contract with DreamWorks. Minus

Margaret Mittleman, in this matter he was hopelessly short of expertise and out of his depth. He was also savvy enough at least to recognise this fact and at last now moved to replace Mittleman. From touring in Europe with the Flaming Lips, he had got to know and like their long-time manager, Scott Booker. Smith reached out to Booker to ask for his help in negotiating him off his record label.

Booker managed the Flaming Lips out of their native Oklahoma City. He had started off running a local record store the various band members frequented and had progressed to promoting shows in the city for the Flaming Lips and also other passing indie-rock groups, Nirvana included. As the Lips' manager, Booker had gained a reputation for securing his band artistic freedom. In 1990, he had signed them from an indie label to Warner Bros and when Mo Ostin and Lenny Waronker were still running the major. As Mittleman did with Smith, Booker had never had a formal contract with the Lips, but based their relationship on mutual trust. He was open to Smith's request. They began to speak regularly by phone, meeting in person whenever Booker came to LA on Lips' business.

'Definitely, I was fully aware Elliott had a drug problem,' says Booker. 'My wife and I visited him at his Disney cottage one time and he brought out a gallon-sized plastic food bag full of pill bottles. He said to us, "This is what I take every day." Personally, I've never really done drugs, but Steve Drozd in the Flaming Lips had drug issues. My attitude with people who have those kinds of difficulties is always to try to just be a constant, normal presence in their life.

'I only really dealt with Elliott when he was good and coherent. At those times, you could have real conversations with him. Elliott just wanted to be off DreamWorks. I loved his records and so I was happy to help. From hearsay, I had heard Elliott had threatened to commit suicide if the label didn't let him go. My first inclination with Elliott was to say, "Look, *why* would you do that?"'

Even on his better days, though, Smith's mind was letting him down. Booker was soon enough made aware of the paranoia others had encountered, the deceptions and confusions plaguing his new client. Best he could, he tried tackling the issue with reason and logic.

'There was one occasion Elliott called me to tell me people at DreamWorks were having him followed,' Booker recalls. 'I said to him, "Here's what I'm going to do, Elliott. I'm going to buy you one of those little portable cameras. I just want you to take a snapshot any time you see someone following you. If you can give me some kind of evidence, I can go talk to DreamWorks." Of course, he never took a picture on the camera I got for him.'

Even so, Smith's capacity for generating moments of wonder was intact. On Good Friday, 29 March 2002, he summoned both Aaron Sperske and Steve Drozd, in town with the Lips, over to Sunset Sound. Smith arrived at the studio with a new friend in tow. Nelson Gary was a writer, poet, spoken-word performer and an addiction counsellor at a treatment centre in Malibu. Smith had tracked him down after reading an article he had written on Lou Reed's recovery from heroin addiction.

They had bonded quoting Kierkegaard back and forth to each other, Gary also being an acolyte of the Danish philosopher.

Smith was stirring together the heaviest song he was ever to record, 'Coast to Coast', and wanted to have it driven by two hulking drum tracks. After setting up two drum kits at opposite ends of the commodious recording room in Sunset's Studio One, he then had Sperske and Drozd play along to the byzantine backing track he had put down already. The two drummers sat facing each other and flailing away, Sperske stacking up a backbeat and Drozd firing volleys in the spaces between. Smith conducted the pair of them from the centre of the room. They made a sound like a legion of bodies falling down flights of stairs. Over the top of their cacophony, Smith had Gary repeatedly read out one of his own poems, on each occasion asking him to change the pitch, inflection and pace of his voice.

'Elliott was wearing his black bellbottom Jimmy Page pants and no shirt, totally topless,' recalls Sperske. 'His hair was long and greasy and he just poured with sweat. He had a very clear, exact idea of what he wanted us to do. Steve and I put our drum parts down fast, in two takes. We just knocked it out the park. It was kind of a magical thing.'

Besides Smith's ongoing contract situation with Dream-Works, there was another issue requiring Booker's urgent attention. Smith was once again running precariously short of ready money. Booker got on the case and arranged a one-off show for him over in Chicago, opening up a hometown gig at the Riviera Theater for Wilco. The headliners were touring a hit album, *Yankee Hotel Foxtrot*, and Booker was able to secure a robust fee.

The Lips' sound engineer and tour manager, Chris Chandler, was based in LA. Booker also arranged to have the redoubtable Chandler chaperone Smith to the gig. Smith and Chandler were due to travel east the day before the show. On the appointed date, Wednesday, 1 May, Chandler pitched up at Smith's Disney cottage to shepherd him to LAX. Valerie Deerin had gone home to Scotland to visit family and Chandler knocked repeatedly on the front door without an answer.

'So I went and got lunch and then came back,' recalls Chandler. 'Our flight was leaving fairly soon by then and I couldn't tell if Elliott was sleeping in or just not there. Finally, a neighbour came by and said, "He's in there, but he's probably not coming to the door." Elliott had a peephole in his door wide enough for me to get my arm through and pop the lock. The house was in a bit of disarray. Elliott was alone in bed. When you show up at someone's house, not really knowing them, they're not coming to the door and you find them in bed, you always kind of assume the worst. But I quickly kind of figured out what was going on, woke Elliott up, got him dressed, packed a bag for him with whatever I could find on the floor and grabbed a guitar.

'We jumped into my car. Elliott said he needed to make a few stops along the way. He was picking up some medications from his doctor. He did those in the car. He had some issues with whatever was going on in his life and did not want to get on the flight. We didn't make it to the airport in time. We went to Elliott's studio instead and I booked us onto the next day's flight. I didn't want to have to deal with him disappearing again, so I locked the studio doors and the two of us spent the night in there.'

Smith barely slept all night, but at the second time of asking, Chandler managed to coax him onto the Thursday afternoon flight to Chicago, although he was still wholly unprepared to do a show. Upon landing in Chicago, Chandler hailed a cab and instructed the driver to orbit the city while Smith figured his way through a setlist, sat in the backseat strumming at his acoustic guitar and singing away. The cab pulled up at the venue just in time for him to walk out onstage. The show itself was a dud. Under the harsh stage lights, Smith appeared lost and confused. He fumbled at his guitar, fluffed songs and ended up cutting his set short. Again.

'After the show, Elliott didn't want to go to the hotel we had booked for him or even to sleep,' says Chandler. 'We spent the rest of the night driving around the city in another cab, while Elliott tried to write songs in the back. The driver looked at us like we were insane. The fare cost hundreds of dollars. Next morning, we were sat outside of the airport before it even opened, waiting to get the first flight back to LA.

'At the gate in the airport, Elliott had an accident. He "went to the bathroom" in his trousers. He was embarrassed, didn't want to stand up and go get on the plane. I just grabbed my glass of orange juice and poured it into my own lap, then said to the flight attendant, "Hey, we've both spilled our drinks. What can we do?" She saw what was going on. She told Elliott people have spills all the time. There was a fire fighter also at the gate. He said to me, "Man, this guy doesn't look good." He helped me walk Elliott onto the plane. Once the two of us were sat on the plane, another flight attendant fetched a blanket for me to put over Elliott. That was my first dealing with Elliott. God, I'll never forget it.'

'I had to call up Elliott afterwards and tell him the promoter in Chicago wanted to reduce his fee because he had played a short set and wasn't so great,' says Scott Booker. 'Elliott retorted, "I *was* great. I don't know what you're talking about." I told him, "That's not the story I'm hearing from everyone."'

The week after the fiasco in Chicago, Jim Fairchild drove down to LA from Modesto to be with Smith for a couple of days. Fairchild spent most of his visit cleaning up the Disney cottage. Without his girlfriend to tidy up after him, Smith had turned the place into a hovel. Scott Booker, meanwhile, continued to work on Smith's behalf with DreamWorks. From the dealings he'd had with him at Warner Bros, Booker had the utmost respect for Lenny Waronker and foremost in his mind was to keep Smith from completely severing another solid bond.

Ultimately, Booker's diplomacy won out over Smith's wrecking ball. Booker proposed a deal to Waronker and Luke Wood whereby DreamWorks would effectively grant Smith a leave of absence. Smith would be free to put out his next record with another label, but DreamWorks would retain their option on him going forward. Waronker and Wood agreed to Booker's terms, seeing it as an opportunity for Smith to re-set himself. As Booker presented the deal to him, Smith was unshackled and freed to do as he pleased with his new music. The next step was for Booker to ensure there actually would be a record and to get Smith back into operating to some sort of reliable order and routine.

Once more, Booker turned to Chris Chandler, tasking him with taking charge of Smith's recording sessions and instilling a renewed sense of discipline into the creative process. Chandler began work at Smith's own studio, but they spent two fruitless days together there being defeated by the Triad board. However, he had a studio of his own just up the road from Smith's, where he had another classic old console, a Neve. He persuaded Smith to move operations to his place. Smith brought with him to Chandler's his Fairchild compressor and Neumann microphones. Once they started up, the sessions at Chandler's studio quickly settled into a familiar pattern. Smith began his working days late in the afternoons and wanted to go on through the night.

'Elliott spent a lot of time just living at my studio,' recalls Chandler. 'He would sleep on the couch and he was not an early riser. He was going through a writing block, too, so we spent a lot of the time with him trying to resurrect older songs. He found a bunch of cassettes of stuff he had written in the past or played live. We would put those on the multitrack and then Elliott would play along to them, trying to recreate the feel for some of these songs.

'There was one newer song we did work on initially, "Don't Go Down". Elliott wanted to play everything on it and we spent four days on recording it, non-stop. We started on a Monday and all of a sudden it was Friday morning. I'm not sure what

Elliott did when he went to the bathroom to keep him going, but he could go for that long. Finally, he went to sleep on the couch and I drove to my home in Venice Beach and just passed out.'

As he had with David McConnell in Malibu, Smith preferred to record in isolation with Chris Chandler, secluded and sealed off from the world outside. There were occasional exceptions to this rule. McConnell dropped by once or twice to sit in with them. At one point, Smith fixated on the idea of having his half-sister, Ashley Welch, play on the record and had her drop by to put down a couple of incidental keyboard parts. Back from Scotland, Valerie Deerin began to call into the studio infrequently to check up on Smith, make sure he was eating. More often than not, he wasn't and soon enough the whole temperature of the sessions at Chandler's studio was fluctuating as wildly as it had done at McConnell's.

'Once Elliott got started he wouldn't want to stop, no eating, nothing,' says Chandler. 'He would eat ice cream only, or drink a couple of Smirnoff Ices instead. Valerie would drop off this thing for him called Easy Mac, which was a macaroni cheese type of thing we could heat up in the microwave. I would get food delivered as well, but he just had no interest in any of it. Three or four days without food or sleep, man, it's a tough way to go.'

'There was one day at Chris's studio that was especially challenging,' recalls McConnell. 'Elliott was partying too much. We were doing a vocal session and he asked me to direct his singing, try to get the best performance out of him. After his first pass, I said to him, "You were flat. You can do this way better, man."

And he lost his shit. He was, like, "Fuck you! I don't sing flat!" It wasn't Elliott and he later apologised, but that was a rough day and those were dark times. He was really struggling.'

The variety and massive volume of medications Smith was consuming were an ever-present, ongoing concern. He would have Chris Chandler run him to his various doctors and wait outside while he went to pick up his regular prescriptions. Back in Chandler's car, Smith would tear open the packaging and immediately set about popping from the bottles of pills he had fetched, apparently indiscriminately. According to Chandler, 'There were something like fourteen different kinds of things he was taking.'

Chandler is convinced Smith was shooting up one of his medications, Dilantin. He had often professed to friends to being terrified of needles, a fear he shared with Nirvana frontman Kurt Cobain. If Chandler is correct and also just like Cobain before him, the strength of Smith's addiction had eventually conquered his phobia.

'The Dilantin pills he would cook up with a spoon,' says Chandler. 'The foam would come up. He would dab it with a cotton ball and then shoot it up, so he got a more powerful dose. He would disappear into the bathroom at the studio for an hour or two at a time.

'Elliott would write out lyrics while he was in the bathroom and then toss them aside. I thought he might want to come back to them, so I would pull his notes out of the trash. He would also write down other stuff, more kind of rambling notes about how he was being followed and his thoughts on how he was not worthy of all of these things he had in his life. Some of these notes were very hard to decipher. Some of them, he'd be writing them out as he was shooting up and so blood would splatter onto the pages. I know it sounds disgusting, but I've saved all of those pages of Elliott's bloodied notes. I just couldn't throw them out, they're a part of the history of the time I was in the studio with him.'

CHAPTER 26

Boy in the Bubble

The pace and intensity of the sessions at Chris Chandler's studio eased up. It was bound to happen. Chandler had other clients to fit in. One of them was a former child actor and star of the TV series *Saved by the Bell*, Dustin Diamond, looking to launch a music career destined never to get off the ground. Also, no amount of chemical stimulation could compensate for just how frail Smith was, both physically and mentally. Besides his pitiful diet, he didn't do any exercise and was bereft of stamina. His mind was by now such a mess of terrors, worries and delusions he was beginning to doubt his own sanity. His writer's block persisted, causing him yet more anguish. As weeks turned to months, he didn't do nearly so many all-night marathons with Chandler and spent more time holed up at the Disney cottage.

On Tuesday, 6 August 2002, Smith turned thirty-three years old. His mother, Bunny, flew in from Texas to spend a couple of days with him. Those were happier days. The first evening Bunny was there, he took her and also David McConnell out for a birthday dinner, eating a rare meal himself and if only to keep up appearances for his mother. Afterwards, they all trooped back to the Disney cottage and watched sitcoms on TV for the rest of the night, mother and son sat side by side on the couch, laughing along with each other.

There were still other kinds of good times when Smith would laugh and joke and fool around, his broad, disarming smile lighting up the whole room. It was just they had become so much further apart. Four days after his birthday, the Flaming Lips were in town to play the Greek Theatre. Smith took Valerie Deerin along with him to the show. They went backstage, where Smith hooked up with Steve Drozd, a bottle of whiskey passing between them. One minute he was in high spirits, the next collapsed in a panicked state. Chris Chandler called an ambulance and paramedics wheeled the stricken Smith out of the venue on a gurney, Deerin at his side.

'Maybe it was a panic attack,' says Chandler. 'Maybe it was Elliott being overwhelmed in a big venue and with all that was going on, mixed with the whiskey and the medication he was on. The paramedics talked to him and got him through what he had to work through.'

'I thought it was some kind of overdose-type thing,' says Scott Booker. 'Serious enough for the ambulance to have to come out, but it didn't seem as if the paramedics treated it as life-threatening. Valerie went with him in the ambulance. That's what Valerie did, she adored him. I thought Valerie was good for him, but I don't know – how do you deal with those kinds of things just as humans? Elliott wasn't going to stop self-medicating.'

Smith had at least, and at last, reached the point of desperately wanting to get off the so-called street drugs, heroin and crack cocaine. Following his collapse at the Greek, he promptly checked himself into a facility in Beverly Hills, the Neurotransmitter Restoration Center, on the promise of a ground-breaking ten-day treatment. The NRC programme was the brainchild of a Dr William Hitt. According to Hitt's pioneering theory, pumping amino acids into an addict's body would flush out their system, stimulate their cells to repair themselves and in doing so dramatically reduce cravings. At the NRC, Smith was to twice take the miracle cure Hitt was touting, at a cost of $10,000 per day. On each occasion, he spent his stay tucked up in bed with a catheter in his arm and on a drip bag.

Speaking about the treatment several months later, Smith told an interviewer: 'It was really difficult . . . It's usually a ten-day process, but for me it took longer. It just bombards your system and kicks all the shit out of your nerve receptors . . . But nobody seems to know about it. There's been, like, 15,000 people treated with it, and its success rate is 80 per cent versus 10 per cent for the normal 28-day 12-step.'[31]

Smith was a convert. He wasn't educated about Dr William Hitt's chequered backstory, though. Before pitching up in LA, Pitt had run three treatment clinics in his native Houston. In 1987, he was sued by the state of Texas for fraudulent practices and all three of his clinics shut down by court order. In court, he was found to have misled his patients and invented the details of his medical qualifications. He was no kind of doctor at all.

Smith left Hitt's care feeling wiped out from the treatment, so weak he could hardly stand, but with a new resolve to change his lifestyle. As always, he acted upon impulse and without pause. The next immediate action he took was to break up with Valerie Deerin and then reach out to Jennifer Chiba to ask for her help to keep him on track. Deerin was heartbroken, but also wrung out from tending to Smith. His behaviour towards her had been abominable.

On 26 August, Smith moved out of the Disney cottage and in with Chiba. She was renting a house set on the steep hillsides of Echo Park, her bustling neighbourhood bordering Silver Lake. The house was small, shaded by trees and on a quiet residential road, Lemoyne Street. Straight away, Chiba took over from Deerin as Smith's nurse and wannabe protector. She fixed his food and cleaned up after him, just as her predecessor had done, but also screened his calls and did her best to keep him close to home whenever he was not at Chris Chandler's studio. She enlisted a musician friend, Robin Peringer, to fetch Smith's prescriptions and run other errands for him. Among Smith's other friends in LA, Chiba's influence on him quickly divided opinion.

'To my knowledge, Chiba was a cold-hearted kind of guard dog,' says Aaron Sperske. 'In the name of protecting Elliott, she was like, "He's mine, everyone else stay away." From what I could see, she was doing her best to insulate him from any other outside influence.

"I'm not aware she helped Elliott with getting clean, or to stay clean. Isolation is an addict's worst enemy. In my experience, addicts need to connect and be part of, not removed from life and other people. I don't think her keeping him to herself helped him at all. To my recollection, everyone around Elliott was annoyed with her at the time.'

'Poor Jennifer,' counters Aaron Espinoza. 'She and Valerie both seemed to me like they cared for Elliott in a major way and did their best to put some guard rails around him. I guess like everybody else tried to do. But it was hard to put your foot down with someone like Elliott. He was strong-willed and could be stubborn, he would tell you to fuck off.

'Jennifer had a reputation in LA. People talked about her kind of having a squat at her house, of parties and musicians going on benders and crashing out there for weeks on end. But Jennifer got clean. She and Elliott were cooking healthy food together. Jennifer got him on wheatgrass. I do know she was almost the only support Elliott had left, because he'd burned so many of his relationships.'

Every other Monday night, Smith did head out of the house on Lemoyne Street and down the hill to frequent yet another bar with a jukebox on Sunset Boulevard. The Short Stop had once served as a kind of clubhouse for local LAPD officers. Until, that is, a number of the cops who hung out there were implicated in an infamous corruption case brought by the city against the LAPD's anti-gang unit, the so-called Rampart Scandal of the late '90s. Among other crimes, the officers were charged with planting evidence, drug dealing and armed robbery. In the wake of the scandal, the Short Stop was put up for sale and one of its new co-owners, Greg Dulli, was a fellow musician and song-writer. Dulli had first run into Smith almost a decade earlier and on the occasions his band, the Afghan Whigs, travelled down from their adopted home in Seattle to play a show in Portland.

With the Whigs having split, Dulli was biding his time also tending bar at the Short Stop on week nights. Mondays was one of Dulli's regular work nights. Often as not Smith would come in on his own and take up a seat at one end of the bar. Over a period of weeks, the two of them fell into a steady round of conversation. Regularly, Smith would stay on after Dulli shut up the bar at closing time and then there would be just the two of them yakking away, the jukebox playing in the background. Mostly, they talked about music and their mutual obsession with the Beatles especially. Dulli had, in fact, sung the role of John Lennon in the 1994 Beatles-in-Hamburg movie *Backbeat*, although this was the rare piece of Fab Four trivia Smith appeared to be unaware of, or else it had slipped from his muddled mind. At all events, he never once brought it up with Dulli.

'Elliott was delightful to talk to,' says Dulli. 'He asked very insightful questions. He was almost like Jiminy Cricket. One of the things he put to me was, "Do people ask you what you do all day?" I knew instantly what he meant. With songwriters, it sometimes might not look as if you're writing a song, but that's what you're doing. You don't have a guitar in your hand, you're not sat at a piano, you might just be walking down the street or in a chair at home, but you're actively making art in your head. That was something Elliott understood in the same way I did.

'For both of us, music was the safe place and the faithful companion. It would never abandon you and it was always there. It was probably not the best time in either of our lives and Elliott could sometimes be grumpy, but I found him to be a really kind, cool, deep cat. I still picture him sat at the end of the bar, by himself, and his smile when I approached him.'

As the summer cooled, Smith found he was able to recover some kind of musical momentum. He was once more plucking songs out of the ether and putting them to tape with Chris Chandler. A rash of titles – 'The Last Hour', 'Little One', 'Dancing on the Highway', 'Circuit Rider', 'Already Somebody's Baby', 'Stickman' and more besides. Over at his own studio, Smith also hosted a couple of sessions with other artists. The first of these was with Blake Sennett, guitarist with a local band, Rilo Kiley. The second was with Neil Gust and his band, who laboured for ten days on a single song. The two old friends were tentative around each other.

'Elliott said he wanted to make another Heatmiser record, go on tour,' Gust related to Autumn de Wilde. 'But he was a mess. I was like, "You need to get healthy first." There was a lot between us that was left unresolved . . . He made his own choices. He chose those weird, dark-sided people.'[32]

Twice in October 2002, Smith ventured out to play solo shows, the first he had done since his crash opening for Wilco, back in May. On 1 October, a Tuesday night, he took a slot at a club also just down the hill from him on Sunset Boulevard,

The Echo. On 13 October, he had a cross-country date over in Minneapolis at the 400 Bar. After delighting the Los Angeles crowd opening his set with 'Miss Misery', he fluffed George Harrison's 'Long, Long, Long' from the White Album. He looked bedraggled, too – unshaven, lank-haired, an ugly trail of what appeared to be cigarette burns snaking up his left forearm.

In Minneapolis, Smith managed to navigate his way through a 22-song set. Second time around, he nailed 'Long, Long, Long', but came unstuck stabbing at Heatmiser's 'Half Right', as an awkward penance perhaps to Neil Gust. Those were the last gigs he was to play all year.

In total, Smith spent six months working with Chris Chandler. By the end of their time together, he was veering off in yet another direction, recording fifteen- and twenty-minute-long instrumental jams with no fixed points of reference. Formless pieces made up of the pulsing drum and bass tracks Smith put down first and then the screeds of keyboard noise he layered over the top. Likely, he meant to go on and mine actual songs from these meanderings. None of them ever came to light outside of Chandler's studio.

'The recordings Elliott did with me were definitely made from a dark place,' says Chandler. 'Trying to communicate with him, other than on the simplest, most basic of things, simply wasn't possible. Then, every now and again, he would surprise me. I would be in total despair, thinking I couldn't do this with him anymore, and he'd wake up and say, "I have an idea." He would grab a guitar and, holy shit, he would play and sing something and it would be frigging amazing. You'd think, "Where the fuck did *that* come from?" He just wasn't able, no way, to do it all of the time.

'I would have loved to have seen him get out of the space he was in but the amount of medication he was on, all of the drugs he was doing, I just didn't see any other way than to try my best and hope to have these glimmers of Elliott pop out every now and then. He was a smart guy, no getting around it. He was a beautiful songwriter and he cared a lot about people. He didn't want to be perceived as this guy who got signed to a major label and was too good for everybody. He was very uncomfortable in those shoes and maybe that was part of his trouble. He also talked about his stepdad and his family a lot. Those struggles came through and that stuff starts young. If you don't take care of those things, they keep building up, and on and on.'

Chandler was back in LA as soon as Monday, 25 November. The Flaming Lips were opening for Beck at a 6,000-capacity venue in Hollywood, the Universal Amphitheatre. Smith came out to see the gig with Jennifer Chiba. They ran into Joey Waronker backstage before the Lips played. Waronker hadn't seen Smith in months, but his first impression was one of pleasant surprise at how much more like his old self he appeared. Smith was in his regular uniform of T-shirt, jeans and sneakers, but he had shorn his hair and initially seemed to Waronker bright-eyed, clear-headed and engaged.

'He looked like the old Elliott, maybe even a little better than old Elliott,' recalls Waronker. 'I had seen him looking like he was about to die, so it was all good. We were shooting the shit and it felt really comfortable. Then, oh my God, the conversation just turned. It was like a schizophrenic type of thing. Elliott started to talk about his studio and he was losing track of what he was on about. There was clearly something wrong. I kept talking to him for a while longer, before I said I had to leave. It was a little bit heartbreaking.'

After saying his goodbyes to Waronker, Smith went out into the venue with Chiba to watch the Flaming Lips' set. The band was still playing when Scott Booker got a knock on the door of his production office backstage. It was someone from the venue, rushing to tell him that one of his artists had managed to get himself arrested. It took Booker a moment to establish the messenger meant Smith rather than any of the Flaming Lips. In so far as Booker was quickly able to piece things together, Smith had happened across two cops confronting a kid smoking a joint and promptly intervened.

Within minutes, Booker was given two different accounts of what happened next from eyewitnesses. The first came from Paul D'Amour, bassist with the hard rock band Tool. In D'Amour's telling, Smith had simply stepped in between the kid and the police officers and begun arguing on the young lad's behalf. According to Shon Sullivan, Smith had waded into the fray, hitting out at the two cops. Sullivan told Booker the cops had sprayed Mace in Smith's face, wrestled him to the ground and handcuffed him.

'I had to go talk to one of the police officers to see if we could prevent Elliott from going to jail,' Chris Chandler recalls. 'Elliott always had a heart for the underdog, I would say. He would want to help out anyone who was being taken advantage of, or was getting bullied.'

'The police officers weren't bothering Elliott, they were bothering someone else,' says Booker. 'But Elliott did not like the police. I mean, Elliott *did not* like the police. I called up the manager of the theatre and said to him, "You've got Elliott Smith in your drunk-tank, which is embarrassing for him but also for you guys. Do you think we can work something out?" He told me they were going to let Elliott calm down and would then release him.'

However, Smith wasn't to get off scot-free. The LAPD subsequently went ahead and pressed charges against both him and Chiba for unlawfully obstructing a police officer and disturbing the peace. Chiba seems to have been charged for having had the misfortune of being present at the scene with Smith. The case was to linger over Smith for months, yet another unwanted menace. He had also got himself injured in the altercation with the cops. The week following the Universal Amphitheatre show, he turned out to see a screening of Steve Hanft's and Ross Harris's film *Southlander*, in which he and Chiba cameoed. Harris could see he was uncomfortable and in pain. Smith told Harris he had damaged his back and collarbone and how he couldn't move his neck and was having difficulty swallowing. He was being prescribed a course of powerful painkillers, he said – as if he needed to be put on yet more heavy-duty drugs.

At Christmas, Beck threw a house party over at his Silver Lake home. Smith got an invite and went with Chiba. Mark 'E' Everett was there, too. Everett also hadn't seen Smith for many months. A couple of times he had asked him along to the backyard croquet game he hosted every Sunday afternoon, but Smith had never showed. They got to talking and Smith mentioned the idea of the two of them writing some songs together. He gave Everett his new phone number and asked him to call to make the arrangements. Everett never did get back in touch with Smith.

'We had a really nice conversation and I was excited about writing with him,' says Everett. 'It's a great regret of mine it never happened but I was also aware things were going awry for him and he didn't look so great.

'From early on knowing Elliott, I didn't know if he was made for surviving this world. From what I heard, his childhood was quite horrific and ultimately, I have to think it's the biggest culprit in his story. I was always insecure, and I still am, from my own childhood issues. To me, Elliott seemed so fragile it was almost like he was someone from another world.'

CHAPTER 27

Tick, Tick, Tick . . .

The New Year of 2003 began with Smith fretting over the two charges standing against him from his arrest at the Universal Amphitheatre. There was a court case now pending and with it, the very real threat of jail time. Smith was petrified by the prospect of incarceration. Another wave of paranoia swept over him as he speculated on the kinds of murderous characters he might have to face down in prison, imagining all the dangers and indignities he would be subjected to.

Such was his fearful, agitated mood going into his first show of the year, scheduled down the road at Spaceland on Sunday, 12 January. On the night, he showed up late at the Silver Lake club, appearing to onlookers dishevelled and distracted. His hair was greasy and matted. All down his left forearm, he had inked the words 'KALI the Destroyer' in dense blocks of indelible black marker pen. This wasn't body art he was practising, he had done it to cover up another trail of cigarette burns or other evidence of self-harm.

At Spaceland, he played a tentative set. He hadn't bothered to consult Scott Booker about the show, or even inform his supposed manager it was happening, but instead had Jennifer Chiba book it on his behalf.

'That really kind of bummed me out,' says Booker. 'Because it was, like, "You could have just let me know." The night of the gig, I had the manager of the club call me up saying, "Elliott's not here." I said to him, "Well, you know, you should've called me *before* you asked Elliott to play a show."

'After the Spaceland show, I told Elliott maybe he should just focus on making a record. I needed a break. It seemed like everything was getting messed up. I said to Elliott that when he was in a good place with his record to give me a call and I would work out all the deals and everything. It was the last time I ever spoke with him. I heard second-hand he was getting better, figured I'd get a call from him when he was ready, but it never happened. He had some publishing money coming in, so I knew he was going to be able to live fine for a bit. Personally, I never earned a penny from Elliott. I didn't really want to, he needed the money more than I did.'

Smith had lined up a couple of dates at an ornate '20s venue on Hollywood Boulevard, the Henry Fonda Theatre. He rehearsed for these in the small kitchen of the house on Lemoyne Street, accompanied by the faithful Robin Peringer on a solitary snare drum and a couple of ride cymbals. The actual shows were tense, edgy, uncomfortable affairs. Twelve hundred people were willing him on both nights, but the heights he had once scaled with such apparent ease were these days proving all too regularly beyond his reach. Yet again, he fluffed notes on his guitar and seemed befuddled by his own lyrics.

On the first night, 31 January, Smith told the Henry Fonda audience: 'I want to play new songs. They might seem dark . . . But no, I'm fine, really.' He looked anything but, appearing uncoordinated and diminished. For the whole of his set he stayed rooted to a stool, cradling his blue acoustic in his lap as if it were a shield and having apparently forgotten to bring along with him a guitar strap. Stage left, Robin Peringer was sat up next to him at his snare drum. Not so much a musical foil as a kind of human prop, a means of distracting attention from the faltering main attraction.

Halfway through the show a lone voice, a woman's, rang out at Smith from the stalls. 'Get a backbone!' she shouted out to him. Smith blinked back in the spotlights and mumbled a response. Friends of Smith's later speculated his assailant was none other than Valerie Deerin, snuck into the theatre in disguise, baring her scars in public and out for blood. Smith's appalling treatment of her, and the speed he had taken up with Jennifer Chiba, would have given her reason enough.

By then, pretty much anything was credible. As Smith had put it himself, he was living a distorted reality. That night at least, he again kept his own tell-tale, self-inflicted scars hidden from the audience. Once more, he had scrawled 'KALI the Destroyer' down his left forearm in thick black ink. It was an ominous omen.

In 2020, Dr Leah Quinlivan, in collaboration with three colleagues, published a paper detailing a strong link between persons who self-harmed and subsequent suicides. '[Self harm] increases the likelihood that the person will eventually die by suicide by between 50- and 100-fold above the rest of the population in a twelve-month period,' the paper outlined. It went on: 'A wide range of psychiatric conditions are associated with self-harm, such as . . . depression, bipolar disorder and drug-misuse and alcohol misuse disorders.'[33]

'All self-harm, irrespective of motive or intent, is associated with suicide,' says Dr Quinlivan. 'There is evidence to show the more someone repeats a self-harm, the more likely the person will die by suicide. In fact, it's the most strongly associated behaviour you can find to suicide.'

Chris Chandler was still away on tour, but arranged with Smith to have an engineer friend of his, Pete Magdaleno, cover for him. Magdaleno ran the sound at the Henry Fonda Theatre shows. He also set up Smith's studio for him so he could walk in and record at any time, with or without an engineer present. Smith had by now given his studio a name. He christened the place New Monkey, after the song he had cut during the sessions for *Either/Or*. He started to hole up at New Monkey for days at a time, grabbing whatever sleep he needed on a ratty old couch. When he wasn't in the studio, Smith was shut away in the Lemoyne Street house. The inside was almost as much of a mess as the untended front garden, a tangle of weeds and dead flowers. Smith had littered the front room with recording equipment. Jennifer Chiba was either tolerant of this latest intrusion or else close to her wits' end.

One night, a cold one for LA, Smith welcomed a writer into his sanctuary. Markus Kagler was preparing a cover feature on Smith for a new alternative music magazine, *Under the Radar*. The first major interview he had granted in three years, it was also the last one he would ever give. Kagler found Smith to be 'a rather shy and reserved man. He goes out of his way to avoid conflict. Elliott Smith is an odd person to talk to. When asked a question, Smith doesn't really answer it . . . lines of concentration contort his face. He speaks in very slow, almost deliberately childlike responses. He often loses his train of thought.'[34]

Kagler was able to coax some revelations from Smith. How he planned to call his new album *From a Basement on the Hill*, for one. Smith also told him his number-one priority was to establish a foundation for abused children. Reflecting on the gaping span of time since he had finished touring *Figure 8*, Smith said simply: 'Nothing was very good. It touches on drug use. I got caught up in that for almost two years. Then things got better about six months ago . . . I don't think it's important who I am. I really like playing music, but I don't really want to be anything in particular.'[35]

In February 2003, increasingly dissatisfied with the mixes Pete Magdaleno was overseeing, Smith turned again to David McConnell and arranged with him to go back out to Malibu. As before, he turned up at Satellite Park with his car laden with gear and his bags stuffed with clothes and books. The difference was both McConnell and his partner Josie Cotton thought he looked so much healthier than the previous time they had hosted him.

On this occasion the couple were putting him up in the guest house on their property. Smith wanted to start work with McConnell the next day, late on as usual. The following morning while Smith was still sleeping, McConnell got up to prepare the studio and tripped on the stairs, twisting his ankle and bending a toe backwards. By the time Smith eventually rose, McConnell was in agony. He told Smith he was going to have to postpone their sessions for a few days. Smith reacted badly to the news.

'Elliott didn't want to hear it,' says Josie Cotton. 'He didn't want to wait, so he packed up and left the same day. Looking back, I really think him and David would have finished the record together in the end. Elliott left behind all his mixes, his notes and his master tapes. Why would he do that if he wasn't planning on coming back?'

'All I had was Elliott's word he would give me a flat $50,000 when the album came out and I never did get paid,' says McConnell. 'Elliott did give me a guitar, one of his favourites, a Gibson S 3-30. He basically said, "Yeah, it could be a while before I'm able to pay you, so I want you to have this." When he died, his family asked me for it back, so I didn't even end up with his guitar.'

On 4 March, Smith's lawyer, Ed Rucker, filed a not-guilty plea on his behalf to the charges brought against him by the LAPD. Smith didn't personally attend the court hearing. He was hardly in a fit state to. In a scattershot fashion, he had resumed work at New Monkey with Fritz Michaud on the board, or else at home in Lemoyne Street. Monday nights, he was still trooping down the hill to the Short Stop. Greg Dulli arrived at his bar one night in March to find him in a fearful state.

'I came in and someone told me Elliott was in the back there and I should maybe go check on him,' recalls Dulli. 'He was not alone, there were several people with him. There was a manic paranoia about him, which was alarming to me. He was saying the record company were stealing his songs. He didn't seem like he was in a very good place. Probably it was the last time I saw him.'

On 3 May 2003, Smith travelled to Austin, Texas, to play a benefit gig for a local musician and schoolteacher, Glynn Allen Owens, who had died on 2 April of spinal meningitis at just thirty. The show was arranged by Jennifer Chiba's brother, Alex, who was living in Austin. It was Smith's first appearance in Texas for the better part of three years and he performed to a packed house at a club on Sixth Street, the Steamboat, wrapping his eighteen-song set with a cover of Paul McCartney's 'Blackbird'. He appears to have got through the show without incident, by then almost a triumph in itself.

Back in LA, Smith ran into Rob Schnapf one night at Spaceland. Schnapf spotted him sitting in a corner of the club, nursing a beer. He went over, took the beer out of his hand and gathered him up in a hug, then proceeded to sit down with Smith and to tell him a few home truths, how he had hurt so many of the people who loved him.

'We actually kind of cleared the air,' says Schnapf. 'He listened, he heard me. Afterwards, he tried to call me but I was out of town. He called me maybe two weeks before he died. I didn't call him back.'

In June, Smith undertook a run of six shows over on the East Coast. The first was a return to Maxwell's in Hoboken on a Thursday night, 5 June. He had Aaron Espinoza's band, Earlimart, open for him. Short of a dressing room or backstage, the musicians hung out down in the cellar of the bar, sat on beer kegs.

'It was fun and Elliott was very sweet,' recalls Espinoza. 'He said to us, "You guys were so great tonight. How much did we pay you?" I told him we had got $500, well paid for an opening band, but he was like, "Oh no, no, you've got to take more." He started trying to hand out money to us. It was the kind of thing he would do all the time. His booking agent, Ellen, intervened. She said to him, "Elliott, it's fine. This is business, it's all been taken care of."'

The next night, Smith revisited another of his old stomping grounds, Brooklyn, to play the Northsix club. On Saturday, 7 June he drove through the Lincoln Tunnel and back into New Jersey for an altogether bigger event, the Field Day Festival at Giants Stadium, East Rutherford.

At the show, Smith seemed incongruous, out of place, sat up there on a vast stage before a gawking stadium crowd in the middle of the afternoon, yet he temporarily recovered his bearings. The huge crowd hushed as he dug into his ten-song set. He sang soft, his fingers finding all the right notes. The years rolled back to any one of the many nights of his pomp. The other acts on the bill – Beck, Radiohead, Bright Eyes – congregated in the wings to watch him play, catching him now when he was the magic man just once more.

★

Jennifer Chiba had joined a punkish all-girl band, Happy Ending. They had struck a deal to make a single for a small indie label in the UK, Org Records. As soon as he returned to LA, Smith put himself forward to produce the track for them. The sessions commenced at New Monkey in the first weeks of summer 2003 and were to drag on for the next three months. The atmosphere in the studio soon turned toxic, Smith at loggerheads with the rest of the band and Chiba caught in the crossfire. Even after Happy Ending were done with the recording, Smith refused to let go of their song, remixing it over and again, never hearing it right.

Speaking in 2004 about his experience with Smith and Happy Ending, Sean Worrall, owner of Org Records, said: 'One of the girls in the band broke into Elliott's studio, took the tapes and sent them to me. Then it really went off. People started yelling. I was pretty much like, "Let's just shelve it." The worst thing that ever happened to Happy Ending was Elliott getting involved, to be honest . . . People described Elliott and Jennifer as a Sid and Nancy couple, constantly arguing, splitting up and getting back together again.'[36]

Late one night around the same time, Smith brought a couple of friends back with him from the studio to the Lemoyne Street house. He left them in the kitchen while he went off to talk with Chiba in the living room. An argument broke out between the two of them. Chiba ran and locked herself in the bathroom. When his friends slipped out of the house, Smith was at the bathroom door, pleading with her to come out.

'Jennifer Chiba has been painted by a lot of people who don't know anything about her in an unfavourable way,' says Scott McPherson. 'To me, she was one of the best things ever to happen to Elliott. I know she loved him so much and she went through so much, too. She needs to be hugged. Who else was going to nurture someone *that* sick? Normally, a healthy person would have to get themselves out of a situation like that, because it was just insane.'

On 3 July 2003, Smith turned up to court in downtown Los Angeles to plead no contest to the charges of assaulting a police officer and disturbing the peace. He was sentenced to eighty hours' community service and fined $150. He would not be going to jail.

On the 29th, Dorien Garry arrived in Los Angeles to do a show with a band she had begun playing with, Ted Leo and the Pharmacists. On the afternoon of their gig, Garry visited Smith at the Lemoyne Street house. She was struck at first by how positive and upbeat he sounded. Smith told Garry he was planning to have a child with Jennifer Chiba and of his determination to be completely clean and sober before becoming a father. However, the longer he went on talking, the more Garry became scared. Smith revealed to her his intention to not only come off all of the prescription drugs he was still taking, but to do so in one fell swoop and without consulting his doctors. Going completely cold turkey, the risks to a habitual, long-term and heavy drug user were dangerously high.

'At this point, rightfully so, Elliott had a growing mistrust of the medical profession and doctors,' says Garry. 'He had gotten pretty heavily medicated under the watch of doctors. The fucked-up flipside was he was also Elliott, which is to say stubborn and impatient. He was like, "I want to do this and I want to do it my way," which was totally frightening. The biggest part of our conversation was me pleading with him. Like, "I know how you feel. I know this sucks and I hear you, but you have one last thing to do with these doctors, which is to follow their advice for weening off all this shit. You can't just do it yourself. It could have terrible repercussions."

'I don't know for sure if this was part of it, but I think there had already been a little bit of him trying to tell his doctors he wanted off his medication and having pushback from them. That might have set things up for more of a fight from him. Whatever the case, he went and did it his way. If Elliott didn't want to do something, you couldn't make him. He was on so much medication my belief is it put him straight into a state of psychosis.'

'On the kinds of medications Smith was taking, his body wouldn't have had to produce healthy levels of serotonin or dopamine for so long because he was artificially adding them into his system,' says chartered psychologist Dr Rachel Gillibrand. 'You can self-medicate to the point your brain no longer functions in a healthy way. The body also can't instantly start reproducing the natural level of neuro chemicals it would have typically. To come straight off everything completely, your body would go into shock. Psychosis could be a result of that. The withdrawal, I think, would be vile.'

The day of his thirty-fourth birthday, 6 August 2003, Smith enacted his plan, coming off all his psych meds at once. At the same time, he also swore off alcohol, caffeine, sugar, red meat and cigarettes. This, too, ran counter to standard medical advice and practice. For an addict trying to kick their habit, a drink, a smoke, or a shot of caffeine is seen as a powerful crutch, a means towards them coping with their withdrawals.

'Oh God, that can't have helped,' says Dr Leah Quinlivan. 'It sounds as if he was really trying to get himself back in line. But going through all the withdrawals and also taking away every other coping source, he would have been pretty much in a vacuum.'

In the place of these coping sources, Chiba mixed him a smoothie made of green Kava plants. The debilitating effects of Smith's extreme withdrawal, though, soon became glaringly apparent. According to Chiba's later account, his moods veered dramatically. He grew anxious, agitated. He told her he was starting to recall events from his childhood, supressed memories, the worst secrets and the ones he had buried the deepest. One night in mid-September, Chiba recalled, she returned home to find him curled up in their bed, sobbing.

'I pulled back the covers and he had a knife in the bed, and his arm was all cut up,' Chiba said. 'I called a psychiatrist and made the next possible appointment, and we went . . . The doctor rec-ommended he go in-patient somewhere. Go off everything in a safe environment, a medically controlled environment, and then start over and figure what he actually needed. And Elliott was like, "No hospital, no hospital."[37]

On 19 September, Chiba arranged a solo show for Smith at the University of Utah. He performed clean and sober for the first time in years and for the final time altogether. The last words he would ever sing to a live audience were George Harrison's from the Beatles' 'Long, Long, Long': 'How I want you . . . Oh, I love you.'

CHAPTER 28

Curtain Call

However adrift he ever got, whatever storms were baying, the music remained Smith's safe harbour. He moored himself to it again now, something solid to hold on to through the turbulence of his withdrawals. At New Monkey, he began to sift through the more than fifty songs he had collated on tape and hard drive over the past two and a half years, mulling on which ones to include on *From a Basement on the Hill*.

The stockpile included the tracks he had put down with David McConnell, Chris Chandler and Fritz Michaud. Songs from before then he had recorded in Rob Schnapf's garage and with Jon Brion. Others he had put down himself at the Disney cottage, or in the house on Lemoyne Street. Still more he had cut with Aaron Espinoza and other friends and even one or two stretching back to the *Either/Or* sessions with Schnapf and Tom Rothrock. As a whole, it was both the litany of his recent life and a testament to his whole being.

Smith continued to record new material at New Monkey, too, with Fritz Michaud and he also started up a round of rehearsals at the studio with a new band he assembled. Robin Peringer was on bass, Ariana Murray of Earlimart on keyboards and Shon Sullivan and Scott McPherson alternated on drums. Together, they set about working up Smith's motherlode of new songs, readying for a tour never to happen.

'Elliott was kind of back and present,' recalls Scott McPherson. 'His mind wasn't working against him. The fact of him cleaning up was really happening. For the first time, I actually had hope for him. He was in a different place to when he wrote those songs. He would have the lyrics on a stand next to him and he would be like, "I can't even sing these words." He would cross them out. It was almost like he'd woken up.'

On Smith's reels and discs, there was a surfeit of instrumental tracks. All of them unfinished songs awaiting his vocals and which his voice, scorched to a husk from smoking crack, hadn't previously been up to. Eager to get these tracks over the line, he turned to Larry Crane. He'd had very little contact with Crane over the past few years and was apprehensive about calling him. Too anxious, in fact, to pick up the phone himself and so instead he had Jennifer make the overture to Crane. Chiba asked Crane if he would be open to the idea of coming to LA at the end of October 2003 to run vocal sessions with Smith at New Monkey. Crane was reticent at first.

'I was worried about going down there because of the stories I'd heard,' Crane says. 'I said to Jennifer Chiba, "Look, I don't want to come down and waste my time. If I show up and he's not in working shape, you're going to have to pay me and I'm leaving." I was very much living moment to moment back then and it could just have destroyed me. Eventually, Elliott came on the phone. I said to him, "I don't want to find you're strung out." I was told I wouldn't get left holding the bag. Of course, as it happened, I didn't get to go down there at all.'

But Crane wasn't the only old friend Smith reached out to. He spoke with Sean Croghan, told him how he was thinking of asking Jennifer Chiba to marry him. One day, during band rehearsals, Smith had even excused himself from the studio to go shopping for an engagement ring. From their own contacts with Smith, each of Garrick Duckler, Autumn de Wilde and Tony Lash would speak later of their impressions of him being more steadied at the time, not so much in harm's way. To so many of the people who knew him the best, it was as if he had a renewed purpose.

'People who experience severe depression actually do come out of it, but that's when they're at most risk,' says Dr Rachel Gillibrand. 'At bottom, they haven't the energy or willpower to do anything at all. There's much more likely to be something like a suicide attempt as the person starts to get better.

'For one thing, they have got the psychological capacity to think of doing it. For another, other people start to leave them alone. They forget about any of the cares they've been doing, such as hiding knives or pills, so there's opportunity. Then there is also the fear of ending up in a depression again, an, "I don't want to go back there" feeling. It's the hardest thing for other people to deal with, because when somebody is really, *really* low, it almost makes sense. You kind of think, "Okay, I get it."'

'Suicidal thinking and distress can also fluctuate,' says Dr Leah Quinlivan. 'Someone may feel well, but then drop and start to experience suicidal thinking again. Some suicide attempts may involve careful planning, but others may be decided quickly or impulsively and be facilitated by easy access to means.'

There were other stories swirling around about Smith at the same time, ugly rumours and bleaker conjectures. In their telling, he was beginning to slip and slide back into older habits. Conceivably, these may have arisen from misinterpretations of his mental state. On not knowing about, or else fully appreciating the potentially massive destructive force he had set upon himself from so recklessly junking all of his medications. One tale had him appearing outside of Largo on a weekday at noon, banging on the door of the club and begging to be let inside. In this account, Smith was in an agitated, sweaty, paranoid state, convinced there were drug dealers pursuing him in a car.

One thing is for certain, Smith was running from something he wasn't ever able to shake. The hauntings of his childhood, the spectre of his stepfather and of all the things he believed he had been subjected to at the hands of Charlie Welch. Nothing has ever been proven and whatever happened did so out of anyone else's sight, but neither was it ever out of Smith's mind.

In an article published in *Spin* magazine in December 2004, journalist Liam Gowing reported Smith had finally confronted his mother with his belief he had been sexually abused by his stepfather during a telephone conversation with Bunny Welch on the occasion of her sixtieth birthday, 30 September 2003. 'Incredulous, she suggested they spend the upcoming Thanksgiving holiday together in LA,' Gowing wrote. 'And so the two men could discuss Smith's allegations face to face.'[38] Dorien Garry contends Smith raised the matter much earlier, with other members of his family at least, and when he was still lodging at her apartment in New Jersey.

'Elliott went to his family and said, "I want to talk about this, I want to be heard, I want validation in what was done to me,"' says Garry. 'For the most part, everybody just pushed him out and told him to go away. I don't even think it was an apology he was looking for, I think he just wanted to be believed by the people who were supposed to take care of him. And they failed him, which is a gigantic thing when you're a child. For a long time I felt very protective of this story and Elliott's relationship to his family. In recent years I've gotten angrier both at the situation and then also at myself for feeling like I'm the secret keeper.

'Because fuck that and fuck them. In my mind at this point, there are people in Elliott's family who are totally responsible for his death. He might not be the happiest man on the planet, he might still have a lot of shit he carried around with him, but I believe he would be here still if certain people in his family had not abused him the way they did. I mean, he told me he suffered physical, emotional and sexual abuse and I believed him 100 per cent. I believed him from when he first spoke to me about it and I believe him to this day. I don't know how humans come back from, or survive that. They do, obviously, but it's what broke Elliott.'

★

Late on the Sunday afternoon of 12 October, Smith went into New Monkey, Jennifer Chiba at his side, and cut his lead vocal track for 'King's Crossing'. His voice was still rougher around the edges than it had once been, chipped like old paintwork, but the finished track was magnificent. The song bloomed from a chatter of disconnected voices into a swirling, kaleidoscopic head rush.

'I can't prepare for death any more than I already have . . . Give me one good reason not to do it.' He could not have been any more explicit.

'It's stunning to me when I look back now – it was all right there in front of me,' says Aaron Espinoza. 'I think, "What the fuck was I doing?" I feel like I just didn't have the tools. I don't know how many times you need to talk about suicide, or abuse, for someone to believe you. Look at the whole of that record. Elliott's talking about killing himself. It was right there in front of all of us.'

On 16 October, Smith met up with film director Mike Mills. Smith had agreed to contribute three songs to the new movie Mills was preparing, *Thumbsucker* (2005), a pitch-black comedy, one a cover of an old Cat Stevens' tune, 'Trouble'. He put in a call, too, to Aaron Espinoza. Smith hadn't been in touch with Espinoza for some time, but he was angling to do some vocal tracks over at his studio, the Ship.

'For some reason, I had been off the call list again,' says Espinoza. 'I'd left Elliott messages, but he hadn't been calling me back. Earlimart were about to go off on tour and I thought, "Fuck him, I'm not going to answer his call. Let's see how he feels." He left me an awesome message, but I decided to play it out a little bit. A couple of days later, I left town with the band.'

The next day, the 17th, Smith received in the mail a typewritten letter from Charlie Welch. The letter was an acknowledgement from Welch of his deficiencies as a father and an apology. According to Smith's half-sister, Ashley Welch, 'Elliott really took it to heart, but it allowed him some closure. I think Elliott really appreciated that, and I think it helped.'[39]

Aaron Sperske ran into Smith on the evening of the 19th at a neighbourhood sushi joint. Smith and Jennifer Chiba were out together having a meal. A couple of weeks prior, Sperske had gone over to New Monkey to borrow some guitar cables from Smith. On that occasion, Smith had given him the gospel of his newfound sobriety. When Sperske went over to say hello to Smith and Chiba in the restaurant, Smith immediately offered him a beer.

'I was, like, "Are you sure this is good?"' says Sperske. 'Elliott said, "Oh, I'm fine. I just have one hit here and there to calm my nerves. I'm not doing anything else."'

With both of Ariana Murray and Scott McPherson going off on the Earlimart tour, Smith put the band rehearsals on hold. They would reconvene in mid-November, he told the group. In the meantime, he meant to carry on putting down his absent vocal tracks at New Monkey. He had a new sense of urgency about getting the record done. Having sunk the greater part of his remaining savings into the studio, he needed to be back on the road and working, too.

The evening of the 20th, he went into the studio to add vocals to a track he had originally started out on at Abbey Road during the very first sessions for *Figure 8*. He had just recently rediscovered 'Tiny Time Machine', having initially abandoned it for sounding too much like a George Harrison song. The musical track was upbeat, engaging, and he had written a fresh set of lyrics. He put his lead vocal down fast. These were the last couple of takes he would ever record. When he was done, he logged the song under the new title he had also given it, 'Suicide Machine'. The final lines Smith sang in a recording studio were these: 'But everybody's trying to turn me into a suicide machine. Everybody's trying to turn me into a suicide machine.'

On Tuesday, 21 October, Smith and Chiba both had medical appointments scheduled. Chiba was due to see her doctor for a check-up and later the same afternoon, Smith had a session booked with a psychiatric therapist. Neither of these dates was kept. The only living person able to testify to what actually transpired between the two of them on that fateful day is Chiba. According to her 2019 account to film-maker Gil Reyes, Smith woke up earlier than usual and in a fitful, aggravated state. He had been fretting over his mother's and stepfather's impending visit for Thanksgiving and couldn't get his mind in order. They were soon running late for Chiba's doctor's appointment. Neighbours on Lemoyne Street heard a loud argument break out in the house around noon.

'We were arguing about several things,' Chiba said. 'One being . . . I had said out loud in the house what our plans were for the day. [Elliott] was angry at me, because he thought the house was bugged. He would go in and out of this kind of paranoia. It didn't make sense to me. I just needed a break. I needed some reality. I mean, I felt like I was going crazy myself.'[40]

As she had done during a previous argument witnessed by friends, Chiba said she fled from the kitchen and went and locked herself in the bathroom. Smith, she said, followed her and once more began to knock on the bathroom door, apologising profusely and begging her to come out. Chiba refused to open the door. The house fell silent. Five, ten minutes at most passed. Then, Chiba told Reyes, 'I just heard this horrible noise from the kitchen. I came out of the bathroom, went to the kitchen and he was standing at the kitchen sink with his back to me. I just knew something was awful.'[41]

When Smith turned towards her, Chiba recalled, she saw he had a kitchen knife sticking out of his chest, embedded to the hilt. Reflexively, she said, she pulled the knife out. Chiba described how Smith ran past her, out onto their balcony, where he collapsed, blood pouring freely from his unplugged wound. At 12.38 p.m., Chiba made an emergency 911 call. Smith was still clinging to life when the ambulance arrived at the scene. He was rushed to the LA County Hospital on the University of Southern California campus, 6 miles south and an eight-minute drive at speed from Lemoyne Street.

A friend of Chiba's alerted Smith's half-sister, Ashley Welch, who also dashed to the house. By the time Welch got to Lemoyne

Street, police officers were already in attendance and in the process of questioning Chiba inside the house. Chiba presented the officers with a Post-it note she had left stuck up in the kitchen for Smith to read. Underneath her message to him, Smith had apparently written: 'I'm so sorry – love Elliott. God forgive me'.

Ashley Welch hurried on to LA County Hospital. At the hospital, she pleaded in vain to be allowed to see her half-brother. He was in surgery, the attending doctors battling in vain to save his life. Smith was pronounced dead at 1.30 p.m. and from not one but two lacerating knife wounds to his chest. It was an hour later when Chiba finally made it to the hospital. She had changed out of her blood-stained clothes and was wearing an Elliott Smith T-shirt.

Chris Chandler was with Steve Drozd and Wayne Coyne of the Flaming Lips, backstage at the Key Arena in Seattle, preparing to open another show for the Red Hot Chili Peppers, when a friend called to tell him the news. The band went onstage within minutes. Wayne Coyne announced Smith's death to the Seattle audience and dedicated a song to him.

On tour with his band Earlimart in Columbus, Missouri, Aaron Espinoza fielded a series of phone calls, refusing to believe the substance of any of them, until he turned on the TV in his hotel room and watched an *MTV News* report of Smith's death. Espinoza still hadn't returned the call he had got from Smith five days earlier.

Pete Krebs was playing an early-evening show at an English pub, the Moon and Sixpence, up in Portland when he also took a call from a friend. 'He said he'd just heard Elliott had died,' says Krebs. 'I said thank you and I sat down and had a shot of Irish whiskey, because that's what the two of us would always drink. It was kind of my wake for Elliott.'

Sean Croghan was at his grandmother's funeral in Boise, Idaho, when Neil Gust phoned from Portland to tell him Smith was gone. As soon as she got the news, Allison Wolfe put in a call to Dorien Garry in New York. 'Dorien was crying so hard she couldn't speak, or hardly even breathe,' recalls Wolfe.

The date – 21 October – also happened to be the birthday of Rob Schnapf's and Margaret Mittleman's son, Sonny. It was four years to the day since Schnapf had passed the long hours waiting for his wife to give birth, wandering the hospital corridors with Smith.

For those closest to Smith, everyone who loved him so dearly, the extent of their reckoning was almost immeasurable. They had not only the numbing shock of his passing and their own shuddering grief to contend with, but also to weigh the immensity of his pain and then again to make sense and find a reason for the appalling, unfathomable circumstances of his death. So much of a tally, however could anyone not leap for an answer, stretch for a scenario to fit? Something, anything perhaps, but for the awful truth.

'What we're talking about is the darkest possible place somebody could be in,' says Dr Leah Quinlivan. 'And some of the things people do in the midst of such darkness are unimaginable.'

CHAPTER 29

Aftermath

The week following Smith's death, Gary Smith held a memorial service for his only son at the family home he and Marta Greenwald had moved to in north-west Portland. The right side of the city tracks now. Smith's body was cremated and his ashes shared between his father, his mother, Bunny, and his half-sister, Ashley Welch. The service at the Greenwald-Smith house was a small, sombre affair for close family and Smith's Portland friends – Sean Croghan, Pete Krebs and Jason Mitchell among them. The mourners congregated out on the backyard patio. Gary Smith was beside himself with grief.

Two days later, Martyn Leaper, who sang with Joanna Bolme's band, the Minders, hosted a second and bigger gathering for Smith in Portland. Jennifer Chiba flew in from LA with Aaron Embry to attend the second memorial. It passed off more like an old-school Portland house party and with everyone spilling out into Leaper's backyard. There was, though, an undercurrent to the proceedings. Whirling eddies of anguish, anger and despair, both felt for and also directed at Smith. It was the sum of all of their grievances and confusions at how he had left them behind, when he had departed Portland in the first place and now for good. Sam Coomes stayed away. Several of the guests cold-shouldered Chiba as if she were the totem of his undoing, the lightning rod for his wreck and ultimate ruin.

'People didn't have the best feelings towards her,' says Pete Krebs, who also attended the Leaper gathering. 'She tried to talk with folks and a lot of them just didn't want to deal with her. It made the whole thing so much more surreal, to have the one person who was there when Elliott died at a wake for his friends. I don't even know who would have invited her.

'At some point, she and I got into conversation. I was drunk. I was probably one of the few people there that was nice to her. She kind of poured her heart out to me. Honestly, I felt like I was getting her side of the story and her intention was to set the narrative a little bit. I never saw or spoke to her again.'

On 3 November, a tribute concert was held for Smith in LA, back at the Henry Fonda Theatre. Among the artists performing covers of Smith's songs on the night were Beck, Rilo Kiley, John Doe of X and Beth Orton. The proceeds from the show were donated to organisations helping abused children. Beck, Smith's closest contemporary in so many aspects, yet so self-assured-seeming he was like his polar opposite, sang 'Clementine'. The words Smith wrote out eight years past sounded right there and then like his own epitaph to himself, an apology for all he was and everything he could never put right: 'You drank yourself in slo-mo, made an angel in the snow . . . Oh, my darling, Clementine, dreadfully sorry.'

On 6 January 2004, an otherwise ordinary Tuesday, LA Deputy Medical Examiner Lisa Scheinin published her autopsy report into Smith's death. Scheinin's text was dry, considered, understated, but also proved explosive. The spark was contained in the second paragraph of her report, in which she stated the cause of Smith's death was 'undetermined at this time.' Noting the absence of hesitation wounds to his chest and making no definitive judgement on whether Smith had stabbed himself or not, Scheinin recorded an open verdict. The LAPD investigation into his death was also to remain open. Summing up, Scheinin qualified: 'The undetermined node is NOT an indictment of the girlfriend.' Yet this much was wholly lost in the furore of conspiracy theories and accusations her report generated at the time and persist to this day.

One outlandish-sounding theory, rooted no doubt in the gossiping of Smith's paranoid appearance at Largo that noon day in September 2003, posited he was slain by drug dealers breaking into the Lemoyne Street house and as retribution for unpaid debts. However, the overwhelming weight of alternative theory was brought to bear and remains visited upon Jennifer Chiba. The small, incised wounds noted by Scheinin on Smith's right arm and left hand were taken by the conspiracy theorists to be defence wounds, no matter his history of self-harm. The fact of Chiba pulling the knife from Smith's chest was perceived as damning evidence of her guilt, rather than her sheer, blind panic.

The Post-it note Chiba presented to police officers at the scene gave rise to yet another theory. There were claims Smith's Christian name was misspelt on the note and so it read, 'I'm so sorry – love Elliot. God forgive me'. Doubts cast as to whether he himself could ever have made such a mistake. In fact, there was no such error on the actual note. The missing 't' was a slip in the coroner's report.

In the immediate aftermath of Scheinin's report, Chiba went on the defensive, telling *MTV News* how Smith's family 'knew the truth'. The Smith family's response was quick and devastating. On 14 January, the attorney hired by the family to act as executor of Smith's estate, Conrad Rippy, issued a statement on their behalf. Rippy stated, 'Elliott's family has every confidence the ongoing police investigation will determine the actual circumstances of Smith's death.' For good measure, he qualified, 'Neither Elliott's family or anyone else can claim to know "the truth" about Elliott's death, and any statement to the contrary mischaracterises the family's position.'

Taking shelter from the storm blowing up around her, Chiba fled LA for New York, where she hid out at the house of a friend, the comedian David Cross. The sheer volume of people using the Happy Ending band website to direct death threats at Chiba forced Org Records to shut it down completely. An LA music writer and fan of Smith's, Alysson Camus, started up another, campaigning website, Justice for Elliott Smith, upon which she continues to cite Chiba as the chief, and only, suspect for his killing. In the intervening years, the opinions of Smith's friends and associates have either split down the middle, for and against Chiba, or else occupy a muddled territory in the space between these two points, conflicting and conflicted as Smith was himself.

Garrick Duckler remains convinced Jennifer Chiba murdered Smith. He wrote me: 'There was really no indication that Elliot was any more suicidal than he ever was, but there is a tonne of evidence this was another – and most extreme – instance of how, throughout his life, Elliott would pull for being attacked, especially by the people who he got to love him . . . Most of us, of course, didn't resort to knifing him . . . '

Both Aaron Embry and Scott McPherson, however, are just as firm in their advocating for Chiba's version of events. Embry says, 'Jennifer told me the entire story and I believe her every word. We all knew what happened. It wasn't the first time Elliott tried to do that.' McPherson notes, 'Elliott was tough, he could take the pain. He could take the punches. It makes complete sense to me that the way he did it would be so painful to his own self.'

Even at a remove of twenty years, neither of Scott Booker nor Pete Krebs has resolved the matter in their own minds one way or another. 'I'm not convinced Elliott committed suicide,' says Booker. 'To stab yourself in the heart . . . Would I put it past Elliott to *say* he would do that? No. Do I believe he had been suicidal before? Absolutely. Was I surprised when I heard he'd committed suicide? No. I mean, he had said he would kill himself if he didn't get off DreamWorks.

'All the indications I got from the people I knew around him at the time were he was in a pretty good place right then. But I'm not a therapist, or doctor. I'm not saying Jennifer Chiba did it either. I don't know, it just seemed weird to me.'

'The way Elliott supposedly died didn't square with me at all,' says Krebs, too. 'Some sort of suicide wouldn't have surprised me, but that scenario . . . I still don't really understand how it happened. It still doesn't make sense to me.

'From what I understood, Elliott and Jennifer fought a lot. I could see Elliott, if he was really strung out, or whacked out on this or that, not dealing with reality too well. But he must have been really out of his mind . . . I've never really bought the story, but as grisly as it sounds, there is some poetic symbolism in the idea of Elliott stabbing himself in the heart.'

There are these and so many more countering opinions just like them and others besides. Two decades' worth of convictions without conclusive proof, questions to which no answers are forthcoming. Except for the fact that, in 2013, Lisa Scheinin, expanding upon her autopsy judgment, wrote to the author William Todd Schultz: 'It would have been much easier to call it a suicide, but I do not call anything a suicide unless I am absolutely certain. If there is anything irregular, I am constrained to be cautious.'[42] This, and also another salient fact of the LAPD never yet having found sufficient evidence to bring charges against Jennifer Chiba, or anyone else in connection with the death of Elliott Smith.

Then again, there is the body of Smith's own work to take into account. The unbridgeable span of his own pain, and of the torments visited upon him, measured in the words he wrote and sang, set down on record and disc, the indelible, immutable artefacts of his suffering. Put out there, shared, admitted to, foretold, blatant and obvious. The hardest of truths, impossible still for any of us to fully comprehend, much less accept, and so instead we look away, seek other justifications and perspectives.

'In the case of suicides, there's a thing some people who knew the person tend to do, which is a biographical reconstruction,' says Dr Leah Quinlivan. 'People will reconstruct the biography to develop a narrative about why the person has died and to try to understand why this thing has happened. Often in this narrative, there's a player who has to take responsibility. Sometimes it's another family member, or an employer. And other times it's the partner.'

EPILOGUE

Legacy

The turbulences of Elliott Smith's life carried on even into his death. Time didn't, and hasn't healed the deepest cuts. As soon as July of 2004, Jennifer Chiba filed a claim in the LA Supreme Court against Smith's estate for 15 per cent of his earnings from August 2002 and up to his passing. During this time, Chiba contended she had an oral agreement with him to act as his manager and agent. Four months later, Chiba filed a second complaint against the Smith family, claiming they had breached another promise Smith made to her, which was for him to provide her with financial support for the rest of her life. In this second case, she sought damages of $1 million. In October of 2007, both cases were dismissed on appeal in a California appellate court.

To mark the first anniversary of Smith's death, Chiba hosted a Thanksgiving dinner for a group of Smith's LA friends at her new home in the city. It was, recalls Aaron Embry, 'a really beautiful evening. We all sat around the piano, playing songs we had listened to together with Elliott.' These days, she lives in Texas with her husband, Alex Whomsley. She returned to playing music with a three-piece band, Hello Menno. At the time of writing, their Facebook page has not been updated since August 2021 and at which point it had 155 'likes'. The LAPD investigation into Smith's death stays nominally open. For so long as it does, Chiba's version of the events at the Lemoyne Street house on the morning of Tuesday, 21 October 2003 will be doubted, contested and scorned.

'It became impossible for Jennifer to stay in LA,' says Embry. 'There was this question mark that wouldn't go away. With all she has been through, I don't really know how she's managed to cope.'

In the wake of his death, Smith's family set up a memorial fund in his name. To date, the Elliott Smith Memorial Fund has donated in excess of $50,000 to a non-profit organisation, Free Arts for Abused Children, based in Los Angeles. A 2021 post from the family to the *Sweet Adeline* website updated on the fund, stating: 'There are tons of other very worthy causes that we'd like you to know about . . . Elliott was vocal about helping abused kids.' In its original form, the post was signed off 'Charlie'. As of August 2022, the sign-off had been amended to 'Elliott's Family'.

On 18 October 2004, *From a Basement on the Hill* was finally released on ANTI- Records. Or at least, a version of the record Smith was still working on at the time of his death came out. Smith's family hired Rob Schnapf and Joanna Bolme to mix the tracks he had completed. Fifteen songs feature on the album, a single and not the double he had intended. Songs as wrenching as 'Strung Out Again', 'A Fond Farewell' and 'King's Crossing' made Schnapf's and Bolme's final cut, but not 'Suicide Machine'. Well-reviewed, *From a Basement on the Hill* in America became the highest-charting record of Smith's career, a top-twenty hit on the *Billboard* Hot 200. In the liner notes to the album, David McConnell was credited with 'additional recording', alongside the likes of Fritz Michaud, Jon Brion, Chris Chandler and Pete Magdaleno.

'The way Elliott and I would have mixed the record would've been different, but I think they did a great job with what they had,' McConnell says. 'Our version would have been mixed for headphones. Elliott and I would have done this crazy stereo imaging stuff we had been working on. We had figured out a way to do vocals that had never really been done before, where it sounded like his voice was in your head. It didn't get mixed that way, but that's okay. It's probably 90 per cent representative and still an incredible record.'

'David never could bring himself to destroy the masters, but I wish he had,' opines Josie Cotton, now separated from McConnell. 'He thought he would be robbing the world of something great.

'The family came for all of the recordings Elliott made with David and David just let them take them away. David felt bad for Elliott's mother. He never dreamed they wouldn't credit him as the main producer on the record. He trusted they would release the mixes Elliott wanted, but they didn't. I've heard people say it's the best record Elliott ever did, but it's not the record Elliott wanted. David was never the same afterwards. Eventually, he stopped making music altogether.'

Smith's music has kept on coming. Mike Mills' film, *Thumbsucker*, starring Keanu Reeves and Tilda Swinton, was eventually released in 2005, with Smith performing three songs on its soundtrack – his own 'Let's Get Lost' and his versions of Big Star's 'Thirteen' and Cat Stevens' 'Trouble'. The Stevens' track was one of the last he ever put down at New Monkey. On behalf of Smith's family, Larry Crane in 2007 curated a compilation album featuring twenty-four previously unreleased studio recordings made by Smith between 1994 and 1997. The album, *New Moon*, was released as a double by Kill Rock Stars.

A year ahead of *New Moon*, a three-disc bootleg appeared, compiling a treasure trove of unreleased tracks and alternate studio outtakes. *Grand Mal: Studio Rarities* employed the title Smith had originally intended for *XO* and extensively testified to his prodigious output and relentless meticulousness. This was even more the case when it later on appeared in an expanded format, ranging across eight CDs and a whopping 131 tracks. Among them were the quietly vengeful 'No Confidence Man', the aching 'True Love' and such final, immolating outpourings as 'Stick Man' and 'Suicide Machine'.

Ever since his death, too, Smith's reputation and influence has grown exponentially, year on year. At the time of his passing, his best-selling record was *XO*, which was nudging up towards 200,000 sales. Today, *XO* has sold more than 500,000 copies worldwide, but also, it's been overtaken by Smith's imperious third album, *Either/Or*, a record still never to have charted. The splendour of Smith's music, the sheer scale of his songwriting prowess has proven to be unique and unblemished, awe-inspiring like the most precious of jewels. His flame has been kept burning by disciples of singer-songwriters and bands. Artists such as Justin Vernon of Bon Iver, Phoebe Bridgers, Conor Oberst of Bright Eyes, Jenny Lewis, Julien Baker, Beirut and the National, all of whom continue to pay homage to, and preserve the essence of, his sound.

A multiple Grammy Award winner, Phoebe Bridgers has described herself as an 'Elliott Smith nerd'. On the title track to her garlanded second album of 2020, *Punisher*, Bridgers imagines a conversation between herself and Smith at the site of the old *Figure 8* Sound Solutions mural on Sunset Boulevard, which fast became a place of pilgrimage for Smith's fans. On the song, as hushed, haunted and delicately rendered as one of Smith's own, Bridgers sings: 'Hear so many stories of you at the bar. Most times alone and some looking your worst – but never not sweet.'

'His music is like the Beatles to me, and I mean that in every way,' Bridgers said soon after *Punisher* came out. 'If someone doesn't like his music, I actually feel like I'm not going to agree with them about anything . . . *Figure 8* totally feels like something that could come out today and everybody would freak out. But, also, I think music would sound a lot different if it hadn't come out. *My* music would definitely sound different.'

★

In totality, Smith released just five full-length solo albums during his lifetime and one posthumously. Three of these records are undeniable masterpieces – *Either/Or*, *Figure 8* and *From a Basement on the Hill*. Taking *New Moon* also into account, over 100 of Smith's songs have officially come out and not a single duff one among them. So many of them continue to resonate, to strike chords and touch hearts. Smith mined some of the darkest and most impenetrable recesses of the human condition and time and again, made something beautiful and exquisite out of the rawest materials he excavated.

'I did feel like because he took his own life, or whatever it was happened, that it took so long for Elliott to be redeemed,' says Margaret Mittleman, still his champion. 'That's the hardest part. It was as if it was, like, "See, we all told you. We all knew this was where it was going to go." That really hurt me.

'No, that wasn't where it was supposed to go. I really didn't think it would end up the way it did. I felt bad for his career, and his talent. It was the wrong message, the wrong outcome. I couldn't even play his music for a very long time. It's still very hard for me to play it in the house.'

Therein lies the heartbreak of Elliott Smith's story. There is the magnificence of his music, his wonder and glory. How even amid the excruciating pain he was fighting against, the agonies he felt to his bones, the immensity of his talent rose and stood tall. It will go on shining, too, a secret treasure awaiting discovery and to be pored over and passed on from one generation to the next. Because incontestably, Smith was, and will remain, one of the true, all-time greats in his field. A near-peerless soul apart. Then again, there is also the fact of his legacy, like his life, being so compacted and horribly ended. Nothing like as much of it as there should have been. So much he could have gone on and brought into the world, but never will. An overriding sense of tragedy and of sheer, hopeless waste.

New Monkey, too, has survived Smith. In August 2004, two friends, Joel Graves, who had played with Aaron Espinoza in Earlimart, and his friend and business partner Robert Cappadona, bought Smith's precious studio from his family. They continue to run it to this day out of Valley Center Studios, just off Van Nuys Boulevard. The old Triad Trident A-Range console is still there, fully operational now. Graves and Cappadona have also preserved several other vintage items from Smith's collection, as well as the last Post-it notes he left stuck up around the place as reminders to his self, trace elements of the work he left unfinished.

Aaron Espinoza, Ariana Murray and Scott McPherson were among the first clients to book into New Monkey under its new regime. Jim Fairchild of Grandaddy has made a couple of pilgrimages to record there, along with his wife, Natasha.

'It's like we're somehow able to extend Elliott's memory, and his legacy,' says Fairchild. 'If you're lucky to have affected people's lives like Elliott did, there's still that energy people carry around with them and it spreads out in the world. That's what immortality is, right?'

ACKNOWLEDGEMENTS

This book would simply not have been possible without . . .

My representative on earth, Matthew Hamilton. Pete Selby, the most attentive publisher. My wonderful editor, Melissa Bond. And everyone at Nine Eight Books.

For their time and graciousness in sharing their memories and insights with me: Kevin Denbow; Tony Lash; Pete Krebs; Larry Crane; Jason Mitchell; Janel Jarosz; Margaret Mittleman; Rob Schnapf; Greg Dulli; Mark 'E' Everitt; Jason Lytle; Jim Fairchild; Mike Doughty; David McConnell; Marie Tak; Megan Pickerel; Tim Foljahn; Allison Wolfe; Glynnis Fawkes; Bill Santen; Denny Swofford; Scott Booker; Chris Chandler; Joel Graves; Joey Waronker; Aaron Espinoza; Chris Slusarenko; Mark Buchanan; Josie Cotton; Aaron Embry; Andy Factor; Aaron Sperske; Scott McPherson; Andy Prevezer; Ted Cummings; Russell Warby; Dr Rachel Gillibrand and Dr Leah Quinlivan.

JJ Gonson, Garrick Duckler and Dorien Garry – for going above and beyond.

364

ACKNOWLEDGEMENTS

Jennifer Baichwal – for fact-checking and filling in the blanks.

My beloved Denise, Tom and Charlie – for their unending patience, tolerance and support.

Elliott Smith – for the gift of his music.

Thank you, thank you, a thousand times over, all of you.

Anyone feeling suicidal can call the following services for support:

Samaritans
Telephone: 116 123

Campaign Against Living Miserably (CALM)
Telephone: 0800 58 58 58

NOTES

1. Sourced from the documentary film *Heaven Adores You*, directed by Nickolas Rossi, 2014.

2. Sourced from 'You've Got to Hide Your Love Away' by R. J. Smith, *Spin*, February 2004.

3. Sourced from 'Pretty Barfly' by Keith Cameron, *NME*, 1 May 1999.

4. Sourced from 'What's New at Frisbee U?' by Chip Brown, *New York Times*, 10 June 1990.

5. Sourced from 'See You Later: Heatmiser Looks Back at Last' by David Greenwald, *The Oregonian*, 8 October 2012.

6. Sourced from 'He's Mr Dyingly Sad, and You're Mystifyingly Glad' by R. J. Smith, *Spin*, January 1999.

7. Sourced from 'Walkin' after Midnight' by M. Bates, *JIMZine*, November 1997.

8. Sourced from *Elliott Smith* by Autumn de Wilde, Chronicle Books, 2007.

9. Sourced from 'Elliott Smith: Better Off Than Dead' by Marcus Kagler, *Under the Radar*, March 2003.

10. Sourced from 'The Lost Boy' by Keith Cameron, *Q*, January 2011.

11. Sourced from *Torment Saint: The Life of Elliott Smith* by Professor William Todd Schultz, Bloomsbury Publishing PLC, 2013.

12. Sourced from 'Keep the Things You Forgot: An Elliott Smith Oral History' by Jayson Greene, *Pitchfork*, 21 October 2013.

13. Sourced from *Elliott Smith* by Autumn de Wilde, Chronicle Books, 2007.

14. Sourced from 'Keep the Things You Forgot: An Elliott Smith Aural History' by Jason Greene, *Pitchfork*, 21 October 2013.

15. Sourced from the documentary film *Searching for Elliott Smith*, directed by Gil Reyes, 2019.

16. Sourced from *Either/Or* album review by Ian Watson, *Melody Maker*, 30 May 1998.

17. Sourced from *Elliott Smith* by Autumn de Wilde, Chronicle Books, 2007.

18. Ibid.

19. Sourced from 'Elliott Smith: Emotional Rescue' by Jonathan Valania, *Magnet*, 2 January 2001.

20. Sourced from the 'Adverse Childhood Experiences Study' by Dr Vincent Felliti et al., 1998.

21. Sourced from the documentary film *Heaven Adores You*, directed by Nickolas Rossi, 2014.

22. Sourced from the *MTV Live with Carson Daly* interview, broadcast 5 March 1998.

23. Sourced from 'Logarithms and Biorhythms Test a Young Janitor' by Janet Maslin, *New York Times*, 5 December 1997.

24. Sourced from *Elliott Smith* by Autumn de Wilde, Chronicle Books, 2007.

25. Sourced from 'The Lost Boy' by Keith Cameron, *Q*, January 2011.

26. Sourced from *Elliott Smith* by Autumn de Wilde, Chronicle Books, 2007.

27. Sourced from *XO* album review by Rob Sheffield, *Rolling Stone*, 12 August 1998.

28. Sourced from *Figure 8* album review by Jon Pareles, *Rolling Stone*, 27 April 2000.

29. Sourced from *Figure 8* album review by Ryan Schreiber, *Pitchfork*, 31 March 2000.

30. Sourced from *Elliott Smith* by Autumn de Wilde, Chronicle Books, 2007.

31. Sourced from 'Elliott Smith: Better Off Than Dead' by Marcus Kagler, *Under the Radar*, March 2003.

32. Sourced from *Elliott Smith* by Autumn de Wilde, *Chronicle Books*, 2007.

33. Sourced from 'Patient Safety and Suicide Prevention in Mental Health Services: Time for a New Paradigm' by Dr Leah Quinlivan, Donna L. Littlewood, Roger T. Webb and Nav Kapur, *Journal of Mental Health*, January 2020.

34. Sourced from 'Elliott Smith: Better Off Than Dead' by Marcus Kagler, *Under the Radar*, March 2003.

35. Ibid.

36. Sourced from 'The Mysterious Death of Mr Misery' by Alexis Petridis, *The Guardian*, 18 March 2004.

37. Sourced from the documentary film *Searching for Elliott Smith*, directed by Gil Reyes, 2019.

38. Sourced from 'Mr Misery Revisited' by Liam Gowing, *Spin*, December 2004.

39. Sourced from the documentary film *Heaven Adores You*, directed by Nickolas Rossi, 2014.

40. Sourced from the documentary film *Searching for Elliott Smith*, directed by Gil Reyes, 2019.

41. Ibid.

42. Sourced from *Torment Saint: The Life of Elliott Smith* by Professor William Todd Schultz, Bloomsbury Publishing PLC, 2013.

SELECTED BIBLIOGRAPHY

BOOKS

Elliott Smith and the Big Nothing by Benjamin Nugent (DeCapo, 2004)

Tormented Saint: The Life of Elliott Smith by William Todd Schulz (Bloomsbury, 2013)

Elliott Smith by Autumn de Wilde (Chronicle Books, 2007)

331/3: XO by Matthew Le May (Bloomsbury, 2009)

Heavier Than Heaven by Charles R. Cross (Sceptre, 2019)

Shakey: Neil Young's Biography by Jimmy McDonough (Anchor Books, 2003)

The Biography of Nick Drake by Patrick Humphries (Bloomsbury, 1997)

Hotel California: Singer-Songwriters and Cocaine Cowboys in the LA Canyons 1967–1976 by Barney Hoskyns (Harper Perennial, 2005)

Waiting for the Sun: Strange Days, Weird Scenes and the Sound of Los Angeles by Barney Hoskyns (Bloomsbury, 1996)

Music, Mayhem and Bad Decisions: Three Years in the Portland Punk and New Wave Scene by Sharon E. Cathcart (Create Space, 2017)

Our Band Could Be Your Life: Scenes from the American Indie Underground 1981–1991 by Michael Azerrad (Little, Brown, 2001)

Meet Me in the Bathroom: Rebirth and Rock and Roll in New York City 2001–2011 by Lizzy Goodman (Dey St, 2017)

The Storyteller: Tales of Life and Music by Dave Grohl (Simon & Schuster, 2021)

FILM

Heaven Adores You directed by Nikolas Rossi, 2014

Searching for Elliott Smith directed by Gil Reyes, 2019

PODCASTS

Happiness (Episode 5) by Charlie Ramirez and Jeff Cohen, November 2022

Life of the Record: The Making of 'Elliott Smith'

XO: To Elliott Smith from Brandon